IN
COURT

IN COURT

JACK BATTEN

Macmillan of Canada
A Division of Gage Publishing Limited
Toronto, Canada

Canadian Cataloguing in Publication Data
Batten, Jack,
  In court

ISBN 0-7715-9717-7 bound
    0-7715-9761-4 pbk

1. Lawyers — Canada.   I. Title.

KE395.B382   349.71'092'2   C82-094653-2

DESIGN: Brant Cowie/Artplus

Original hardcover edition published in 1982 by
Macmillan of Canada
A Division of Gage Publishing Limited

Paperback edition published 1983

Printed in Canada.

*The author wishes to acknowledge the indispensable assistance
of the Canada Council and the Ontario Arts Council.*

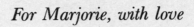

For Marjorie, with love

CONTENTS

INTRODUCTION

IN A REAL SENSE, this book is about the renegades of the Canadian legal profession. It tells the stories of true-life Perry Masons, lawyers who perform in courtrooms, cross-examining witnesses, coaxing juries, foxing judges, scrapping for their clients. They're called "counsel" in the usual legal nomenclature, and they are, as I discovered in working on the book, a nervy, smart, colourful, witty, sometimes gaudy bunch. As I also discovered, they're regarded by many of their fellow lawyers in other disciplines as slightly suspect, as outlaws of a sort. Lawyers who practise in the more mainstream and respectable areas — corporate lawyers, real-estate lawyers, lawyers concerned with wills and trusts and estates — tend to look on counsel as the profession's necessary evils, only to be summoned from the back rooms on those dreadful occasions when a client gets himself into a fix that can only be resolved by writs and briefs and defences against prosecution. Courtroom lawyers don't mind the patronizing attitude. They hardly notice. They're too busy rejoicing in the challenge and chaos of litigation.

Roughly speaking, there are two kinds of courtroom lawyers — criminal counsel and civil counsel. The surface distinction is clear enough: the first kind defend clients who are charged with a criminal offence, and the second kind act for either the plaintiff or the defendant in a dispute that needs to be settled by a lawsuit or the threat of a lawsuit. But below the surface, getting down to the nitty-gritty of practice, the differences between the two sorts of courtroom work are so marked that most counsel specialize in

1

one or the other. Some lawyers are equally adept at both — John Robinette, arguably the most accomplished North American counsel of this century, provides a glorious example — but the majority stake out their territory in one field at the beginning of their careers at the bar. The differences, criminal versus civil, are not only legal but social and tactical and psychological. Civil-litigation specialists deal with more paper than do criminal lawyers. They handle writs and pleadings and transcripts from examinations for discovery (these are pre-trial hearings in which the lawyers on each side are permitted to examine the parties from the other side under oath), and they use all this paper as a basis for attempting to settle the case before it proceeds to trial. Civil counsel love the thrust and jab of an exhilarating courtroom battle, but, recognizing the considerable expense of a trial to their clients, they first negotiate with the other side. It's part of a counsel's skill to work the angles on behalf of his client. He persuades and cons and cajoles in an attempt to get an out-of-court settlement, but if the parties remain adamant and apart, then, gloves off, they proceed to court.

Criminal lawyers are more concerned with human problems than with paper. To be sure, they confront their share of documents — everything from legal-aid certificates that authorize them to act on behalf of impecunious clients to informations that set out the charges alleged against the accused person to transcripts of evidence at a preliminary hearing that sends the accused to trial. And, like civil counsel, they wheel and deal outside the courtroom. In criminal law, the process is commonly called "plea bargaining," and it involves the defence counsel and his opposite number, the crown attorney who is handling the prosecution, in discussions that may lead to an agreement whereby the accused pleads guilty to a lesser charge. The trade-off is fair: the crown gets a sure conviction, the accused receives a lesser sentence, and the public is saved the expense of a trial. But more than paper and bargaining, a criminal lawyer must condition himself to the agony of crime. An enormous percentage of the people who are charged with an offence are guilty of *something*, maybe not of the specific offence with which they're charged but of *some* offence. Many real criminals, especially the old professionals and the long-time hoods, are diverting characters. However, most people who come before the criminal court are simply people in trouble. Maybe they're sad, perhaps they're confused and troubled, or, worse, they may be evil. The criminal lawyer is the single link to the rational world in his client's time of grief and distress. That's a heavy load for anyone, but criminal lawyers are unusual people who relish the burden.

Criminal lawyers are also the people who must answer that habitually asked question: how can a counsel defend a person who is most likely guilty? How can he take pride in beating a conviction for rape or assault or murder? Counsel who are unable to reply to these questions can't and don't practise criminal law. They stick to civil work. Criminal lawyers have no trouble with the answer. It's all a matter, they say correctly, of the system. In Canada, as in the United States and Britain, a man or a woman is innocent until he or she is proved guilty. It's up to the prosecution to establish the accused person's guilt. It's the defence counsel's role to ensure that his client has been proved guilty beyond a reasonable doubt. That's the system. Conscience isn't a factor. The system applies to everyone who appears before the courts. Thus, the criminal lawyer acts for the marijuana-smoker, the break-and-enter artist, the rapist, the murderer, the Mafioso. But fundamentally he acts for the system.

Of the ten lawyers who appear in the ten chapters of this book, ten lawyers who told me their stories and allowed me to hang around with them in and out of court, eight deal with criminal cases and two deal with civil cases. Some of the cases come from the recent past and some from the ongoing present. All, I like to think, are instructive and entertaining, sometimes tragic, frequently funny (though the humour is usually of the gallows variety), and almost always tinged with suspense. I wasn't looking for any morals to draw from the stories of the cases, though occasionally they crept into the telling. Nor was I poking after secrets to courtroom success, though, willy-nilly, they, too, surfaced from the stories. Rather, I wanted a whiff of the courtroom, a sense of the drama of the trial, and a taste of the personality of the counsel in action. I set out to learn something about the methods and style of those honourable outlaws of the legal profession. And what follows in the next ten chapters is what I found.

THE ENTERTAINER

"SOME CASES, a counsel can laugh out of court," Dave Humphrey, criminal lawyer, was saying. "In some cases, even a smile is out of order. Some cases call for a display of righteous indignation. And a hell of a lot of cases require a plea of guilty. If your client is guilty and is clearly going to be proved guilty, the last thing he wants is a trial. The crown's got him by the short hairs, and what he needs is a hell of a good plea-bargainer."

It was a bright morning in late winter, and Humphrey was holding forth in his office in a handsome renovated brownstone on Sultan Street in midtown Toronto. Humphrey, in his mid-fifties, is a raconteur of the flamboyant school. Tales and opinions, epigrams and sermonettes rattle from his mouth like bullets from a Gatling gun. Off duty — and sometimes on duty — he's the Great Entertainer among lawyers of the criminal defence bar. And he looks the part, a husky man with a broad, expressive face and eyes that can nail a witness or an audience at thirty paces. With his sharp suits and his repertoire of gestures that underline punchlines, he's the sort of natural comedian — an upbeat Rodney Dangerfield — who could work one of the high-roller rooms on the Strip at Vegas.

"I had a rape case," he said in his office. "There wasn't much evidence against my man, and the crown's case looked pretty weak. But sometimes it's the weak cases that slip out of your hands if you're not careful. All the witnesses had testified, and it was the night before the crown and I were to present our arguments to the jury. I was sitting at home, getting ready to write out my address, and I thought to myself, instead of a long harangue, I'll keep this thing tight. So next day in court I got up, walked over to the jury box and I said, 'Members of the jury, if this case is rape, then I'm a monkey's uncle, and though the resemblance may be amazing, I ain't.' Then I went back and sat down.

"Herb Langdon was the crown, and he had such a hard time to keep from falling down laughing that he didn't address the jury for longer than fifteen minutes. The judge was just about as brief. The jury went out, and we barely had time to light a cigarette when they were back with a verdict of not guilty.

"Now, suppose I hadn't used that one-line address. Suppose I'd given a long, impassioned speech. That might've made the jury stop and think, hey, if Humphrey's so serious about this thing, maybe there really is a case against his guy. As it was, this was one of those times to laugh a charge out of court."

Humphrey abruptly switched topics. He was in a mood to scattershoot his views on the courtroom process, and his next subject was entitled How Clients Perceive Lawyers.

"I had a guy charged with murder. He'd escaped from the reformatory and whacked his girlfriend over the head with a brick. Killed her dead. So it's first-degree murder. The guy and the girlfriend had a little nine-month-old baby, and the crown tipped me off not to mention the baby when we got to court. It seems the police had found a note from the guy when he was in reformatory telling the girlfriend to throw the baby in the Don River. That wouldn't have sounded nice in court. Anyway, I huddle with the crown and negotiate the charge from murder to manslaughter, and I take the news to my guy.

" 'No way,' he said.

" 'If you don't take it,' I said, 'you'll go down for murder one.'

" 'I wanta fight the charge,' he said. 'I'll get off.'

" 'Goodbye,' I said.

"The guy got himself another lawyer who was glad to fight the murder charge. This lawyer shouted at the judge, shook the crown attorney by the neck, and made all kinds of noise. He may even have mentioned the nine-month-old baby. The result was the guy got convicted of murder and was sentenced to life. But all the time he's sitting in jail, he's gonna be saying what a terrific lawyer he had, somebody who stood up and told those bastards in court where they could get off, not like that Humphrey who only wanted to *negotiate*."

Humphrey lit a cigarette and blew a ribbon of smoke. "A legal-aid case I had, a French Canadian charged with manslaughter. This guy had already done four bits for armed robbery. His girlfriend was cheating on him, and one night he beat her up in a drunken fight and killed her. The guy phoned the cops to tell them about it. He was crying on the phone, the whole remorse thing. It was genuine, and I got the crown to reduce the charge from manslaughter to assault with bodily harm.

" 'No,' the guy said when I told him. 'I won't go for it. I can get off. I was drunk when I hit her.'

" 'If you were drunk,' I said, 'then the law says that's manslaughter.'

" 'All right,' he said. 'She was cheating on me. I was provoked into hitting her.'

" 'That's manslaughter, too,' I said.

" 'I wanta fight,' he said.

" 'Look,' I told him. 'You're a toothless Frenchman who killed an Ontario girl. You got a record stretching your whole adult life. Any jury's going to put you away.'

" 'No,' he said, and he hired himself another lawyer who ranted and raved on his behalf. The guy got eight years for manslaughter, but he figured the other lawyer, not me, was the hero."

Humphrey let out another smoke stream. "The point is, you can go into court and say very little and be more effective. Arthur Martin — now there was a *great* criminal lawyer — he'd speak very quietly and be very polite to everyone. He'd ask a few questions and make a couple of soft-spoken arguments to the judge. First thing anybody knew, he'd have his client's confession ruled inadmissible or he'd impugn a key crown witness's testimony or he'd accomplish something else just as crucial, and the case against the client would collapse. It was all so simple and low-key that the client would say, 'Hey, why'd I hire an expensive counsel like Arthur Martin? Any lawyer could've done that.' The hell *any* lawyer could have."

Humphrey's phone rang.

"Seymour!" Humphrey said, hunching forward as he talked into the receiver. "How nice to hear from you. . . . You've been *arrested*? What for? . . . Book-making. Is a police officer there? Let me talk to him. . . . Good day, officer. It's too nice a morning to be out arresting people. What plans do you have for Seymour? . . . I see. Just booking him. Well then, he'll be out by the time night falls. That's fine. Thank you, officer, most kind of you. . . .

Do I have any message for Seymour? Tell him to save his money for the lawyer's fee. Good morning, officer."

Humphrey had a case in the Supreme Court of Ontario that took up most of the first week of March 1981, and each day he he wore the same tie, a dark four-in-hand decorated with little pigs and the repeated letters "MCP," which stood for Male Chauvinist Pig. Humphrey was defending a muscular extrovert named Gord Knowlton who had played linebacker for nine years in the Canadian Football League. The charge was rape. But Humphrey figured that the complainant, the woman who claimed that Knowlton had raped her, was being less than straightforward in her accusations, and the necktie with the little pigs and the MCPs struck him as entirely appropriate to the occasion.

Nobody disputed the hard facts, neither Knowlton nor the complainant, whose name was banned from publication by court order. Knowlton had met the woman, a twenty-five-year-old airline stewardess, almost four years earlier when she was a cheerleader for the Toronto Argonauts and he was an Argo linebacker. Their relationship was instant and, in Knowlton's word, "lustful." Once, on a short boat cruise, they kept score of the number of times they had sexual intercourse. The score was entered on a piece of paper tacked to the wall of their cabin, and it had reached fifty-five before the boat returned to port. Knowlton's burden was that he wanted to marry the stewardess, but she had doubts about long-range commitments. She preferred to cast around for a broader spectrum of male companions, and it was on a night when she was engaged in a little casting that events leading to the alleged rape occurred.

The stewardess arrived home at two a.m. after a night of drink and dance at a disco. Knowlton showed up at the door of her apartment. She was in pyjamas, he was in a Tarzan mood. He carried her in his arms to his car, drove to his apartment, and ripped off her pyjamas, tops and bottoms. She hurled abuse and a punch at him, and he aimed a slap at her. It landed. For the next twenty minutes there followed what Knowlton described as a "quiet period," which gradually gave way to a round of familiar love-making.

"She enjoyed it," Knowlton said. "As she always did."

"Gordy," she said after the sex, "that's the last time."

"But I want to spend the rest of my life with you."

The stewardess put on her pyjamas, and Knowlton drove her

home, where, after reflecting on the evening's events, she decided to lay the rape charge.

Humphrey took a shot at plea bargaining. He'd plead Knowlton guilty to a lesser charge, assault causing bodily harm. "The appropriate charge," said the crown attorney on the case, Margaret Browne, after reviewing the evidence, "is rape." Humphrey wasn't surprised. "That woman," he said of Browne, "is dying to nail Knowlton."

The trial began before Mr. Justice Thomas Callon of the Supreme Court sitting without a jury, and when Humphrey's turn came to cross-examine the stewardess, he weighed in with a heavy but skilful hand. In examination-in-chief the woman had testified of her reluctance to have sex with Knowlton on the night in question. She hadn't consented to the act. It was rape. Humphrey moved to establish the highly sexual nature of her previous relationship with Knowlton. How about the boat cruise? How many times did she and Knowlton make love? Fifty-five? Could she check the score sheet? Humphrey's cross-examination wasn't intended to blacken the stewardess's reputation. Its aim was to emphasize her fondness for the act of love and the length and variety of her sexual history with Knowlton.

As a witness in his own defence, Knowlton followed Humphrey's deft questioning, and his testimony was at once canny and emotional, a wondrous mix of the sincere and the self-serving. He appeared to be in agony as he testified, perspiration staining his suit jacket, and when he finished, he gave way to tears. But he was candid and effective. "I know I'm not an intelligent person," he said from the box, "but there's no way you rape someone you're going to marry." Under Humphrey's lead, Knowlton relived his three-and-a-half-year affair with the stewardess, underlining most significantly its stormy nature. The couple often argued, Knowlton testified, but the bitterness invariably dissolved in bed, where the sex was frequently "rough." What happened on the night of the alleged rape — apart from the slap, which Knowlton said was a regrettable reflex action — was all of a piece with the couple's previous relationship.

In his address to Mr. Justice Callon, Humphrey didn't kid around with one-liners. His buttery summing-up projected a flow of logic and common sense. Knowlton was a man obsessed by the complainant. "Obviously he is terribly immature and so totally and hopelessly in love with her. She was truly his queen and he was her devoted subject." But Knowlton made a terrible mistake. "The accused for the first time in their unusual relationship of three and a half years slapped the complainant. That's why he is here. It's not because they had sexual intercourse. That, indeed, is old hat." The slap coloured the interpretation of events that the complainant offered in her testimony. "She was dramatically distorting the facts in her favour. She was presenting facts of the case deliberately to get revenge on the man she hates." What does the law say about this bizarre set of circumstances, Humphrey asked. "The accused believed she was consenting to have sexual intercourse with him, even though she may have been pretending to consent. In law, Knowlton cannot be convicted of rape if he believed she was consenting unless it can be established that the consent was brought about by violence."

As far as Mr. Justice Callon was concerned, Humphrey had rung the right bells. His judgment squared with Humphrey's reasoning. Knowlton, Callon said, made "the credible witness," while the stewardess's testimony was "inconsistent with her conduct and inconsistent with any reasonable understanding and assessment of the circumstances." As to the key matter of the complainant's consent — did she or did she not give it? — Callon pursued a winding line. "There was no general reluctance on her part to accompany the accused to his apartment." Once inside the apartment, she may have been "somewhat at odds with her feelings," but there was "no attempt to escape the situation." In fact, Callon said, "she still retained her desire for sexual gratification from the accused." Hence, consent existed and rape did not. Knowlton was acquitted.

"In my thirty years of being a lawyer," Humphrey said after Callon announced his decision, "I've never heard a judgment where the complainant is in effect called a liar."

"*He* lied," the stewardess said of Knowlton as she left the courtroom.

Humphrey accompanied Knowlton and his friends to a small victory party at a table in the bar of a nearby Holiday Inn. He had a gift for Knowlton, something that Humphrey said would aid Knowlton in remembering the difference between good women and evil women. It was Humphrey's tie, the one with the little pigs and the MCPs.

A couple of weeks later, Knowlton dropped in to Humphrey's office. He was ebullient. The Montreal Alouettes had offered him a fat contract. His boss at the executive-management recruiting firm where he worked had a better idea. He wanted Knowlton to forget about football and concentrate on the firm. The boss would reward him with a piece of the business. Everything was coming up roses for Knowlton. Down in Florida on a holiday after the rape trial, he'd picked up a piece of paper from the floor of a bar. It was a hundred-dollar bill. In the office, Humphrey passed the time of day with Knowlton, who soon left on his happy way to have a few celebratory drinks with friends from a radio station.

Much later that night, an attendant at a waterfront parking lot called the police. Someone, he complained, had beaten him up. The attendant, a thirty-year-old named Salahudin Khawaja, said that a customer had objected to paying a one-dollar parking fee. This customer had punched Khawaja in the face, kicked him in the groin, and thrown him over a parked car. Then the man jumped in his own car and accelerated out of the lot. Another customer caught a glimpse of the fleeing automobile's licence. He memorized the letters and numbers and passed them on to the police, who checked the car's ownership.

It belonged to Gord Knowlton. The police charged him with assault causing bodily harm.

At first, Humphrey said he'd have nothing to do with Knowlton's fresh round of trouble. "Discretion, they tell me, is the better part of valour," he said, "and discretion says I should give Gordy a pass this time round." A young criminal specialist named David McCombs took over the case, a sensible second choice for Knowlton. Almost immediately, however, Knowlton discovered that he needed a second lawyer, a civil-litigation man, because the parking-lot attendant announced that he was launching a civil suit against Knowlton for damages suffered in the assault. Knowlton consulted a lawyer named Ron Dash, who entered into negotiations with Khawaja's lawyer. A deal was struck. Khawaja would accept $5,000 for punitive damages and for assorted other complaints including loss of income while he recuperated from his hurts. In return, Khawaja agreed not to pursue the assault charge. The various lawyers contacted the crown attorney who was handling the case, Norm Matusiak, and he, too, gave his blessing to the plan. All seemed to be in order for a swift resolution of the affair except for clearing a final hurdle. Since an assault charge had been laid and since it was listed for hearing on a court docket, a judge's approval was necessary for the formal withdrawal of the charge.

The case was scheduled before Judge Charles Cannon in Etobicoke Provincial Court on August 18, 1981, and Knowlton's lawyers thought the presence of a senior counsel by their client's side would be at least helpful to their cause.

Which senior counsel?

Dave Humphrey, of course.

Humphrey agreed to re-enter the case. "You have to feel a little sorry for Gordy," he said. "After he pays the five grand, he'll have nothing left in the bank." Humphrey's services were on the house.

The appearance in Judge Cannon's Provincial Court lasted all of five minutes. Matusiak, the crown attorney, explained the circumstances, and the judge nodded his head. "I commend all participants and counsel concerned for the view they have taken in this matter," he said. "Justice has been served." Humphrey smiled. His job, mostly a matter of lending his silence and his weight to the proceedings, was done.

Six days later, the *Toronto Star* raised the Knowlton case for fresh examination. "Was justice cheated this week," the paper's story began, "when an assault charge against an ex-football player, Gordon Knowlton, 31, was dropped when he paid $5,000 in damages in an out-of-court settlement of a related civil suit?" After several hundred words of looking at the matter from all sides, quoting lawyers with varying views, the *Star* arrived at no particular answer to its question.

"Maybe an arrangement like that smacks the wrong way," Humphrey said in his office, speaking of the Knowlton settlement, "but it's not illegal or immoral."

Then Humphrey told a story. It was all about the lawyer's son who got himself so stoned on drugs and liquor that he tore through a friend's house, wreaking havoc to the tune of $15,000. Police charged the boy with the offence of causing wilful damage. But when the boy's father, the lawyer, anted up $15,000 to cover the cost of repairs to the ravaged house, the wilful-damage charge was dropped.

"This kind of thing," Humphrey said, "is unusual but not unheard of."

He paused to light a cigarette.

"All the same," he said, "I trust Gordy'll keep himself out of any more trouble. *I* can't stand the excitement."

Dave Humphrey laughed.

At the 1957 Grey Cup game between the Hamilton Tigercats and the Winnipeg Blue Bombers at Varsity Stadium in Toronto, a Hamilton defensive back with the onomatopoetic name of Bibbles Bawel intercepted a pass and was hotfooting down the sidelines toward a certain touchdown when a man lingering on the edges of the field impetuously stretched out a leg and tripped Bibbles. The man with the outstretched leg was Humphrey. When Maria Callas, on her farewell world tour, concluded a concert at Toronto's Massey Hall on the night of February 21, 1974, the sell-out audience hailed her with a host of bravos — and one boo. Humphrey was responsible for the jeer. "Her performance," he said later, "was a disappointment." No one would mistake Humphrey for a shrinking violet. As a young man, he drove a taxi to pay his room and board and joined the U.S. Navy to see the world. He once flew planes, he used to sail a racing Albacore, and he still takes to the road on one of his motorcycles. Humphrey is a man to touch all bases. He's a knowledgeable opera buff, and an ardent golfer, and his understanding of the Bible is long-standing and intimate. For years he taught Sunday school at a Presbyterian church.

In the late 1970s he was elected to serve on the Discipline Committee of the Law Society of Upper Canada, the august body that oversees the profession in Ontario. The appointment meant that Humphrey qualified as probably the only lawyer in the province's history who has both served on the Discipline Committee and been reprimanded by it. The reprimand came in March 1964 when the Law Society penalized Humphrey $1,500 for "unbecoming conduct." What was unbecoming in Humphrey's conduct, according to the Law Society, was his fraternization with a couple of gents named Vincent Feeley and Joseph McDermott. The two happened to be leaders among Ontario's gambling community, and Humphrey's reason for associating with them seemed to him to be perfectly natural. They were occasional clients whose company he enjoyed. The Law Society was not amused.

But, utterly consistent with Humphrey's free-form ways, and his philosophy of live and let live, the companionship with Feeley and McDermott led him to good works as well as temporary trouble. It came about that in the summer of 1963 Feeley and McDermott were serving time in Toronto's Don Jail while they waited an appeal on their convictions for bribing a police officer. In prison, they struck up an acquaintance with a little man named Donald Coston, who was facing trial for murder. Coston's story was grim. He and his wife and a younger, bigger man had been drinking together. Coston passed out. When he came to, his wife and the young man lay on a couch. They were making love. When Coston objected, the young man began beating him with his fists. Coston looked for protection. His hand fell on a kitchen knife, and he stabbed the young man, who died.

Murder, said the police.

"What you need," McDermott and Feeley said to Coston, "is a good lawyer."

"I've got no money," Coston said.

"No sweat," said McDermott and Feeley.

The gamblers' pal, Humphrey, took the case, argued self-defence, and won an acquittal.

"I'm free," Coston said after he walked out of the courtroom, "because of a fair trial — and three good men."

From the rough and tumble of Humphrey's life, driving cabs, sailing the seven seas, and hanging out with gamblers, from the four years he put in at the beginning of his legal career as a crown counsel matching wits with the giants of the defence bar, and from his own long experience as a defence giant, he has evolved a few maxims that he follows in his conduct of court cases. Humphrey's maxims, it's not surprising, aren't the sort of principles that law schools normally embrace.

"The cabs and the navy were the best preparation I could've had for the legal profession," Humphrey says. "Doing that kind of thing, you get to meet pimps, prostitutes, cops, thieves, and drunken lawyers, and you get an insight into what's going on with people who aren't part of the grey middle classes. You learn about the kinds of individuals who are likely to get themselves into trouble. You figure out their strengths and weaknesses. You get a feel for these men and women, and without the feel, it'd be difficult, probably impossible, to take the measure of a court case. It's a matter of atmosphere, that's what a trial is, and unless you can assess the atmosphere, your client can kiss his chances good-bye."

Another Humphrey maxim centres on simplicity. "I see counsel going into court, and they've got twenty defences they're arguing for their clients. They wrap themselves up in these twenty defences, a bunch of legalisms and textbook stuff, and they're thrashing around, talking their heads off. All right, somewhere in the twenty defences there's one good defence, one possible winner, but when a counsel's arguing twenty defences, what's going to happen is that the good one's bound to merge with the other nineteen and head straight down the drain. The smart route is to arrive at the one winning defence out front and concentrate on it. I mean, people make a big deal out of me reading a motorcycle magazine while a trial's going on. That's nothing to get excited about. All I'm doing is waiting for the useless technical arguments to pass by until I can get down to business with my one solid defence.

"Besides, I like motorcycle magazines."

"A cold-blooded murderer," John Hamilton said.

Humphrey, imperturbable, didn't move an eyeball.

"The police had the right man," Hamilton said a moment later.

Humphrey sat rock-steady in his chair.

"A cold-blooded murderer," Hamilton said a second time.

That made Humphrey react, calling Gordon Allen a killer *twice*. He raised his head in Hamilton's direction and gave him a long, fishy look.

"Hell, John," he thought, "you're *really* shooting from the hip."

This was on an astonishingly warm afternoon in April 1981, and it was John Hamilton, not Humphrey, who was generating the controversy. The two men — Hamilton is a criminal lawyer with a fast-talking style — were appearing side by side before Metro Toronto's executive committee with their hands out. They were asking Metro to pay the legal bills they'd racked up in defending two Toronto policemen. Humphrey had acted for Staff-Sergeant Gerald Stevenson, Hamilton for Sergeant Robert McLean, and both cops, alas, had been found guilty of using a false affidavit.

The circumstances were curious. A woman named Lauralee Lorenz and her lover, Gordon Allen, were suspected of having bumped off the woman's husband in March 1978. Stevenson and McLean, two members of the homicide squad, took on the case, and as an aid in pushing toward a conviction they had confronted Allen with an affidavit apparently signed by Lorenz in which she implicated Allen in the murder. As Stevenson and McLean hoped, the affidavit drew a response from Allen that they believed to be incriminating. That came as good news for the two cops. The bad news was that the affidavit was a phony, concocted by Stevenson and McLean, who forged Lorenz's signature, and when their ruse was discovered they were charged and convicted of a criminal offence, while Allen and Lorenz, with Allen's statement ruled inadmissible as evidence at their trial, were acquitted of murder.

Humphrey's bill for his services to Stevenson amounted to $9,093, Hamilton's for McLean to $8,906, and payment of the bills out of public funds hinged on approval of Metro's twelve-member executive committee. The committee was sitting in session on this warm April afternoon in the large, sumptuous council chamber at Toronto's city hall, and it parcelled out five minutes each to Humphrey and Hamilton to make their pitches. Humphrey, looking spruce in a medium-grey suit, light-grey shirt, and deep-red tie, exuded reasonableness in his address to the committee.

"The officers committed a technical breach of the law," he said, "and I'm not suggesting that council should support the police in disobeying the law. But in this case, Stevenson and McLean were employing an imaginative investigative technique. I'd remind you that the offence was so technical that neither officer was aware he was committing it. I'd also point out that at the officers' trial, even though they were found guilty, the judge gave them an absolute discharge, and they have no criminal record.

"Look," Humphrey went on, "I took the case because I approve of Gerry Stevenson and what he did to try and solve this particular murder. If I'd won for him, then I'd automatically be paid by the city. That's the policy — to pay police officers' legal bills when they're acquitted. But since Stevenson wasn't acquitted, if you people decide not to pay me out of the public purse, I won't charge him a penny."

Hamilton came out firing during his allotted five minutes. McLean and Stevenson, he said, "had the right man. The court that acquitted Allen didn't have all the evidence before it. It didn't have Allen's statement to McLean and Stevenson or the police wire-taps of calls between Allen and Lorenz. All that evidence was ruled inadmissible."

The committee members seemed uneasy and baffled under the blizzard of information — and accusations — that Hamilton and Humphrey served up to them. "Do you mean," one puzzled alderman from the Borough of North York asked Humphrey, "that the policeman signed his *own* name to this affidavit?" "No, Lorenz's name," Humphrey said as he ran down the facts once again in primary-school fashion. The committee chairman, growing impatient, called for a vote. Hands flashed in the air, six in favour and six against paying the lawyers' bills. The tie meant a loss for Humphrey and Hamilton, since they needed a majority vote to win approval of cash from Metro's funds. The two lawyers picked up their briefcases and left the council chamber, radiating mild disgust.

Next day, trouble dropped on John Hamilton. Gordon Allen made noises about suing for libel over Hamilton's characterization of him as a "cold-blooded murderer." Allen's counsel at his murder trial, a high-profile criminal lawyer named Eddie Greenspan, got into the act by dumping on Hamilton's statement as "the kind of comment I would expect from someone without any knowledge of the law." Hamilton appeared to laugh off the attacks. "The next time Mr. Allen drives down from his home in Orillia," he told one reporter, his tongue stuck deep in his cheek, "I'd like him to come by my house and babysit my children." But he was sufficiently concerned to consult a lawyer friend who specialized in libel matters, and the friend devoted two weeks to planning a defence against Allen's threatened suit. Other criminal lawyers rallied to Hamilton's cause, criticizing Greenspan among themselves for breaking an unwritten rule of the inner circle of criminal counsel by going public with a knock at one of their own. Then, swiftly, the fuss evaporated. Greenspan voiced no further criticism of Hamilton's remarks, and Allen decided against raising the old murder issue in a libel action. Hamilton was off the hook.

"It's very satisfying to defend cops against criminal prosecutions," he said in his office one day a few weeks later, "which is why guys like Humphrey and me handle any cop cases that come along. And lately, believe me, a lot are coming along."

Hamilton is a lean, stripped-down man in his mid-forties with the ascetic look of a long-distance runner. From the beginning of his career as a defence counsel in 1963, he's carried a reputation as a bright, brash, aggressive battler. Within five years of his call to the bar, he had taken two cases to the Supreme Court of Canada that established leading decisions on their subjects, one setting limits on police entrapment, the other defining a common bawdy-house. Hamilton has known a share of rounders in his time — and a share of cops.

"A police officer's whole career is in the balance when he's tried," Hamilton said. "If he's guilty, he can never again be an effective cop. Look at McLean and Stevenson. Both of those guys are working desk jobs now. They couldn't handle a homicide investigation, no matter how good they are at it, because they'd have to go to court to testify, and the first question a defence counsel would ask them is, 'Aren't you one of the officers who was convicted of faking an affidavit?' Their credibility would be shot. But with a bandit, if he's in the break-and-enter business and he gets convicted, the conviction doesn't interfere with his profession, apart from the temporary nuisance of serving a jail sentence."

Hamilton, restless and in perpetual motion, paced around his office. "It's a nice change of direction to defend cops," he said. "You know that, with them, you're on the side of the good guys for a change."

Humphrey, meanwhile, was fed up with the business of Stevenson and McLean.

"I've had it with the case," he said in his office. "I'm never going to appear before another civic body for the rest of my life. The six people on that committee who voted for us were right and the other six didn't understand what the hell John and I were talking about."

Humphrey let out a sardonic laugh.

"It's easy to figure out why the six turned us down," he said. "Number one, it isn't popular to do anything nice for lawyers. Pay a lawyer's bill? Are you crazy? Number two reason is just as plain. It's not a good idea these days for a politician to appear too enthusiastic about the police. Which is ridiculous."

"The reason the Bencardino and de Carlo case was so interesting," Humphrey reminisced one afternoon, "was that nobody could figure out at first whether they were really guilty or not guilty."

The case began late on a March night in the early 1970s when four young men — Moretti, Quaranta, Presta, and LaGamba — let themselves into a supermarket in the sprawling northwest section of Toronto known as Little Italy. The four young men came equipped with two large cans of gasoline. They had arson in mind. Presta and LaGamba left the store before the fireworks began, assigning the other two to carry out the mechanics of the job. Moretti applied himself to his chores zealously, sprinkling gasoline over a large area of the store. He was, as it turned out to his misfortune, over-zealous. When he lit a match to the gas, the supermarket went off like a bomb. Moretti was killed, and

Quaranta, standing by the door to the street, suffered cuts and burns and broken bones. One other person was an unexpected victim of the blast, a cleaning lady named Maria Simone, who, unknown to the arsonists, was working on the second floor of the building next door to the supermarket. Maria Simone died almost immediately, and her death made the crime not merely arson but murder.

When Presta and LaGamba heard of the plot gone wrong, they caught a plane for their old home town in Italy. They expected to find sanctuary, but what they received instead was a jail cell. Italian police learned of the crime in Toronto from their Canadian counterparts, and they arrested Presta and LaGamba under an Italian law which gives the country's courts jurisdiction over any Italian-born citizen who commits a crime anywhere in the world against another Italian-born citizen. Unfortunately for Presta and LaGamba, Maria Simone was a daughter of Italy.

Paolo Quaranta, the wounded arsonist, stood trial for murder in Toronto and, despite an enterprising defence by his counsel, Eddie Greenspan, was convicted. The sentencing judge came down hard on Quaranta, putting him away for life with no parole for twenty-five years. But Quaranta, even as a jailbird, was a talkative fellow, and he had an intriguing story to tell anyone who would listen. The police listened, because Quaranta's tale was that the four arsonists had been put up to the job by Raffaele Bencardino and Giuseppe de Carlo, who happened to be the owners of the supermarket and who wanted the place burned for its insurance money. Bencardino and de Carlo were accordingly charged with Maria Simone's murder, and in February 1973 they stood trial, Arthur Maloney acting for Bencardino and Dave Humphrey for de Carlo.

"Weird case," Humphrey mused. "Quaranta came down from the Don Jail and testified for the crown that Bencardino and de Carlo had hired the four guys to burn the supermarket. Even worse, he said that he saw the owners at the store around the time of the fire and he heard one of them say something like, 'Do a good job, boys.' It looked bad for our people. Well, the night after Quaranta testified, I got a phone call at home from the wife of a former client of mine named Bruno Pisani who was currently residing in the Don. The word from Pisani was that he'd been talking to Quaranta, and Quaranta wanted to change his testimony. With that news, Maloney and I tried to get the crown,

Frank Armstrong, to recall Quaranta to the stand. That failed. We tried to get the judge to call Quaranta as *his* witness. That failed. So we ended up calling Quaranta as *our* witness, which was a mistake for a couple of reasons."

First reason: "The only part of Quaranta's testimony that he changed was the part about seeing Bencardino and de Carlo at the supermarket the night of the fire. It was nice he said he lied about that little item, but the fact was that we could already place our guys with their wives at a steak-house miles away from the supermarket throughout the entire evening. It happened to be the Feast of St. Joseph that day, and the two couples were out celebrating Joe de Carlo's feast day. We had witnesses. Quaranta changed that part of his story, but he didn't change another part, the part where he said he heard the two owners talking to Moretti about burning down the place. Thanks a lot."

Second reason: "Since we called Quaranta as our witness, that gave Frank Armstrong the opportunity to cross-examine Quaranta on the reasons for his sudden change of testimony. I mean, here was Quaranta on the stand, tears in his eyes, scared silly, and looking clearly like he'd been recently beaten up. Armstrong wanted to know what Bruno Pisani had to do with the situation, Bruno Pisani who was Dave Humphrey's old client. Armstrong went to town on the guy."

So he did, as the trial transcript indicates.

ARMSTRONG: "Did Bruno tell you he had been convicted of possession of counterfeit money?"

QUARANTA: "Well, I believe he did say that, but he had about ten dollars false money. That is all, and that was the end of it."

ARMSTRONG: "Mr. Humphrey had acted for him in that matter?"

QUARANTA: "What do I know?"

ARMSTRONG: "Didn't he tell you that Mr. Humphrey acted for him?"

QUARANTA: "I don't believe so."

ARMSTRONG: "Never had any discussion about the fact that Mr. Humphrey had defended him on this charge of possession of counterfeit money?"

QUARANTA: "No, sir."

ARMSTRONG: "Because if he had, it would be pretty surprising to you, would it not, that Bruno was befriending you, a major witness against one of Mr. Humphrey's other clients?"

QUARANTA: "What do I know?"

ARMSTRONG: "What did Bruno Pisani say to you that prompted you to tell him that you lied about this matter?"

QUARANTA: "That is not the way it went. That talk did not happen."

ARMSTRONG: "Didn't he say anything to you?"

QUARANTA: "I just said those two words to him, and that's all."

ARMSTRONG: "What words?"

QUARANTA: "I said I lied at certain points."

ARMSTRONG: "Without him asking you?"

QUARANTA: "Was he a judge to ask me questions?"

ARMSTRONG: "I put it to you, Paolo, that Bruno Pisani told you that you had to change your evidence on that one material point, and that was that you did not see the owners in the store on the night of the fire, and as long as you tell that story they will let you live to at least rot in jail. Isn't that true?"

QUARANTA: "Not true."

"Armstrong's argument," Humphrey went on, "was that Pisani had beaten up Quaranta and made him change his story. We said that, hell, everybody in the jail knew Quaranta was a rat who was testifying for the crown and, ergo, he was fair game for a beating from any of his fellow inmates. The judge got excited and ordered Quaranta to be held in a safe place, which turned out to be the women's section of the jail in the town of Whitby forty miles east of Toronto. It was supposed to be a tremendous secret, but there wasn't a lawyer or a convict or a guy on the street who wasn't aware within five minutes that Paolo Quaranta was the only prisoner in the women's section of the jail in the town of Whitby. Not that it mattered any more. Quaranta had done his damage to us."

But, as the trial unfolded, it was not the twisting testimony and eccentric adventures of Quaranta that proved to be a pivotal element in the ultimate fate of Bencardino and de Carlo. It was another issue, a point of pure law.

"There was evidence," Humphrey went on, "that our two guys had bought six thousand dollars' worth of stolen goods on a previous occasion from some or all of the arsonists. These goods, mostly cigarettes, were in a garage out back of the supermarket. Well, when the judge came to charge the jury, he said that the evidence of the purchase of the goods, *stolen* goods, was capable of corroborating the evidence of Quaranta on the arson and murder. Maloney and I said that was wrong, that the evidence of the stolen goods didn't connect our guys with the arson. Maloney objected to the charge like crazy. After a while I told him not to bother. My reasoning was that, ethically, we were obliged as defence counsel to bring errors in the judge's jury charge to his attention. We'd done that. Why press it further? Suppose we got the judge to change his mind on the corroboration point and he redirected the jury, but then the jury went out and still found our guys guilty. If that happened, we wouldn't have an error in the judge's charge that we could use as a basis for asking the Court of Appeal to give us a new trial."

Which was precisely the sequence of events that followed. The jury convicted Bencardino and de Carlo, not of murder but of manslaughter, and the judge sentenced them to fifteen years in prison. Maloney and Humphrey proceeded to the Court of Appeal and succeeded in obtaining an order for a new trial. On what grounds? On the grounds, the Court of Appeal held, that the trial judge had erred in telling the jury that the mere existence of the stolen goods offered enough corroboration of Quaranta's testimony against Bencardino and de Carlo.

Two more trials followed. The first, before a judge who was cautious and painstaking, was washed out in mid-trial when the judge grew so cautious and painstaking that he made himself ill and was unable to continue. The third trial finally resolved the fortunes of Bencardino and de Carlo, but not before other strange and comic episodes intervened. For example, the trip to Italy.

"Frank Armstrong," Humphrey said, "decided to take commission evidence from the other two arsonists, Presta and LaGamba, which meant we packed off to Italy, the whole cast of us: Armstrong, Maloney, me, Leybourne, who was the cop on the case, the court interpreter, a shorthand reporter, and an Italian-speaking professor from the University of Windsor Law School. All that crowd, *plus* our spouses. This entourage arrived at the courthouse in a little town south of Rome where Presta and LaGamba were being held, and it was bedlam. The judge, Garoffolo by name, wore shades in court and ran the place like a dictator. He had a guy sitting in front of him, a strange person — sleeveless sweater, long, dirty fingernails, a 1935 Corona typewriter. That was the court reporter, and he'd only start typing when Garoffolo dictated something to him. Maloney asked what the hell was going on, and Garoffolo told him to shut up or he'd throw him in the cells for contempt. That's the Italian system.

"The prisoners were brought in, Presta and LaGamba. They

were wearing ancient handcuffs made of wood and iron, and they had the worst case of jailhouse pallor I've ever seen. Those guys were so pale you could practically see through them. By then, they'd been in the can a couple of years without being tried. Italian courts are permitted to hold prisoners for five years before somebody makes up his mind whether to put them on trial or not, and in Italy nobody appears to have heard of bail.

"Anyway, these guys came into court and Frank Armstrong put some statements and questions to them. They clammed up. Silent. Mute. They'd decided their best strategy was not to get involved in any Canadian trial. Armstrong was so mad he was blowing smoke out his ears, and Garoffolo threatened to bury Presta and LaGamba in prison for the rest of their lives. But the two guys stuck to their silence. *Omerta* was the order of the day. That meant there was no new evidence against our guys, and the last I saw or heard of Presta and LaGamba, they were being led to their cells in that old courthouse. Maybe they're still locked up. Who knows?"

Back in Toronto, at the third trial for Bencardino and de Carlo, Humphrey and Maloney called a witness who turned out to be crucial — Mrs. Bencardino, the wife of one of the two supermarket owners.

"She had a story," Humphrey remembered. "She said one day she went down the basement of the supermarket where her husband and the other owner were talking to a guy. This guy was two things. He was one of the arsonists and he was one of the people that the supermarket owners had bought the stolen goods from. He wanted to peddle more stolen goods, and according to the wife, the owners were saying, 'No more stolen goods. Forget them. They're more trouble than they're worth.' The guy got mad. He flashed a gun, and he said, 'You don't buy any more stolen goods from us and we're going to get you for it.'

"And that was the story we emphasized to the jury. We said that the motive for the fire was revenge. It had nothing to do with insurance money. It had nothing to do with personal gain for our guys. The four arsonists set the fire because they wanted to get even with the two owners for not buying any more stolen goods."

When the jury at the third trial retired to consider the Humphrey-Maloney version of the crime and to arrive at its verdict, Humphrey telephoned his mother.

"She's not Catholic, my mother," he said. "but she was educated in a convent and to this day she says her beads. Can't break the habit. I phoned her and said, 'Mother, we got a tough case here, and I think you better do something about it. Get on those beads. Give those things a workout.' Then I sat around with the Bencardinos and the de Carlos waiting for the verdict."

The jury members deliberated for several excruciating hours. But when they returned to the courtroom, it was clear that they'd gone for the revenge theory as the motive for the crime. Bencardino and de Carlo, they announced, were innocent.

"So what happens?" Humphrey said. "The families go crazy with joy. Laughing. Weeping. Hugging. Mrs. de Carlo comes up to me and says, 'Oh, Mr. Humphrey, there's one person we owe this to.' 'Who?' I ask. 'Your mother,' she says. My *mother*? 'It was the beads,' she says."

Bencardino and de Carlo — "two hard-working guys who'd never had a record of any kind" — returned to the grocery business in Toronto. Moretti was dead. Presta and LaGamba, for all anyone knows, languished in an ancient Italian jail. But Paolo Quaranta and his saga were scheduled for a longer run.

"The prison people shipped Quaranta to a penitentiary in British Columbia to serve his sentence," Humphrey said. "They figured he'd be safer out there. That's where Quaranta foxed them. He put in a couple of years. Then he escaped. He made his way to New York City, and after a while everybody knew he was there. The police knew, the RCMP knew, the jail people knew. But nobody cared, because they felt sorry for him. Under all the circumstances of the crime, he should never have been convicted of murder. Anyway, a couple of years went by, and I got a phone call from a lawyer in New York. He said he was acting for Quaranta, and Quaranta wanted to come back to Toronto. What did I think?

"'Well,' I said to this New York lawyer. 'I'm sure nobody is excited about your client. Out of sight, you know, is out of mind. But if Quaranta returns to Toronto, somebody from the police is going to have to remind him that he hasn't finished his sentence. However distasteful it may be to all concerned, they're gonna lock him up.'

"Quaranta's New York lawyer thanked me and hung up. That was the last word I heard on the case of Bencardino and de Carlo."

Though Humphrey couldn't have guessed it, when John Papalia

sent a Scotch and water over to Max Bluestein's table at the Town Tavern one night in March 1961, the stage was being set for one of Humphrey's small classics in criminal defence. Papalia, aka Johnny Pops, was a Mafia enforcer. Bluestein was a gambler who ran a string of floating crap games around Toronto. The Mafia wanted a slice of Bluestein's action as a replacement for its own gambling clubs which were being phased out of operation by diligent police work. Bluestein had so far refused the mob's overtures, and on this March evening at the Town — a now-defunct nightclub near the corner of Yonge and Queen streets in downtown Toronto favoured by jazz musicians, assorted villains, and diners who recognized a culinary bargain, $1.20 for a delicious repast of roast beef and mashed — he was receiving his last chance to co-operate. If he accepted Papalia's offer of a drink, he was signalling that the mob was in. Turn it down, and he was keeping the crap games to himself.

A waitress approached Bluestein's table and began to set the Papalia drink in front of him. Bluestein's action was unequivocal. He waved away the waitress and Johnny Pops' Scotch. Bluestein rose from the table and made his way to the Town's lobby. Papalia followed, motioning four or five mob cohorts to accompany him. In the lobby, they fell on Bluestein with fists and various blunt instruments. Bluestein lashed back with a stiletto he carried for just such occasions and managed to sink six stab wounds into one attacker, a hood named Frank Marchildon. But sheer numbers — five or six to one — made Bluestein a certain loser, and he was left bleeding, battered, and barely conscious on the floor of the Town lobby while Papalia, Marchildon, and company scattered down Queen Street.

The police eventually pieced together the facts of the case and obtained convictions against three of the attackers, including Papalia, who was sentenced to eighteen months, and Marchildon, who got four months. But the case was difficult to prosecute, mainly because the habitués of the Town, understandably nervous about getting in the bad books of the mob guys, made reluctant witnesses. Most reluctant of all was the Town hat-check girl, Eva Anderson, whose post in the cloakroom off the lobby gave her a clear and shocking view of the bloody events. Shortly after the attack, Miss Anderson was heard in a nervous conversation on the cloakroom telephone. "No, Johnny," she said. "No, no, I can't do that. No. *No!*" Presumably her caller was Johnny Pops, the Mafia enforcer, advising her to forget about his presence in the club that night, and by the time Eva Anderson arrived in court as a witness for the crown against Papalia and the others, she had been struck dumb.

"Miss Anderson," Joseph Addison, the magistrate presiding at the trial, said in some anger, "could have given complete identity of the attackers because the assault took place in front of her desk." Addison ordered the poor hat-check girl charged with perjury.

At which point, enter Dave Humphrey as the Anderson defence counsel.

"Ah, Little Eva," he remembers. "I liked her. I liked the Town, I liked its roast beef. What I didn't care for was the case against her. It looked tight."

But Humphrey, for all his talk of feel and intuition in handling court cases, had acquired a fairly sophisticated understanding of psychiatric concepts, and he elected to apply some of his knowledge on behalf of Little Eva.

"Hysterical amnesia," he says. "Nobody talked much about that sort of thing twenty years ago, but I figured that maybe something so traumatic could happen to somebody that they'd forget all about the event. Erase it from their memory so that it no longer existed for them."

Humphrey contacted a psychiatrist by telephone and put the thesis to him, hysterical amnesia as it applied to Eva Anderson's situation.

"Yes," the psychiatrist said, "it's perfectly possible. But I'd like to speak to Miss Anderson myself."

"Oh no," Humphrey said, not anxious for the psychiatrist to get too close to his client. "She's so upset that she can't deal with anybody before the perjury trial."

"Well, all right," the psychiatrist said. "I guess I could testify for her about the likelihood of hysterical amnesia."

"When it came to the day of the trial," Humphrey remembers, "I couldn't keep the psychiatrist from talking to Eva while we were waiting out in the courtroom corridor. But that turned out to be a benefit for us because the psychiatrist really warmed to Eva and her predicament, and when he got in the witness-box, he came on like the world's greatest authority on hysterical amnesia. The crown was sceptical as hell. *Hysterical amnesia?* But the tougher he got in cross-examining my psychiatrist, the more positive the psychiatrist became. He was so convincing that the judge said, well, sure, Little Eva simply couldn't remember what happened at the Town that night. She was acquitted."

Eva Anderson returned, secure, to a normal existence, which was more than Max Bluestein and John Papalia were able to claim. Bluestein, left slightly paranoid by his beating, became convinced that grief was hounding his tail. His paranoia deepened in October 1973 when he parked his car in a suburban Toronto shopping plaza and returned to find sticks of dynamite wired to its ignition. Two months later, in December 1973, he shot and killed a man whom he suspected of plotting against him. The man, entirely innocent of evil intent, was Bluestein's best friend. The court found Bluestein to have been legally insane at the time of the shooting.

As for Papalia, he served seven months on his sentence in the Bluestein case, then was whisked to New York City, where he pleaded guilty to a Mafia drug conspiracy charge. He spent four years in the Lewisburg, Pennsylvania, prison before returning to his home base in Hamilton, Ontario, where he kept a low profile. That lasted until 1973, when he was sentenced to six years for a $300,000 extortion scam. One of Papalia's co-accused in the extortion was a Montrealer of dubious repute named Paolo Viola. Along with Papalia and a couple of others, Viola was convicted at the trial, but his conviction, unlike Papalia's, was overturned by the Ontario Court of Appeal. Viola's counsel, both at the trial and at the successful appeal, was none other than Dave Humphrey.

There seems to be something else about Humphrey — he inspires affection. That's not an altogether common quality among criminal lawyers, people who by the very nature of their profession are essentially hit-and-run operators. But Humphrey, relaxed and funny and good company, generates loyalty and friendship among his peers. And so it was that in the late spring of 1980, Mike DeRubeis, a former articling student of Humphrey's, and now busy in his own litigation practice, got together with a few other grads of the Humphrey office and organized a night of tribute, a celebration of thirty years at the bar for Humphrey. They carried it off in style. Seventy lawyers and judges gathered in black tie at Toronto's Royal York Hotel. There were cocktails in the Royal Suite. Vintage wines and witty speeches with dinner in a private banquet room. Presentation to Humphrey of a Karsh portrait of himself. But from the evening, with all its glitter and distinction, Mike DeRubeis prizes most the memory of a conversation he had over dinner.

"I was talking to John Robinette," he says. "I mean, this was John Robinette, the greatest of all the counsel, and he said, well, the way Dave had performed in court over the years, he had probably turned out to be the smartest and most effective criminal lawyer at the bar today."

CHAPTER 2

BEGINNINGS

CAROLINE LINDBERG'S FACE belongs on a cameo. It is pale and heart-shaped and serene. Her hair is light brown and pulled loosely back from her forehead. She has a long, graceful neck and she wears white blouses. She is ladylike, a young woman whose presence has a naturally civilizing influence. She is a lawyer, called to the Ontario bar in the spring of 1981 when she was twenty-five years old. Her appearance suggests her practice would run to wills and trusts and pieces of property, perhaps assisting a senior partner in a large firm in advice to elderly gentlemen on the disposition of their estates. But appearances deceive. Caroline Lindberg is a criminal lawyer.

"A couple of years ago," she says, "I didn't think I'd be spending my time alone in a room talking to a guy who's charged with incest or indecent assault or eight counts of intercourse with a female under fourteen. But those kinds of people are my clients now. I'm happy with them as my clients. And I worry about them. Especially I worry about the ones in custody waiting for their trials, the ones who can't make bail. Sometimes I can't stop from going over in my head all my clients who are somewhere in a jail."

Lindberg practises on her own. After her call to the bar, she negotiated a line of credit from the Royal Bank for fifteen thousand dollars and spent part of the money to rent space in a small downtown Toronto firm. For about a thousand dollars a month she gets the use of the firm's library, part of a secretary's time, and an office not much bigger than the cells that are home to some of her clients. She lives alone in a tidy one-bedroom apartment near the University of Toronto. Once in a while, when she finds a spare thirty minutes, she walks up to the university's athletic complex for a swim. She enrolled in a yoga class but made it to only half the sessions. She used to see two or three movies a week; now it's one or two a month. Her criminal practice and those worrisome clients have somehow moved into the space she once called her own.

Richard White is a James Dean throwback in looks, all sulky face and wavy hair. He's nineteen years old, and by the time he became Lindberg's client early in the summer of 1981, he showed seven convictions for theft and for breaking and entering, and he'd done one stretch of three months in jail. He had a record, and he wasn't very bright.

"He's like so many of my clients," Lindberg said of White. "I don't act for master criminals. The people I get are the kind who answer 'I don't know' to most of the questions I ask them. They're not very good at articulating their thoughts. But intuitively they have a lot going for them. They remind me of characters from a William Faulkner novel."

The police figured they had a case of assault and robbery nailed shut on White. According to their scenario, the crime began when two fifteen-year-old girls hailed a taxi in downtown Toronto about three a.m. on a late-spring morning. The girls directed the cab driver on a route that ended in the underground garage of an apartment building. One of the girls got out of the cab, leaving the second girl in the front seat with the driver. The two were alone for a few minutes — during which time some sexual activity may or may not have commenced — when two men jumped into the cab, one through the left rear door and the other, scrambling over the girl, from the front passenger door. The man in the rear held the cabbie around the neck while the other frisked him for his money — about $100 — and his wallet. The mugging of the cab driver was shocking and swift, and within ten seconds the two men and the girls had vanished from the garage.

One night a couple of weeks later, as the same cabbie was tooling through the same downtown streets on the lookout for a fare, he spotted the two girls. They were passengers in a car directly in front of him. He radioed his dispatcher to summon the police and set after the car in a surreptitious chase. Six miles later, a police cruiser joined the pursuit and pulled the girls' car to the curb.

"Yeah," the cab driver said, "they're the right broads."

He checked the other passengers in the car.

"Hey!" he said, pointing to a man in the back. "It's the guy from the garage. He's the one that grabbed my cash."

The guy was Richard White.

While the two girls were taken away to be dealt with by juvenile court, White was held overnight in a cell at a midtown police station. At 8:30 the next morning, two officers questioned him. Nah, White said, I don't know about any underground garage. We got a positive identification on you, the officers said, and they told White they were laying charges of assault and robbery. At three o'clock that afternoon, White was driven a few blocks to Metro Toronto Police Headquarters, where he sat alone on a bench on one of the upper floors waiting to be photographed and fingerprinted.

"Hi ya." It was a policeman in uniform. He joined White on the bench, and according to the policeman's later story, he and White fell into an open and easy chat.

"You're gonna be printed in a couple of minutes," the policeman said.

"What am I charged with anyway?" White is supposed to have asked.

"Assault and robbery," the policeman answered. "Two counts of each."

"*Two*? I never assaulted another guy."

"Well, this one guy, the cab driver," the policeman said. "Did you get both the money and the wallet?"

"Yeah, I did," White said. "But, y'know, he was just out to get himself fucked by the girls, so he deserved to be ripped off."

No one, neither family nor friends, would put up bail for White, and he passed seven weeks in jail waiting until his trial date. The York County Legal Aid Society assigned him a lawyer, a man in his early thirties, and on the morning of the trial in Provincial Court, he appeared on White's behalf. The crown attorney called two witnesses, the cab driver, who said he had a "momentary glimpse" of White in the garage, and the uniformed policeman, who repeated the conversation he claimed to have had with White at police headquarters. When the crown had completed its case,

White's lawyer asked for more time to prepare a defence. The judge gave him a week, but a day later, for reasons known only to White, he fired his lawyer.

The Legal Aid Society assigned Lindberg to pick up the pieces. She interviewed White in jail, a couple of long and thorough sessions, and the night before the case was scheduled for completion, she sat late in her office organizing her presentation. She struggled to feel hopeful, but the odds against her seemed formidable. She had no witnesses except White, and he wouldn't strike an impressive figure. She knew that Toronto judges traditionally come down hard on the accused in cases of violence against cab drivers. And she thought the judge on the White case presented special difficulties, a crown-oriented judge who had once been a crown attorney himself and before that, early in his career, a cop.

At 1:30 in the morning, still at her desk, Lindberg phoned the White home. When he wasn't in jail, Richard lived in the suburbs with his parents, who ran a janitorial service which Richard worked for. Lindberg spoke to White's younger brother, a seventeen-year-old who had one theft conviction of his own. Lindberg was fishing, trying to get a handle on White and his background, looking for anything that might give her an edge in her arguments to the judge. She was eager. She talked to the brother for an hour but ended up learning little that was new or helpful, and it was three in the morning before she put aside her papers and her disappointment and went at last to bed.

The trial was at the Collegepark Courts on the second floor of the building that was once Eaton's College Street department store. It's a 1930s art deco creation, and the courts, makeshift and homely, seem an intrusion on the building's graceful architecture. The courts — Provincial Courts — are in effect poor people's forums, hearing-places for desperate and low-life crimes, shop-lifting and mugging and breaking in, and the air in the corridors and the courtrooms is leaden with tension and bad breath and the stink of poverty.

Lindberg called White to the witness stand. His answers came in monosyllables, but in his five minutes of halting testimony, Lindberg got him to deny that he'd committed the assault and robbery. He agreed that he'd talked to the uniformed policeman at headquarters but he hadn't said anything that implicated him in the crime. White returned to the prisoners' box.

"Make your presentations, Miss Lindberg," the judge said. He was a man in his mid-fifties with a rubbery, humorous face and a flat voice.

Lindberg's manner in court, the product partly of her personality and partly of her inexperience, blends intensity and reserve in an attractive mix. Her voice is soft, but some quality in it, a sense of urgency, demands that it be heard. She comes across as undeniably sensible when she stands in front of a judge. She may be young and new to the game, so her manner says, but she carries the credentials of dedication and sound thinking and concern for the right legal principles. That, it's implied, ought to count for something.

On Richard White's behalf, she went straight to the weaknesses in the crown's case. Purposely she avoided much reference to the identification evidence, intuiting that the cab driver's "momentary glimpse" of his attacker wasn't by itself enough to convict White. She analysed the uniformed policeman's testimony. Did it make sense, she asked, that White, who had been told earlier on the day of his arrest that he was charged with assault and robbery, would ask another policeman what he was charged with? And why, come to that, would White speak so frankly to a policeman at all? Especially to a policeman in uniform? And what about the wording of the policeman's question to White, "Did you get *the* money and *the* wallet?" Doesn't that sound suspect? Doesn't it smack of coaching?

"As to the identification of the accused," the judge said, giving his verdict as soon as Lindberg had finished, "it doesn't satisfy me beyond a reasonable doubt. However, I'm accepting the police officer's evidence. It goes beyond a reasonable doubt, and there'll be a conviction against the accused."

Lindberg asked that sentencing of White be put over until the following morning, and that night she read through earlier assault-robbery cases, checking the jail time that judges handed out in such crimes. It was heavy, usually more than the two years needed to send a man to the penitentiary. She made notes for her remarks to the judge, and around midnight she phoned White's mother.

"I'd like you to come to court tomorrow," Lindberg said.

"Can't help you," the mother answered.

"Look, I don't want you to testify or anything. I just want to be able to tell the judge you're sitting in court. Your son could go to the pen, and one thing that might keep him out is if the judge knows you care enough to come to court."

"Can't," the mother said. "We're moving to a new house tomorrow and it's gonna take all day."

Next morning in court, the judge seemed impatient, and Lindberg spoke quickly. Richard White is too young to be sent away to a penitentiary, she said, only nineteen. The most time he's ever done in jail until now is three months. This is his first violent crime. And he's already spent seven weeks in jail waiting for his trial. Lindberg got it all out, all her points, in a smooth, even rush of words.

"Twenty-two months," the judge said. Since the sentence was under two years, it would put White in a reformatory, not the pen.

Lindberg spoke briefly to White in the holding cells before he was taken away to begin his time.

"He didn't show any reaction," she said when she came out of the cells. "He *never* shows any reaction. But twenty-two months is a very good sentence."

Lindberg went back to her office, balancing her optimism.

"Working for people like Richard," she said, "I'm beginning to feel distanced from just about everybody else in the world. Like, my mother will read of a crime in the newpapers and say, oh, look at the horrible thing this person has done, and I think, well, that person could be my client. But I don't make judgments about the person, not about Richard or any of my clients. What happens is that when I'm somebody's lawyer and he's charged with a crime, I'm the most positive element in his life at that point. That means my relationship with him develops in good ways, and it becomes difficult for me to identify with the rest of society who think the forces of law and order are working for the common good and these other people, the criminals, are evil. That isn't necessarily true. The police don't always deal with my clients in straight ways. Look at Richard and the policeman who testified against him."

Lindberg's mind scurried between ideas. She's given to close analysis of her thoughts and emotions, and she was keen to put her reactions to the events and people of her lawyer's life — cases, trials, bail hearings, clients, cops, crown attorneys — in immaculate perspective.

"Most of my clients aren't entirely rational. Maybe if they were,

I'd find the work boring. My clients are people who act impulsively. They hardly ever sit down and plan what they're going to do. They just act, and it's always the things people do impulsively that get them in trouble. Those kinds of acts are never in a person's own best interests. So why do my clients pull these impulsive crimes? I'm fascinated to find out. I talk to them and ask questions and get involved. And I like it. My friends say to me, oh, you'll get over *that*. They think when I have an emotional response to my clients it's inappropriate and undesirable. They think I'll be happier when I get *over* these feelings. But there are things in life that I don't want to get over, and being fascinated by my clients is one of them."

Lindberg flashed back to Richard White. "What made me feel the worst all day about his case was telling him that his parents wouldn't be in court. Parents are always saying to me how much they love their children and then they don't show up in court to support the kids. It's common, but that doesn't make it any easier to tell a person like Richard that he's on his own."

Lindberg brightened.

"Twenty-two months, though, that's an okay sentence. I feel good about that."

Lindberg used two thousand dollars of the Royal Bank's loan to buy a second-hand car. It was a yellow Volks Beetle, and on a Monday morning in midsummer four days after she took possession of the car, she set off for the East Mall Courthouse, where she was to plead a client guilty to one charge of breaking and entering. The East Mall Courthouse is in the Etobicoke suburb of Toronto close to Highway 427, and as Lindberg came off 427 by way of an exit ramp, she saw a red light against her up ahead at the three-way intersection of the ramp and a four-lane main street. She pumped her foot on the brake. Nothing. The brake had failed. The pedal plunged to the floor, and the Beetle hurtled through the red light, past four lanes of oncoming traffic, and bounced over the curb on the far side of the main road. Lindberg was headed in a direct line for a brick house. The house's garage had wooden doors. Lindberg aimed for the garage. She crashed through the doors. Would there be a parked car on the other side? Lindberg braced herself. No parked car. But the garage was stacked with furniture and boxes. The Beetle crunched against them and came to rest in the litter. Lindberg checked herself.

Nothing broken or bruised. But she could hear a funny fluttering sound in the garage. She opened the Beetle's door and looked up. The garage was filled with frantic pigeons. They'd been nestling in cages hung from the ceiling until the Beetle disturbed their peace. Lindberg got out of the car and stood amid the crushed boxes, the fluttering pigeons, and the forlorn Beetle. She felt less like a lawyer and more like an extra from a Laurel and Hardy movie. She telephoned the police and a tow truck and hurried to the courthouse. Too late. Her client's case had been called, and when Lindberg failed to appear, he was remanded back into custody. Lindberg took a taxi downtown and ordered two fast drinks for lunch.

"It's so bad about my client," she said. "He's come up for sentencing four times already, and every time something happens to put it off. This, though, *this* was the worst."

Lindberg didn't feel an early mission to practise criminal law. When the call came, it arrived late, more or less out of the blue in her third year of law school. There seems to be a pattern in her life, she thinks, of apparently random choices that turn out to be definitive discoveries about herself.

She chose an arts course at Carleton University because, as someone who had grown up in many parts of Canada — Prince Albert, Saskatchewan; Sudbury in Northern Ontario; Toronto — she liked the notion of Ottawa's stability and tidiness. "But when I got there," she says, "everybody looked and acted like everybody else in the city. I discovered I can't stand uniformity." After two years of Carleton and a few months of bumming around South America, she chose the University of Toronto Law School. "But I hardly looked into the future. It wasn't until I took my articling year in the Ontario Attorney General's office that I knew I wanted criminal law. What I didn't enjoy was law school itself, and after I discovered my feelings about criminal, it was a relief to realize that it seemed to have been worth while taking law after all."

At the Attorney General's office, she worked on a complicated fraud case, the prosecution of a Mafia figure, a couple of murder trials, several appeals to the Ontario Court of Appeal, and three appeals to the Supreme Court of Canada. She absorbed a lot of law. "I didn't get much court experience of my own, but that was okay. The crown attorneys wanted me to become thoroughly familiar with the cases they were working on so that I could sit down with them and talk the cases through. That way, they could pick up on the holes and weaknesses in their prosecutions. And me, I was getting exposed to case law and statutes and interpretations and court strategy of all kinds."

It was this intense experience that helped Lindberg land a role in a high-profile trial a mere four months after her call to the bar. The work that came her way in the first weeks of practice was confined, as she expected, to cases like Richard White's and other relatively minor-league matters. But on a Monday in mid-August, a Toronto defence lawyer named Will Hechter took her on as his junior counsel in a case that was definitely major league.

"Caroline bowled me over," Hechter says. "I've never met anyone so young who has such a terrific knowledge of the law. Mention a legal point and she'll quote you a case. The other thing about her is that it was *she* who approached *me* about this job. She learned about it and phoned me and insisted that nobody else could handle it except her. I'd never heard of her before the call, but she talked her way on to the case."

The case, as it happened, was murder: Lindberg's first homicide trial.

On December 30, 1980, Gary Fitzgerald and Joe Schoenberger, eighteen and seventeen years old respectively, left their homes in Windsor, Ontario, in Schoenberger's 1974 Dodge Duster and headed for the Mattawa area in the most northerly tip of Southern Ontario, where, according to Fitzgerald's plan, they would steal some guns and sell them to raise money for a trip to Hawaii. "I hate cops," Fitzgerald said at a party before the trip, "and if one gets in my way, I'll kill him." The two reached George Richards' home near Mattawa on New Year's Day — Richards was a second cousin of Fitzgerald's — and later, about eleven p.m., while several other people in the house slept, they loaded the Duster with guns and knives that belonged to Richards and drove into the night. One of the weapons was an AR-7 Explorer semi-automatic twenty-two. Over the following few hours, Fitzgerald would use it to kill two men and wound a third.

Shortly after midnight the Duster pulled into the Ultramar Gas Bar in Emsdale, about seventy miles down Highway 11 from Mattawa. Chester Blackmore, the station's fifty-year-old attendant, pumped $16.01 in gas into the car's tank. Neither Fitzgerald nor Schoenberger had any money, and when Blackmore moved forward to collect his payment, Fitzgerald shot through the open window and hit Blackmore twice in the face.

The Duster sped further south on Highway 11 until an Ontario Provincial Police cruiser signalled it to pull over. Constable Richard Verdecchia, thirty-five and alone in the cruiser, hadn't heard about the shooting back in Emsdale. What attracted him to the Duster was its broken tail-light. He stepped out of his cruiser, and Fitzgerald shot him through the chest. Fitzgerald walked to the fallen body and fired three more shots in a cluster around Verdecchia's right eye.

Several more miles down Highway 11, OPP Constable Neil Hurtubise was next to spot the Duster's broken tail-light. Hurtubise, forty-five and also alone in his cruiser, knew of the Blackmore shooting and was aware that Verdecchia wasn't answering radio calls for some inexplicable reason, but he didn't associate the Duster with either Blackmore or Verdecchia. On foot, he approached the driver's side of the Duster. Fitzgerald opened fire.

"You don't have to shoot me!" Hurtubise screamed.

He turned back to the cruiser. Fitzgerald's shots caught Hurtubise in the side and the shoulder, neck and cheek. He stumbled to his car radio.

"Officer shot!" he called as the Duster pulled away. "Officer shot!"

Hurtubise's signal set off the largest police hunt in Ontario history. Several dozen officers, a fleet of cruisers, a helicopter, and a tracking dog named Max set after the car that Hurtubise described. Three hours later, police found it in the parking lot of the Sundial Motor Hotel on the outskirts of Orillia twenty-five miles south of the spot where Hurtubise was shot. The Duster was empty — apart from nine guns, some rounds of ammunition, four knives, and two bayonets. Max, the dog, caught a scent and led his masters down a nearby set of railroad tracks and across a field to Kerr's Auto Body Shop. Fitzgerald and Schoenberger were asleep in the back of a dilapidated Volkswagen van on the lot, Fitzgerald with the AR-7 Explorer beside him. The police woke and arrested the boys. It was 7:08 on the morning of January 2, 1981, barely eight hours from the time the two left George Richards' house in Mattawa.

The crown attorney's office charged both Fitzgerald and Schoenberger with first-degree murder in the killing of Constable Verdecchia because he was a policeman and with second-degree murder in the Chester Blackmore case. (The crown laid charges of attempted murder of Constable Hurtubise, then withdrew them; the charges would, however, resurface several months later.) The crown's case against Fitzgerald seemed open and shut; he had, as he admitted to the police with a touch of pride, fired all the shots from the AR-7 Explorer. But under a complicated section of the Criminal Code, Joe Schoenberger was equally guilty of murder if the crown could prove that he had aided or abetted in the shootings and knew or ought to have known that death would follow from Fitzgerald's actions.

Will Hechter thought he could head the crown off. Schoenberger's parents retained him to act for their son a few days after the shootings. Hechter was an energetic, friendly man in his late thirties who had entered private practice only six months earlier after experience as a crown attorney in both Winnipeg and Toronto, and he formed an early opinion about his new client from which he never wavered in the tough weeks ahead.

"I decided," he says, "that Joe had been nothing more than a boy who happened to be in the wrong place at the wrong time."

Schoenberger's background showed him to be a model teenager. No criminal record, solid student at school, popular among his peers. He held down a job in the shoe department of a Windsor store after school hours, and he played drums in the Scarlet Brigade, a local marching band that performed during the half-time show at the 1980 Grey Cup football game.

"Joe met Fitzgerald only a couple of months before the killings," Hechter says, "and somehow got caught up in his orbit. In the end, on the night of the murders, Joe was so afraid of Fitzgerald that he thought he might be the next victim."

Gary Fitzgerald's lawyer, a sleek, worldly defence counsel from Toronto named Clay Ruby, had a more complex, less appealing personality to deal with. Fitzgerald had been born the fourth illegitimate child of a twenty-one-year-old woman. He was adopted at fifteen months, but his adoptive parents, after a short period of lavishing Gary with affection, turned sour on him. They strapped and beat him, and in reaction, Gary, a loner, began to lie and steal and set fires. A school for emotionally disturbed adolescents diagnosed him as suffering from "a fear of being lost and abandoned." But he was a clever kid, manipulative, and he found a special satisfaction when he joined the Royal Canadian Service

Corps. "Fitzgerald," an army report said, "is a credit to his unit." Gary liked guns. He handled them expertly, and he developed into a crack shot.

"My guy's a psychopath," Ruby said after Fitzgerald had undergone a lengthy examination at the Clarke Institute of Psychiatry in Toronto. "The times he's truly happy are when he's killing somebody. His big regret in life, this eighteen-year-old kid, is that he missed fighting in the Vietnam War. He's ill, and he ought to be found not guilty by reason of insanity. But I don't know if we've got enough to meet the Criminal Code definition of insanity. He's not schizophrenic and he's not paranoid, which would meet the definition. He's a plain psychopath, which probably won't."

The trial of Fitzgerald and Schoenberger was held in Barrie, a small city sixty miles north of Toronto and the principal centre for the County of Simcoe, where the killings had taken place. Barrie's courthouse is a new building in gaudy red brick and has an abrupt and graceless look as if it had been put together from a Meccano set. Another building, ancient and grey, a miniature fortress, squats at the rear of the courthouse. It's the county jail, and from the time of the killings, it made a stern and forbidding home for Fitzgerald and Schoenberger, especially for Fitzgerald.

"Don't let that boy escape," Fitzgerald's adoptive mother had said, making a nervous joke to the guards on a day when she visited Gary.

The guards, all too aware that they had possibly the most notorious killer in Simcoe County history on their hands, took Mrs. Fitzgerald at her word. They locked Gary away from the other prisoners in solitary confinement, and he lived there, in "the hole," for several weeks until the end of his trial.

On the Tuesday after Labour Day, 1981, OPP officers patrolled the doors of Courtroom Number Four in the courthouse, checking everyone who entered with metal detectors, and inside, Mr. Justice MacLeod Craig of the Supreme Court of Ontario ordered the trial to begin. Craig, a brisk, balding, no-nonsense man in his late fifties, was a stickler for order and punctuality. ("When he says court will start at ten o'clock," Hechter said, "that means he'll be on the bench and impatient for us to get going at five *to* ten.") The judge came from Owen Sound, several miles northwest of Barrie, and in his youth he had been one of the town's finest hockey players. That gave him two points in common with the crown attorney, who was brought in from outside Simcoe

County to handle the prosecution. He was David Watt, a sandy-haired, deceptively nonchalant man in his early thirties. Watt, who made his reputation in the mid-1970s when he successfully argued the crown's side before the Ontario Court of Appeal and the Supreme Court of Canada in the sensational Peter Demeter murder case, was also a native son of Owen Sound and had been so accomplished at hockey that he played in the professional Central League during his years at law school. Watt and Craig spoke the same language.

In their company, the two defence counsel, Hechter and Ruby, seemed the outsiders, both from Toronto, both dark and Jewish, both clever and fast-talking. Hechter had misgivings about Craig's presiding at the trial because Craig had heard the defence's applications for bail and for a change of venue and had rejected them both. The two hearings meant that Craig was already aware of many details in the crown's case, possibly prejudicing him against the defence. Hechter considered a motion to ask that another judge be assigned to the case. But he abandoned the idea, and now, on the first Tuesday in September, he and Ruby sat in court ready to proceed. Hechter was flanked by his junior, Lindberg, and Ruby by his, an engagingly open young man named Michael Kamen. Schoenberger and Fitzgerald sat in the prisoner's box to the right of the defence table and behind a bullet-proof shield. Both were short and brown-haired and neatly dressed in shirt, tie, and suit. Schoenberger had small, pinched features. He wore glasses and a worried expression. Fitzgerald seemed relaxed, on the edges of boredom. He had baby-faced good looks and a pouty upper lip. When he grinned, his mouth glinted with the silver of the braces on his upper teeth. Neither boy's appearance suggested he was a killer.

Jury selection came first in the order of the trial's business, and from the start, it was a slow, painstaking process, mostly because the defence was wary of the wide-ranging publicity that the murders had received in Simcoe County. Would they find twelve local jurors, good and true, who could react impartially to Fitzgerald and Schoenberger? Hechter and Lindberg drew up a list of twenty test questions that they put to the prospective jurors. Had they contributed to the fund for Chester Blackmore's family? Did they or their relatives attend the dance held in support of Constable Hurtubise? The questions also tried to pin down the prospective jurors' biases. Would they find a police officer's evidence more credible than that of other witnesses? As the defence worried along the selection process, Watt was at the same time indicating the sort of jury that the crown aimed at. He rejected for jury service a psychiatric social worker, another woman who counselled mentally retarded adults, even a chef who was retired from the kitchens at a mental institution. Watt, it was clear, wanted no one on the jury who might be versed in psychological concepts. The selection ground through two and a half days, and 103 members of the jury panel were examined by the counsel before seven women and five men were finally agreed on late Friday morning.

"In some ways the jury stuff was my favourite part of the trial," Lindberg said later. "Will let me take some of the questioning of the jurors, and it was the first time I'd stood up in my gown in a courtroom before a Supreme Court justice."

The rest of Lindberg's duties took place more behind the scenes. She had worked on research from the Monday three weeks before the beginning of the trial when Hechter hired her, digging out the relevant case law on the issues that Hechter expected to come up during the trial — the use of character evidence, areas of duress, the relationship between parties to an offence, crown disclosures. Lindberg prepared long memos of law for Hechter on all the points. And when the jury selection ended and the crown began calling its witnesses, she took up another part of a junior counsel's slogging work — making notes of the witnesses' testimony.

"Damn near verbatim," Hechter says. "If she hadn't written down the testimony in such amazing detail, I don't think I'd have been as successful as I was in cross-examination. That turned out to be crucial."

Watt summoned a parade of witnesses to the stand — arresting officers, experts in forensic medicine, fingerprint experts, pathologists, George Richards and his Mattawa friends, teenagers from Windsor who had heard Fitzgerald's talk of shooting policemen who got in his way. "The crown's calling everybody except Max the tracking dog," Hechter said during a recess one day in the second week of the trial. Watt needed the witnesses. Since no one had been an on-the-scene observer of the two shootings, his evidence was entirely circumstantial, but by patching together a meticulously detailed account of the events of those late December and early January days, by drawing from many witnesses details that blended into a complete picture, he intended to demonstrate for the jury that Fitzgerald, with Schoenberger's knowing aid, had coolly and rationally gunned down Chester Blackmore and Richard Verdecchia.

Watt marshalled his witnesses, and as they testified, Hechter, on cross-examination, began to push his own interpretation of events. He would put space between Schoenberger and Fitzgerald. Fitzgerald was the killer — no one, not even Fitzgerald's own counsel, would dispute that fact — and Schoenberger was the unfortunate bystander, the unwilling sidekick, a captive, even a potential victim. The two, Fitzgerald and Schoenberger, were as different as night and day, as black and white, as guilty and innocent.

"What sort of person is Joe Schoenberger?" Hechter asked one of the crown's witnesses, a teenager named John Alp, who was one of the Schoenberger-Fitzgerald crowd back in Windsor.

"A great guy."

"Well, what about this talk of stealing guns up north?"

"That was Fitzgerald blowing off his mouth," Alp answered. "Fitzgerald was the only one who talked about robbery."

Hechter pulled similar testimony in his cross-examination of Kathy Renaud, another Windsor teenager, but it was Clay Ruby's cross-examination of Renaud that, paradoxically, gave Hechter much stronger material. Ruby was upset at Renaud because she had refused to discuss her evidence with him in advance outside the courtroom.

"Why wouldn't you talk to me?" Ruby asked her as she stood in the witness-box.

"I don't think I should defend a person who would kill anybody," Renaud answered. "I don't think Joe would kill anybody, but Gary would have."

Hechter could hardly keep the smile off his face.

The crown's witnesses gave Hechter the chance, too, to remind the jury that it was Fitzgerald who was the crack shot with guns, that it was Fitzgerald who loved to shoot rifles, that it was Fitzgerald who had acted so murderously on the night of January 2. Always Fitzgerald. Not Schoenberger. Put the space between them. Who was it, Hechter asked one of the arresting OPP officers, who led police to Verdecchia's body? The answer came: Fitzgerald. It was Fitzgerald, not Schoenberger, who knew where Verdecchia's body had been hidden — in a snow bank — after Fitzgerald had pumped the bullets into it.

Sometimes Hechter's small, but telling, victories on cross-examination came through pieces of instant good fortune. When Watt was leading a young woman from Mattawa through her examination-in-chief — a woman who owned one of the guns stolen from George Richards' house — Michael Kamen leaned across the defence counsel's table to Hechter and told him that Fitzgerald had once gone hunting with the woman. "Was Fitzgerald a good marksman?" Hechter asked her on cross-examination. "Out with me," the woman answered, "he shot a rabbit through the head from fifty yards." Hechter glanced at the jury as if to check that they had grasped the point, and later, with another witness, he brought out testimony that Schoenberger, by constrast, was just a city boy who'd never fired a gun in his life. The point had been made — and underlined.

As the trial proceeded, as Watt built his case of circumstantial evidence and as Hechter countered with his cross-examination, life in Barrie for the Toronto lawyers settled into a rhythm. The trial lasted from ten each morning until late in the afternoon. Afterwards the lawyers retreated to their hotel rooms to review the day's evidence and plan cross-examinations for the next day. Dinner tended to be late and leisurely. Ruby, a gourmet who maintains a lovingly selected wine cellar at his home in Toronto, invariably ate at the Lafayette, Barrie's single claim to elegant dining, while the others usually scattered to the city's more humble restaurants. Sometimes all of them would take in a movie, sometimes they'd go to the trotting races, and sometimes Lindberg and Kamen would finish the evening over drinks with the Ontario Provincial Police officers, who were, they agreed, a friendlier bunch that either the Toronto cops or the RCMP.

"Good case like this," an OPP investigator on the Chester Blackmore case said in a bar one night, "it gets you lots of overtime. Me and the wife are gonna take a trip to Acapulco in February on what I'm makin' here."

Everybody at the table laughed.

"What happens at a big murder trial," Kamen said later, "is that everybody develops a kind of macabre streak. It's better that way, better than thinking about all the dead people."

Fitzgerald stories yielded many of the dark laughs in Barrie. There were a couple of new tales each day, sometimes ghoulish, sometimes merely amazing.

"When Fitzgerald was in the Clarke seeing the psychiatrists," Ruby said at lunch one day, "he phoned an old girlfriend in

Windsor. The girl's mother answered and said the girl couldn't come to the phone. 'She's sick,' the mother said. 'Things aren't that good with me either,' Fitzgerald said to her. Now is *that* a blasé kid?"

"Listen to this, it's unbelievable," Kamen said. "That time when the police pathologist was testifying and he said that Blackmore was shot twice in the face, Gary called me over to the prisoner's box, and he said, 'Not twice in the face. I got him *three* times.' He was so pissed off because he thought the pathologist wasn't giving him enough credit as a good shot."

The woman whom the lawyers nicknamed the "Religious Lady" was another source of black humour. She was a handsome, middle-aged woman from the nearby village of Severn Falls, and she'd developed a strange fascination with Fitzgerald. She attended every day of the trial, holding her Bible and occasionally dragging along her husband, a gent whose obvious lack of comfort in the alien courtroom suggested he'd rather be home in Severn Falls. The woman dispatched notes to Fitzgerald, notes of affection and faith and hope. "I love you," she wrote in several of her missives. A couple of times during court recesses she dropped to her knees in prayer, and whenever Fitzgerald entered the prisoner's box, she offered him tiny waves and reassuring smiles.

"She isn't the only one," Kamen said. "At the Clarke, there was a nurse who fell in love with Gary. She wrote him letters after he was sent back here to the Barrie jail. She told him he should escape and run off to Australia with her. The Clarke finally let her go."

"Every big trial gets its own groupies," Lindberg said. "I always see little old ladies at rape cases in Toronto, and any time a bunch of bikers are on trial, that's when you get the adolescent girls. They go crazy."

Lindberg was beginning to feel borderline crazy herself. She couldn't shake a discouraging cold she caught not long after the trial got under way, and she had mixed emotions about leaving behind clients in Toronto. One boy whom she'd previously defended on a break-and-enter charge in the city had left a message at her office; he was charged with two more break-and-enters and wanted Lindberg to defend him. "Hey," she said, pleased at the recognition of her skills, "I'm starting to get repeaters." She was anxious to return to her own clients, but she appreciated the value of the Barrie experience. And she also saw her role as Hechter's junior beginning to shift and change.

"Support seems to be a lot of my job now," she said. "Making things tolerable for the senior counsel. In Will's case, that means reassuring him at the end of the day that his cross-examination made the right points or that his objection to something Craig said would set up the basis for a possible appeal later on. Maybe I'm not the ideal person for that job. I'd prefer just to discuss the issues, but with Will, when I bring up a point, to me it'll be the beginning of the discussion, whereas he'll take it as my conclusion."

Back in court, after Watt had put in the case for the crown, Ruby called witnesses in Fitzgerald's defence. Ruby wasn't challenging the evidence that his client had fired the death shots. His point was that Fitzgerald was insane at the time of the murders, that he was so mentally ill that he could not, in the language of the Criminal Code, "appreciate the nature and quality of his acts." To establish the point, Ruby relied on three witnesses: two psychiatrists and a psychologist who had independently examined Fitzgerald over a period of several weeks. The first psychiatrist told the court that the shootings were no more than "a technical exercise" to the boy. The second psychiatrist testified that Fitzgerald had told him, "I enjoy shooting faces off." He labelled Fitzgerald "unpredictably dangerous." And the psychologist said that "Fitzgerald gave the killings no more thought than brushing his teeth." The boy, he concluded, "has one of the most severe personality disorders I've ever seen."

Watt chose to attack one of the psychiatrists on cross-examination, belittling the tests he'd given to Fitzgerald. He picked up one of the psychiatrist's Rorschach tests and suggested it was of value only as a kind of parlour game.

Ruby got to his feet.

"Perhaps Mr. Watt could tell us what he sees in the test," he said, "and then we'll know if it works."

"I see ink blots, Mr. Ruby," Watt said.

"Well, that says a good deal about you, Mr. Watt," Ruby said and sat down, smiling.

Watt was not amused. Neither was Craig.

At the end of the first psychiatrist's testimony-in-chief, Hechter stood up to question him.

"Mr. Hechter," Craig asked, "are you requesting the right to cross-examine this witness?

Hechter looked stunned.

"M'lord," he said, "in cases where there are two accused, counsel for one accused has an *absolute* right to cross-examine witnesses called by the co-accused."

Craig hesitated, and Watt came to everyone's aid.

"I'm satisfied that the authorities support Mr. Hechter, m'lord," he said.

"Go ahead, Mr. Hechter," Craig said.

Hechter sent Watt a glance of gratitude and proceeded to score value points for Schoenberger in his cross-examination of the psychiatrist.

"Is Mr. Fitzgerald a person who's capable of acting suddenly and impulsively?" he asked the psychiatrist.

The answer came easily. Yes, the psychiatrist said, Fitzgerald would go off on his own tangent. He'd follow whatever impulse seized him. Hechter pushed forward another step. Would the presence of another person, someone like Schoenberger, make any difference in Fitzgerald's actions? Hardly, the psychiatrist answered. Well, could someone in Schoenberger's position *anticipate* what Fitzgerald's next act might be? No, the psychiatrist answered again, and his responses were echoed when Hechter put the same questions to the second psychiatrist and the psychologist. Hechter felt confident that he'd set the picture for the jury: Schoenberger could have had no advance warning that this crazy, unpredictable Fitzgerald was going to shoot Blackmore and Verdecchia.

Hechter called his own witnesses, all of them character witnesses who spoke to Schoenberger's past and the promise he showed for the future. "Joey's always been a good boy," his mother testified. Would Mrs. Schoenberger take her son back into the family home, Hechter asked. "Any time," the mother answered and burst into tears. Three of Schoenberger's schoolteachers and an old family friend took their turns in the witness-box and spelled out Schoenberger's history as an above-average student, a religious kid who attended church with his parents, a diligent worker, a responsible boy. They were baffled, they said, by his involvement in these killings. It wasn't in character for the boy they knew.

Hechter and Lindberg had been debating all through the trial over the wisdom and necessity of using one more defence witness — Schoenberger himself. In the early days they leaned in favour of calling him, but as Watt put in his case, as Hechter winkled favourable testimony out of the crown's witnesses and Ruby's psychiatrists, opinion on the value of Schoenberger's testimony began to switch. "I look at the evidence," Hechter said as the deadline for a decision on Schoenberger's testimony approached, "and I don't think the crown has proved anything that Joe needs to answer." There was another consideration in keeping Schoenberger out of the box — if he testified, Watt might upset him on cross-examination. "Joe's got a lot of explaining to do," Lindberg said. "How well will he stand up to Watt's questions? Watt can get very biting and sarcastic." Hechter made a choice. "It isn't a close enough case," he said. "We don't need him as a witness." He and Lindberg put the option to Schoenberger. To testify or not to testify — the ultimate decision had to be his. Schoenberger made up his mind quickly. He opted out of facing the jury, the courtroom, and Watt's inevitable questions. He elected to remain silent, and late on Friday morning, September 25, with the last of his character witnesses, Hechter closed the case for the defence.

Craig adjourned over the weekend, and on Monday morning, at a few minutes past ten o'clock, counsel made their final addresses to the jury. Ruby went first. "This is a dangerous boy," he began, speaking of Fitzgerald, and for almost thirty minutes, sounding more passionate than he had in all the days of the trial, Ruby argued that, of the two places to which the jury's verdict could ultimately send Fitzgerald, he belonged, not in a penitentiary, but in a hospital for the criminally insane. To place him in a hospital, he said, was "the humane verdict of the two and such a little thing to ask." He reviewed the facts of the killings and described the person who had done them as "a broken item. He needs to be mended. Common sense says a man who kills this way can't be sane. These are insane crimes." He acknowledged that public pressure leaned toward conviction of murder and a life sentence in prison. But the jurors, he said, "should abandon vengeance and intolerance." Besides, Ruby finished, pointing to the braces that Fitzgerald wore on his teeth, this was a very young person whose fate the jury held. "He is," Ruby said, "a boy." Next day, one of the newspaper accounts of his address would describe it as "compelling."

Hechter launched into his address as soon as Ruby sat down. "By the time my turn at the jury came," he said later, "I felt pumped up. Usually I'm nervous, but this time I had the nerves two days earlier. In court, I was feeling so psyched. Almost high." He spoke for forty-five minutes and didn't miss a detail or a nuance. He hit his theme early in the address: "Joe Schoenberger may be naive, but he is not a killer." He dissected the crown's case and concluded that it established just one fact — that Schoenberger was present when the killings took place. It proved no involvement on Schoenberger's part, no complicity, no acquiescence. Schoenberger was "guilty of something — bad judgment." But that failure exhausted his guilt. There was no evidence, Hechter emphasized, that Schoenberger aided or abetted or assisted or encouraged the crimes, nor was there evidence that he knew or ought to have known that Fitzgerald would shoot the two victims. He asked for an acquittal on both charges that Schoenberger faced. "Please," Hechter said, "send this boy back to his family."

Hechter felt confident when he sat down. "I was exhausted," he said later. "I'd lost eight pounds during the trial. But I sensed a strong rapport with the jury all the time I was talking. I got good facial expressions from them." Lindberg agreed. "Juror number six, the youngest woman, did you see her?" she asked Hechter. "Number six had tears in her eyes when you were speaking. If somebody's looking for signs, tears are positive."

Watt, speaking last, concentrated on tearing down the defence counsel's two main arguments — that Fitzgerald was insane and that Schoenberger was an unwitting passenger in the adventure. Fitzgerald, he told the jury, was "crazy like a fox." He was using insanity as a means of escaping justice. "Don't be fooled by such a manipulator," Watt said. And don't treat the trial as "a morality play that should decide whether Fitzgerald would be better off in a mental hospital." As for Schoenberger, Watt pointed out that he knew of Fitzgerald's plans to steal guns and commit robberies and that he supplied the car which made Fitzgerald's plans possible. Schoenberger, he said, "wasn't just along for the ride. . . . He was a helpful and willing tool." Watt wanted convictions on both counts for both boys.

Craig set aside the next day, Tuesday, for his instructions to the jury. "Now he's going to give it to you and me," Ruby said to Hechter that morning. "We haven't been humble enough in this trial." Craig's wife was in court for her husband's performance and so were thirty-nine students from an Orillia high school. "Don't be moved by sympathy for the accused," Craig told the jury as he began the address shortly after ten o'clock. "And don't consider what institution is proper for Fitzgerald." Then he commenced a lengthy recapitulation and analysis of the evidence. He was thorough to a fault, and for some in the courtroom, the fault appeared to be boredom. "I've never seen such a restless jury," Hechter said during a morning recess. The Orillia high school teacher took advantage of the recess to lead his students out of the courtroom and back to class. Craig pressed on. His instructions lasted for almost five hours, the only break in the monologue coming in a testy confrontation that Ruby precipitated before the jury returned to the courtroom after a recess in the afternoon.

"M'lord," Ruby said, speaking in his lickety-split style, "I must point out that in your instructions when you talked of the psychiatric evidence in the crown's favour, your voice was bright and lively, but when you talked about the defence of Fitzgerald's insanity, your voice fell off."

"I don't go for that stuff," Craig answered, clearly angered at Ruby's criticism.

He resumed his charge. "A jury," he said, "stands between the public and people who commit crimes." And finally he was finished. The clock showed a few minutes after four, and the jury was excused to begin their decision-making.

Life over the next few days turned into a grind for the jury. Craig ordered them sequestered in a hotel until they reached a verdict, but the International Ploughing Matches had begun in Barrie that week, and the city didn't have an empty hotel room to spare, let alone twelve of them. The jurors had to spend their nights forty miles away in Collingwood, and each morning, sheriff's officers bussed them back to Barrie to continue their deliberations in the courthouse. "Maybe the idea of all that travelling will make them come in with a fast verdict," Lindberg said. It didn't. The jury deliberated through Tuesday afternoon, all day Wednesday, and into Thursday morning. Their agony was reflected in the number of times — seven — that they returned to the courtroom for further instructions from Craig on specific points. The speculation among defence counsel was that the jury had arrived at an early decision on Fitzgerald and was puzzling over Schoenberger's fate. But no one could know for a certainty.

"The jury's got a verdict."

It was the sheriff's officer on duty outside Courtroom Number Four who broke the news at five minutes past two o'clock on Thursday afternoon to Hechter, Lindberg, and Kamen as the three were returning from lunch. Ruby was in Toronto arguing a case before the Court of Appeal. Hechter and Lindberg took their seats in the courtroom while Kamen hurried to the holding cells on the floor below the courtroom. Fitzgerald and Schoenberger were in separate cells several feet apart but facing one another. Both knew that the jury was ready for them. Fitzgerald reached a hand through the bars of his cell in Schoenberger's direction. "Hey Joe," he said, "good luck."

Craig took his place on the bench at 2:20 and the jury filed in. The court clerk asked the foreman of the jury, a dapper, solemn man named Stewart Christie, for the verdicts on Fitzgerald.

On the first count, second-degree murder of Chester Blackmore. "Guilty," said Christie.

The only sound in the courtroom came from the "Religious Lady" of Severn Falls, who let out a small groan.

On the second count, first-degree murder of Richard Verdecchia. "Guilty."

The clerk asked for the jury's verdicts in Schoenberger's cases. On the first count.

"Not guilty," Christie said.

"The moment between Christie's words on the first count and the second count," Lindberg said later, "were the most tense of the whole trial. Joe could walk. He could go free. There was hope after the first count. But maybe the jury was going to make a saw-off — acquit him on the first count and find him guilty of something on the second. The tension stretched. Really tight."

On the second count, the first-degree murder of Constable Richard Verdecchia.

"Not guilty," Stewart Christie said.

A rush of wind seemed to fill the courtroom, as if everyone in it had simultaneously gasped in air. Schoenberger leaned over the rail of the prisoner's box and hugged Hechter. He took off his glasses, rubbed his eyes, and grinned in the direction of his parents. The Schoenbergers, with tears and laughs, were hugging one another.

Craig called for order — "That's enough," he said — and when Hechter asked that his client be discharged from custody, the judge fixed a stern look on Schoenberger.

"All I can say to you, Schoenberger," he said, "is that you are a very fortunate young man, and you are free to go."

In the corridor outside the courtroom, the crush of reporters, TV cameramen, and radio interviewers waving microphones was so dense that the Simcoe County sheriff talked of invoking the

Riot Act. "I was naive," Schoenberger said over and over to reporters. "I guess I'll have to be a better judge of friends." He had lost his worried look. He was free and ecstatic. But neither his freedom nor his ecstasy would last. Hechter knew there was more grief ahead for Schoenberger.

"David Watt had told me a couple of days earlier," Hechter says, "that if by some miracle Schoenberger was acquitted, there'd be new charges laid against him. Watt was opposed to it, but the Simcoe crown attorney, John Murphy, wanted to get Schoenberger. To me, it was bad taste and sour grapes."

Back in the courtroom, while the press conference raged outside, Craig asked Fitzgerald if he wished to speak before sentence was passed on him.

"I view my conviction as a small obstacle in being helped and possibly changing," Fitzgerald said in the silence of the courtroom. "All I can do now is move forward."

It was the first time most of the people in the room — judge, jury, and spectators — had heard Fitzgerald speak. His voice came as a shock. It made a small, high-pitched sound. Ruby had been right — Fitzgerald was, after all, just a boy. Craig sentenced him to life in prison without possibility of parole for twenty-five years, and the guards took him from the courtroom.

"I don't feel anything," Fitzgerald said a few minutes later when Michael Kamen visited him briefly in the cells. "I should feel something, but I don't."

"That's the same thing Gary told me months ago," Kamen said later. "Right after the killings, back in January when I first talked to him, he said, 'I don't feel anything.' He knew he was supposed to. He knew something was wrong. But he couldn't find it inside himself."

Upstairs in the courthouse, Murphy, the Simcoe crown, led Schoenberger into his office and laid a fresh charge against him for the attempted murder of Neil Hurtubise, the OPP constable who survived Fitzgerald's shooting spree. Schoenberger was taken back to the county jail while Hechter, furious and raising his voice as he never had in the courtroom, railed at Murphy.

"This is goddamned cruel," he said.

"We'll give your man bail in a couple of days," Murphy said, a cool, unmovable customer.

"A couple of *days*?" Hechter shouted. "I want him out now!"

Hechter, Lindberg, and Kamen walked the two blocks to their hotel, where they gathered in Hechter's room and drank champagne and beer.

"What are we celebrating?" Kamen said at one point. "Joe's still in jail."

"Listen," Hechter said, "just don't leave me. I don't feel like being alone right now."

Hechter put in a few calls to Murphy's office, and by late afternoon the two men arrived at an agreement on bail. Schoenberger would be released immediately to his parents on a $25,000 bond.

"That's it," Hechter said to the others. "We can leave Barrie behind."

Among the three of them, the Toronto lawyers had only one car. It was Lindberg's Volkswagen, the infamous Beetle with the quirky brakes.

"Oh my god," Hechter said. "I can see the newspaper headlines now: 'Client Acquitted. Defence Team Wiped Out in Car Accident.'"

The brakes held up, and the three, feeling giddy, whooped and hollered and shouted their way back to Toronto.

"You know what?" Kamen said in a brief sombre moment on the ride. "The jury made a trade-off. They convicted Gary and then they could give themselves a pat on the back for letting Joe go free."

Lindberg delivered the two men to their homes. Kamen made a sandwich and watched film reports of the trial on three different television networks. At Hechter's apartment, his wife had baked a welcome-home cake, and he, too, watched the TV reports. Lindberg went out to dinner with a friend. She didn't bother with television.

"Why should I see it on TV?" she said. "I was right there when it all happened."

The Monday after the end of the Barrie trial began too early for Lindberg.

"I learned something," she said later. "Which is that if someone comes to your door at eight in the morning, don't answer, because who else could it be except the police. This cop served me with a summons for the time my car went through the garage door out by Highway 427. It's crazy. They've charged me with careless driving."

Later in the morning she went to Family Court to look after a case for one of the lawyers in Hechter's office. A mother had taken her thirteen-year-old son on a shop-lifting expedition at a Woolco store. The mother had been convicted in Provincial Court. Now it was the son's turn.

"He's a good kid," Lindberg said to the crown before the case was called. "He really is. Goes to school and has no previous record. The mother's already got a conviction. The best thing is to let the kid go and you'll probably never have him back here again."

Her sweet good sense persuaded the crown, and the thirteen-year-old left the court still without a record. Lindberg left with the feeling that she, too, would never return to the Family Court building.

"Anything to do with family law doesn't interest me," she said. "I'm a defence counsel."

That night, Lindberg and Michael Kamen went to *True Confessions*, a film that gives a gritty, funny, insider's view of relations between cops and hoods and lawyers. Kamen came out of the movie feeling exuberant.

"The movie is exactly the way it is in that kind of environment," he said. "Like, the most exciting part of the Barrie trial for me was when we smuggled the eggrolls in to Joe Schoenberger. This happened on the last Wednesday night. Caroline and I were out for a Chinese meal, and I remembered something Joe once said about the two things he missed most in jail were sex and Chinese food. I was thinking he's up there eating a lousy prison dinner and maybe tomorrow he's going to hear a verdict that'll send him away for twenty-five years. He ought to have his Chinese. So we got the eggrolls in to him, and I had this funny thrill about pulling a stunt like that."

"The part of the Barrie experience that was the best for me," Lindberg said, "was understanding the personal pressures that trial lawyers have to handle. For starters, we had this eighteen-year-old client who could go down for life or he could walk. Then you add a bunch of other pressures."

She ticked them off.

"The fact that it was a policeman who was killed. The fact that the press was constantly looking over our shoulders. And the fact that we were working in Barrie, away from our normal Toronto situation. All those things, they could destroy you."

Lindberg thought it over.

"What I learned," she said, "is I have to develop a resistance to the stresses of this business. I don't want to be one of those counsel who gets an ulcer and dies young."

Later in the autumn, the Barrie crown attorney laid more charges against Joe Schoenberger: accessory after the fact in murder of Chester Blackmore, accessory after the fact in the murder of Richard Verdecchia, and breaking and entering and theft in connection with the removal of the weapons from George Richards' house in Mattawa.

"We may be in court for a long time," Will Hechter said.

On December 23, 1981, Lindberg appeared in Etobicoke's East Mall Courthouse to stand trial on the careless-driving charge. Her lawyer was Mark Kerbel, an associate of Hechter's, and Lindberg was her own star witness. She was uneasy as she gave testimony, and afterwards she said, "It's so much more natural for me to be a counsel than a witness."

The judge dismissed the charge.

Late in January 1982, a leading Toronto defence lawyer named Harry Doan hired Lindberg to act as his junior in a murder case. The crown was alleging that the accused man, Doan's client, had killed a fifty-year-old prostitute, stuffed her body in a blue steamer trunk, sold her collection of Royal Doulton figurines, and fled to Scranton, Pennsylvania.

"I like this case," Lindberg said. "In the Barrie trial, all I got to do in court was examine the prospective jurors. In this one, Harry says I'll be taking some of the witnesses through their testimony. That's good. I'm getting closer to a real criminal counsel's work."

CHAPTER 3

JOE SEDGWICK AND
THE OTTAWA SPY

PROBABLY HE SPOKE the simile a hundred times in his life. A thousand times. Joe Sedgwick was a story-teller of the old school, never tiring of a good line, willing to polish and refine it, intuiting the optimum moment to drop it into a speech or conversation, calculating its risible impact.

"A counsel is like a loaded blunderbuss," he used to say. "Your opponent hires him and he blows your brains out or you hire him and he blows your opponent's brains out."

He would laugh, guttural and merry, a Sidney Greenstreet laugh.

"A client's best advice is to hire counsel and then keep his mouth shut," he might go on. "No sense having a dog and barking yourself."

All this was delivered in a voice with the timbre of Churchill's. Even in his retreating years — Sedgwick was eighty-three when he died on December 27, 1981 — the voice kept its rolling, mellifluous quality. Even after the operation for throat cancer in 1974, it remained a cathedral of a voice. And the laugh, that glorious rumble, made a proper mate for the voice.

Joe Sedgwick liked the Queen and horse races and Teacher's Scotch topped off with Apollinaris. He liked bow-ties and after-dinner speaking and the Conservative Party, the Anglican Church and trains and the portrait of himself that hangs in Campbell House, the 1833 Georgian home in downtown Toronto where members of the Advocates' Society take lunches of chops and wine and trifle and talk of the fun and triumphs of their court-room lives. The Advocates' Society is restricted to lawyers whose practices are at least mainly litigious. It was founded in 1964. Sedgwick gave the money, five thousand dollars, that began the fund to preserve and restore Campbell House. He liked the Advocates' Society. He liked the view from the bedroom of his widower's apartment on the thirty-fourth floor of the Manulife Centre in midtown Toronto, a vista south over the skyscrapers to the islands and the summer sailboats. He liked bridge, poker, the military, Chesterton, and his grandchildren. But, most of all, he liked to laugh.

When Sedgwick, in his courtroom prime through the 1940s, '50s, and '60s, used to arrive by train in Ottawa to argue appeals before the Supreme Court of Canada, his suite at the Château Laurier became the unofficial clubroom to all the counsel in town for the Supreme Court sittings. Sedgwick poured drinks. Tensions eased. Sedgwick told stories. Counsel's minds drifted away from their briefs. Sedgwick laughed. So did everyone.

"My great friend Jack Cartwright has always been the very epitome of courtesy," Sedgwick used to say, launching one of his favourite stories about the Honourable J. R. Cartwright, a Justice on the Supreme Court of Canada from 1949 and its Chief Justice from October 3, 1967, to March 20, 1970, when he retired. "Jack is a gentleman. Isn't he *just*. But, you know, there was a single occasion when Jack was seen to display some unkindness. That distinguished but ponderous counsel, Matthews, was before Jack's court arguing a combines case and he was going on in a very dull and long-winded fashion. Jack kept his patience for an hour or so but finally he interrupted Matthews.

" 'May I ask, Mr. Matthews, if this is the nub of your argument?' And Jack outlined Matthews' point in a very few clear sentences.

" 'Yes, m'lord,' Matthews said. 'That is certainly my point.'

" 'Thank you, Mr. Matthews,' Jack said 'I just wanted to know what to do with my mind while you are talking.' "

Sedgwick's laugh and his stories and his availability brought him friends and acquaintances by the lineup. He was one of those men who seem effortlessly to brush up against history. Somehow he found himself next to famous people. When he began to practise law in Toronto in the early 1920s, he took on his first articling student. The young man passed his spare time in Sedgwick's office writing short stories. He was Morley Callaghan. When Sedgwick joined the Ontario Attorney General's Office for eight years, 1929 to 1937, he assisted in the prosecutions of Tim Buck, charged with the then crime of membership in the Communist Party, and of David Meisner, charged with kidnapping John Labatt, the beer tycoon. Buck got five years, Meisner fifteen. In 1935, Sedgwick and David Croll, then the Ontario Minister of Municipal Affairs, put together the Dionne Quintuplets Protection Act and used it to negotiate a series of commercial deals for the girls. "We made them a million bucks," Sedgwick said. "Without us, they'd have been robbed blind." In 1937, Sedgwick was fired from the Attorney General's Office when Mitchell Hepburn, the Ontario premier, who was given to unexplained purges, cleared house of Croll, Sedgwick, and company. "Mitch phoned me years afterwards when he was out of office," Sedgwick later said. "He wanted a favour. Mitch remembered me all right."

So did they all, Callaghan and Buck and the Dionnes. So did Jack Kent Cooke and Charlotte Whitton. Sedgwick defended the two, successfully, when the Province of Alberta charged them with criminal libel as a result of a story that Whitton, later the mayor of Ottawa, wrote about an Alberta child-adoption system in *Liberty* magazine, which was owned by Cooke, later a California sports tycoon. When Canadians with recognizable names and significant connections got into trouble, Sedgwick was summoned to the scene. In one case, he defended Morris Shumiatcher, a prominent Prairies lawyer and Tommy Douglas's number one advisor during his years as premier of Saskatchewan, and in another case, he acted for Ralph Farris, Vancouver businessman and brother of the Chief Justice of the British Columbia Supreme Court. Sedgwick sued Pierre Trudeau and his Minister of Energy, Joe Greene, on behalf of Steve Roman, the president of Denison Mines, who was sore at the federal government for blocking the sale of a piece of his company. As a personal favour to another prime minister, Lester Pearson, Sedgwick took on a tough chore in 1965, conducting a federal inquiry into the country's immigration policies. A third prime minister, John Diefenbaker, was for a while Sedgwick's *bête noire*.

"Oh, John was all right," Sedgwick said, the lifelong Tory. "He was a loner and that made him difficult. He said he'd put me in the Senate, which I would have enjoyed, but he got cross at me over some imagined slight and never followed through. We were at odds until the day I went up to him and said, 'John, we've known each other for too many years to carry on in such an undignified manner.' This was at [former Ontario premier] Les Frost's funeral, and John and I patched things up."

Sedgwick's conversations were punctuated with the names of his many prominent friends. One of these was Tom Fogden, president of Gilbey's Gin, who went to Sedgwick in the spring of 1946 with a case that will perhaps be remembered as Sedgwick's monument. Fogden's brother-in-law — Fogden's wife's sister's husband — was in trouble. His name was Eric Adams. He was thirty-nine years old in 1946, a man with the suave good looks and tidy moustache of a William Powell. Adams had a degree in electrical engineering from McGill and an M.B.A. from Harvard. Through the 1930s he worked in Montreal for Cockfield Brown Advertising Agency, in the office of the assistant to the president of the CPR, and for a firm of consulting engineers, Coverdale & Colpitts, in New York City. In November 1940 he was summoned to Ottawa to handle a series of assignments for the Foreign Exchange Control Board and the Bank of Canada. Both bodies placed him on loan to various agencies, and he held jobs with the Wartime Requirements Board, the War Inventions Board, the National Selective Service, the Department of Finance, and, beginning in January 1945, the Industrial Development Bank in Montreal. The jobs put him close to the upper reaches of the civil service in wartime Ottawa. He came into contact with mandarins like Norman Robertson, Under-Secretary of State for External Affairs. He sat on committees. He was privy to crucial decisions. He occupied a position of trust and delicacy. And through it all, during his long wartime service in high places, Eric Adams may have been, as the Canadian government now claimed and as Tom Fogden told Joe Sedgwick, a spy for Russia.

Igor Gouzenko began the fuss when he walked out of the Russian Embassy in Ottawa on the evening of September 5, 1945, with 109 documents buttoned inside his shirt. Gouzenko was officially listed at the embassy as secretary and interpreter to Colonel Nicolai Zabotin, who was, in turn, officially listed as military attaché, but Gouzenko served in fact and deed as cipher clerk for Zabotin, who was nothing less than the Soviet's head of Military Intelligence in Canada. Gouzenko and his family were scheduled for return to Moscow in the fall of 1945. However, having grown accustomed to a democratic and congenial lifestyle after their years in Ottawa, they elected to defect, and Gouzenko took along the 109 documents which, he knew, revealed the existence of nine rings of Canadian spies maintained by Zabotin. The rings included several men and women in Canada's civil service. *That*, Gouzenko figured, ought to catch Ottawa's attention.

At first he met rejection. On the night of September 5 and early the following morning, the *Ottawa Journal*, the Ministry of Justice, the RCMP, and Ottawa's crown attorney all turned away Gouzenko along with his story and his documents. But later that morning, word of the Russian who was frantically banging on the doors of official Ottawa reached Norman Robertson. He was sufficiently alarmed by Gouzenko's tale that he carried it to Prime Minister Mackenzie King, whose instant instinct was to reject Gouzenko's plea for asylum. But by a stroke of good fortune for Robertson and Gouzenko, William Stevenson happened to be visiting in the Ottawa area. Stevenson, a Canadian with his base in England, had operated during the Second World War as one of the Allies' master spies, and when Robertson had the presence of mind to tell Stevenson of Gouzenko, his advice was unequivocal. "Take him," he said to Robertson, and on the afternoon of September 7, after speaking again to King, Robertson sent out the word to the RCMP. Gouzenko was given asylum.

Robertson and the other Ottawa decision-makers proceeded cautiously and privately on the Gouzenko revelations of Russian spies in their midst. Mackenzie King favoured a tiptoe approach to the whole embarrassing business. Why should Canada, of all Western democracies, be seen as the country to disturb relations between East and West? Why were *we* afflicted with this awkward situation? King travelled to Washington and advised three Americans — President Harry Truman, Secretary of State Dean Acheson, and FBI Director J. Edgar Hoover — of the Gouzenko situation. The United States, for its own diplomatic reasons, urged King to resist any impulse to go immediately public with the news. And, back home, King's own Ministry of Justice pointed out, correctly, that its lawyers needed time to build cases against the people named in Gouzenko's documents that would lead to convictions in court. Tiptoeing, for all these reasons, seemed a wise policy.

In the end, a journalist forced King to act. On February 3, 1946, Drew Pearson broke the story of the Ottawa spies on his radio program. Pearson was a Washington columnist and broadcaster adept at dishing up inside dope, and his tip on Gouzenko had originated with J. Edgar Hoover, who was anxious to get on with the battle against the Red menace. In Ottawa, King fell back on that most Canadian of institutions, the royal commission. On February 5, after telling his full cabinet of the spy troubles for the first time but continuing to keep his electorate in the dark, he appointed a royal commission with an intimidating mandate: "To Investigate the Facts Relating to and the Circumstances Surrounding the Communication by Public Officials and Other Persons in Positions of Trust of Secret and Confidential Information to Agents of a Foreign Power." The two men selected to preside over the Commission, Justices Robert Taschereau and R. L. Kellock of the Supreme Court of Canada, moved swiftly and secretly. On February 13, after steeping themselves in the RCMP's research on the mess, they questioned Gouzenko *in camera* and were, as they later wrote in their report, "impressed with the sincerity of the man and with the manner in which he gave his evidence, which we have no hesitation in accepting."

Two days after the questioning, on February 15, the King government revealed to Canadians the first official news of the spy rings. The announcement took place in the afternoon. On the morning of that day, at seven a.m., RCMP officers had arrested the first thirteen of the alleged spies on charges that weren't specified. Under the Mounties' original plan, the arrests were scheduled for three a.m., but Norman Robertson insisted on a more civilized hour. Three a.m., he thought, smacked of Russian tactics. The way for the arrests had been paved by an Order-in-Council passed in virtual secrecy back on October 6, 1945, by three cabinet members, King, Minister of Justice Louis St. Laurent and one other minister. The Order-in-Council gave the government authority to detain any spy suspects without the usual requirement of formal charges. Bail, right to counsel, contact with family, habeas corpus — all were denied to the thirteen men and women who were spirited away to the RCMP training centre in the Ottawa district of Rockcliffe where they were held in isolation from the outside world, especially from their alleged Russian masters, who would surely advise them to hold silent.

Eric Adams was one of the thirteen.

"Ahhh, Eric wasn't a communist," Joe Sedgwick later insisted. "He was a pinko, nothing more. What they called in those days a fellow-traveller. Nothing traitorous about the man."

Adams' fascination with Russia, even his affection for it, was undisguised. He journeyed through the Soviet as a tourist for several weeks in 1934. His library was long on Russian political and economic theory. He saved back copies of such left-wing North American journals as the *Clarion*, the *Canadian Tribune*, and *New Masses*. And he served as an active Ottawa member of an organization, admittedly respectable in the wartime context of co-operation with Russia, called Friends of the Soviet Union.

The Royal Commissioners deduced that Adams' Russian connections were rather more sinister. "We have no doubt on all the evidence," they wrote in their 733-page final report, "but that Colonel Zabotin found in Adams a convinced communist who considered the communication of information to Russia in line with his ardent beliefs as a member of the Party." Some of the Commissioners' "evidence" smacked more of anti-Red hysteria than of hard proof. "Adams' library," they wrote, "was literally full of Communist books, including such authors as Marx, Engels and Lenin." But other facts, especially the information that surfaced from Gouzenko's 109 documents, appeared to be altogether more damning.

Several documents identified one of the Canadian spies as a man operating under the code name of "Ernst." Whom did "Ernst" shield? The documents had an answer: Eric Adams. One of the documents was a page of paper with handwriting on it torn from a notebook and ripped in three. The notebook and the handwriting, in Russian, belonged to Nicolai Zabotin. He had ripped the page on a morning in August 1945 and given the pieces to Gouzenko for burning. Gouzenko instead squirrelled away the three scraps against the day when he walked out of the embassy. The page, when put together, summed up Ernst's contributions to Zabotin's spy ring. "He gives detailed information on all kind of industries and plans for the future," the colonel had written. "Supplies detailed accounts of conferences." Zabotin jotted a few more notes, then described Ernst's value in two devastating words: "Good worker."

The Commissioners marshalled other facts that seemed to point to Adams' involvement in the ring. There was a copy of a mailing list that Zabotin sent to Moscow on January 5, 1945, in which Ernst was credited with furnishing pages of printed material during the preceding year, information on the "Despatch of Munitions to England," on the "Invention of Waterproofing," copies of "Correspondence about contracts." And there was the testimony against Adams given by a woman named Kathleen Willsher, another of the thirteen arrested on February 15. Willsher was English, an employee since 1930 in the Ottawa office of the British High Commissioner, and her job as Deputy Registrar gave her access to most of the confidential papers that passed through the High Commissioner's hands. By her own admission to the Royal Commission she saw to it that the contents of many of those secret documents reached Colonel Zabotin, and one of her contacts, a fellow agent who, she testified, acted as a relay between her and Zabotin, was Adams.

"Adams' conduct and associations with Soviet agents," the Commissioners reported, "his personal sympathies dating back at least to 1934 which made him easily receptive to the suggestions of Zabotin, his endeavors to obtain information of a secret nature, which turned out in many instances to be fruitful, as evidenced by the testimony of Miss Willsher, and the documents from the embassy, leave little doubt in our minds that he has conspired to commit offences in violation of the Official Secrets Act, and that he has also committed the substantive offences of obtaining, for the benefit of a foreign power, secret information, and of inciting others to commit such offence."

Adams hardly helped his own cause in the testimony that he gave to the Royal Commissioners before whom, as was the case for all the suspected spies, he was compelled to appear without counsel. He claimed a misfiring memory in answer to many of the questions put to him by the Commission's counsel. Who attended the "study group meetings . . . discussing Communism and Marxism" at Adams' Ottawa home? "I don't recall any people there." How did he happen to know Kathleen Willsher and who introduced them? "I don't recall." And how did a document prepared for the Labor-Progressive Party, the name under which Canada's Communist Party operated, a document entitled "Draft Outline for Research in Province of Ontario" and described in its first paragraph as "of great political importance to our Party," find its way between the pages of a book in Adams' home library? "I don't recall now." The answers left the Commissioners politely sceptical. "We unhesitatingly accept Kathleen Willsher's evidence with regard to Adams, and indeed Adams does not deny that evidence. He merely does not 'recall' the events to which Willsher deposed. That, of course, is incredible. Such evidence is typical of a mind which recalls the facts perfectly, and, while not prepared to admit, takes refuge in the fancied security of an assumed inability to remember."

The case against Adams appeared to grow more secure through the spring of 1946. In late March the government took Fred Rose to court for a preliminary hearing on charges that he had recruited several of Zabotin's spies and had acted as a conduit in passing on secrets. Rose was a Member of Parliament from Montreal representing the Labor-Progressive Party, and a principal witness against him was Kathleen Willsher, who testified that she began handing over to Rose useful information from the British High Commissioner's Office as early as 1936.

Crown counsel to Willsher: "Subsequently did any other person introduce himself to you for the same purpose?"

Willsher: "Eric Adams in 1942 or 1943." She gave Adams, she told the court, material concerning "a general outline about the war, that there would be a second front, generally the prosecution of the war."

When Rose came to trial in May and June of 1946, Adams was called as a crown witness. He was asked questions about Rose's involvement in spying and about his own connections with Rose and others in the ring. Adams gave the same response to all questions. "I decline to answer on the grounds that it might incriminate me at my own trial." The judge presiding over the Rose trial sentenced Adams to three months in jail for contempt of court. Rose was convicted of spying and got six years in prison.

"It was a good tactic on Eric's part not to respond," Sedgwick said. "It meant that his answers at the Rose trial couldn't be read back to him in cross-examination at his own trial. That might have had the potential to be embarrassing."

It wasn't Sedgwick who advised Adams in the tactic — Adams was on his own as a witness — but Sedgwick had taken up his client's cause earlier in the spring when Tom Fogden first approached him. Sedgwick, ever faithful to his concept of counsel as a "loaded blunderbuss," hesitated not for a moment to accept the case. Some friends, however, needed straightening out on his motivation.

"It was the temper of the times," he later explained. "McCarthyism in its early form. George Drew — he was premier of Ontario then — came to me and said, 'Joe, how can you act for such a man, a *traitor*?' George was a good fellow. He served with my brother

Harry in the same brigade of artillery in the First World War. A good fellow but a little stiff. It's been said of the British that they have all the qualities of a poker except for the occasional warmth. That describes George. 'How can you defend this man?' he asked me. George was a lawyer but he had never acted in court. I told him he didn't understand the business of the counsel. 'With the fees we charge,' I said to George, 'we don't get the innocent, but by God, they're innocent once we get them!' "

Sedgwick laughed.

"That may be funny," he went on. "But it's also the truth. Unless you can involve yourself to a personal degree in a client's misfortune, you don't have the right to practise the kind of law I practised."

Sedgwick's major chore before the start of Adams' trial, apart from conferring with his client and building a defence, was to sort out the exact nature of the charges against Adams. The crown had issued two indictments alleging in vague and sketchy wording that Adams had conspired with a group that included six Russians, eight Canadians, and one Englishwoman, the ubiquitous Kathleen Willsher, to collect and communicate information in violation of the Official Secrets Act. Sedgwick needed more. He brought a Motion For Particulars in the Supreme Court of Ontario, and when he succeeded, the crown was compelled to produce a document, called simply Particulars, which succinctly outlined its case against Adams.

The crown alleged that from the beginning of 1942 to the end of 1945 a conspiracy existed in Canada to gather information about the country's military, its war industries and munitions, its development in radar, and its relations with Britian, Russia, and the United States, and to convey this information to Moscow by way of Russian officials in Ottawa. Eric Adams, so the Particulars alleged, joined the conspiracy in 1942 and carried out a number of acts that were conspicuously "in furtherance of the conspiracy." Most especially, he gathered the various pieces of information, correspondence, and research that were set out in Colonel Zabotin's mailing list dated January 5, 1945; he collected information from Kathleen Willsher, usually the contents of letters addressed to the British High Commissioner in Ottawa; and finally, "in furtherance of the conspiracy," in June 1945 he paid Willsher a sum of money, twenty-five dollars, to cover some of her expenses incurred in the act of passing secrets to Adams.

Thus enlightened, Sedgwick pondered his defence strategy.

"As a defence counsel," he always said, "you must have a theory. Otherwise you're up the creek without a paddle. You have a theory, and every question you ask in examination or cross-examination is directed to establishing that theory or demolishing the one on the other side."

Sedgwick went into the Adams defence with a simple theory: when the Canadian government interpreted Adams' actions as traitorous, it was misreading behaviour that could be explained in entirely innocent terms. Adams was not "Ernst." Kathleen Willsher was mistaken in the view she took of her contacts with Adams, which were, for him, merely social. And Adams' fascination with Russia, its economics and politics, sprang simply from his educational and professional interests as a businessman, economist, and civil-service employee.

In the eight days that the trial eventually lasted, Sedgwick's defence — his theory translated to specifics — would not turn on courtroom histrionics and fireworks, or on a surprise witness, or on a piece of sparkling cross-examination. His defence would be a matter of chipping away at the crown's case. It would depend on the manner in which Sedgwick handled the crown's witnesses, casting tiny shadows of doubt on their testimony, shaking their assurance ever so gently, raising questions in the jury's mind about those witnesses' veracity and accuracy and judgment. And it would depend, at the very end of the trial, at the eleventh hour, on an unforeseeable piece of good luck that Sedgwick would manage brilliantly to turn to his client's advantage.

The trial was called for October in Ottawa. Much earlier, back in June, Sedgwick had moved for a change of venue. He argued that the report of the Taschereau-Kellock Commission, so condemnatory of Adams, had received such wide circulation in the Ottawa newspapers that he'd have trouble finding a jury of twelve men from the city who weren't already persuaded of Adams' guilt. Sedgwick's motion came before James McRuer, Chief Justice of the trial division of the Ontario Supreme Court. Sedgwick suggested that Toronto might be more safely neutral. McRuer rejected the motion. Adams, the Chief Justice held, was as likely to get a fair trial in Ottawa as anywhere else in Ontario.

Sedgwick wasn't distressed.

"All part of the waltz," he later said. "You take these steps, motions, and so on, to keep the other side slightly off balance. I knew that if the trial proceeded in Ottawa, as I expected it would, I'd ask each prospective juryman whether he'd read stories about my man in the newspapers. If he had, I'd reject him. If he hadn't, I'd take him. Oh, I was always a great believer in the jury system. Chesterton's essay 'Twelve Men' has it exactly right. The basic goodness of juries is what Chesterton says, and I agree. I've been before hundreds of them and never met one that wasn't fair."

The trial began on schedule in the Ottawa courthouse on a Monday in mid-October. A familiar face peered down from the bench, Chief Justice McRuer's. And a more familiar face looked over from the crown's table, Jack Cartwright's. Cartwright was in private practice as senior counsel at the Toronto firm of Smith, Rae, Greer & Cartwright and had been retained by the federal government to take on the special burden of prosecuting the Canadians charged in the spy conspiracy. Cartwright came from an Establishment background: a member of one of Ontario's oldest families; twice wounded in France during the First World War, aide-de-camp to three generals, awarded the Military Cross; an elected Bencher of the Law Society of Upper Canada; a respected barrister; and a good friend of Joe Sedgwick's. He was slim and elegant and dedicated to linguistic precision. The Oxford English Dictionary was his favourite book. Polite, almost self-effacing, he was, for a barrister, deceptively soft-spoken.

"As a counsel, Jack was deadly," Sedgwick said. "By that I mean he applied himself to the points at issue and didn't wander about. He usually gave his opponents very little to work with."

Cartwright called an array of witnesses for the crown. Most of them were RCMP officers who told the court of their investigations into Adams' activities, their interrogations of Adams and others after the February 15 arrests, the results of their searches of Adams' Montreal apartment and his office when they turned up the "communist" books and other documents that pointed to Adams' leftist connections. The RCMP evidence was largely circumstantial, and it became clear that Cartwright's case would depend for its strength on the testimony of two witnesses who were more intimately linked to the spy ring: Igor Gouzenko and Kathleen Willsher.

Gouzenko, in his late twenties, was short, thick-set, with heavy eyebrows. He testified without the hood over his face that later became his trademark, but, for his protection, four or five Mounties in civilian clothes sat among the courtroom spectators. Another

Mountie took his place near Gouzenko in the witness-box. He was Constable Melvyn Black, Russian born, and his job was to help Gouzenko, who wasn't entirely comfortable in English, when he stumbled on counsel's questions or his own answers.

Prodded by Cartwright, Gouzenko told his familiar story. How he acted out a simple masquerade at the Russian Embassy as a secretary and an interpreter. How, as Colonel Zabotin's cipher clerk, he trafficked, at least on paper, in Canadian spies. How documents crossed his desk that had been filched from Ottawa government offices and were headed for Zabotin's masters in Moscow. How the different members of Zabotin's network of Canadian sneaks and spies were assigned code names. How "Ernst" was the code name for a man named Eric Adams, a spy who was, according to the documents that Zabotin had in his possession and that Gouzenko removed from the embassy on the night of September 5, 1945, a "good worker." And how convinced Gouzenko was, given the paper evidence and given Zabotin's enthusiasm for Ernst, that Adams was one of the indispensables among Canadian spies.

Sedgwick rose to cross-examine Gouzenko. He had outlined his approach in a handwritten note in his confidential file on the case: "Gouzenko merely gives hearsay. He can't say who made the file on Adams, who designated him as 'Ernst.' He can't say who gave Zabotin the information on which Z made his memo — which must have been hearsay and which is false."

"I couldn't do much with Gouzenko on cross-examination," Sedgwick said later. "He hadn't met my man and he didn't know anything that wasn't in those damned files of his."

Sedgwick contented himself with attempting to establish the points in his memo, that Gouzenko's knowledge of Adams as Ernst was of a second-hand nature. It was hardly a searching cross-examination, but Sedgwick, rightly or wrongly, felt he'd run up a point or two with the jury in his client's favour.

Kathleen Willsher took the stand. She was, in Sedgwick's description, "not a colourful person." She was in her forties, quiet-spoken, bland in looks, a woman who would blend invisibly into any crowd. She had pleaded guilty to violations of the Official Secrets Act on May 3, 1946, and received a sentence of three years in prison. From the date of her plea, she co-operated with the crown and gave evidence at the trials of the other alleged conspirators with whom she claimed to have had contacts. One conspirator she insisted to have been in constant touch with was Eric Adams.

Adams approached her, she told the court at his trial, as early as 1942 and asked her to pass to him any information from the British High Commissioner's Office that might be "in the interest of the Communist Party." Willsher, fascinated by communism and attracted to Russia's cause, agreed. She provided Adams with details from letters, briefings, and other communiqués on a continuing basis from 1942 to 1945, making the meetings of an Ottawa study group, often held at Adams' home, the usual occasions for relaying her secrets. And what was the subject under study by the Ottawa group? "The theory and practice of socialism and communism and the party program."

Cartwright asked Willsher for examples of the information she had conveyed to Adams. Well, Willsher said, there were the contents of two letters dated November 3 and November 11, 1945, that came through her office for the High Commissioner's attention, letters from the Canadian ambassador in Moscow to the Canadian prime minister dealing with matters confidential to the Canadian government. And there were other pieces of information. Willsher listed them. Then, also in November 1944, Lord Keynes, the British economist, visited Ottawa to discuss financial arrangements between Canada and Great Britain after the war. Willsher got her hands on the reports of the Keynes meetings and rushed their contents to Adams.

Her contacts with Adams didn't end when he moved out of Ottawa to his job with the Industrial Development Bank in Montreal early in 1945. Adams often met her back in Ottawa for the usual purpose of taking delivery of the High Commissioner's secrets. And on a couple of occasions she travelled to Montreal to meet Adams. Once, Adams and his wife invited her to their apartment for a meal. And another time, Adams gave her twenty-five dollars. What was the explanation for this sum? It was money to cover Willsher's train expenses between the two cities when she was on her nefarious business for the Party, the business of passing on government secrets to Eric Adams.

On cross-examination, Sedgwick took the tack that Willsher was naive, confused about her relationship with Adams, and just possibly intimidated by her dealings with the RCMP and the Taschereau-Kellock Commission. Part of the tone for his approach was set in a memo that Adams made for Sedgwick in the weeks before the trial. Adams referred to the questions put to him by the Commission counsel as "attempts to trick me into false admissions" and speculated that "I found it difficult to combat this kind of attack, so what chance had someone like Willsher?" In a later note, Adams offered Sedgwick more on Willsher's likely state of mind: "A friend of Willsher's saw her since [her] trial and she said the RCMP had frightened her by saying that unless she said exactly what she told them and the Commission, her sentence would be increased."

In cross-examining Willsher, Sedgwick affected his most concerned and tender and understanding persona. He *knew* what Willsher had endured, his manner and voice kept saying, and he felt *compassion* for her predicament. Hadn't her appearance before the Royal Commission unnerved her? Wasn't the prospect of a jail sentence a terribly disturbing influence for her? Wasn't she anxious to please the RCMP and the crown in her testimony? And, oh yes, wouldn't it be true to say that all these forces and factors conspired to help her to misconstrue her dealings with Eric Adams? Willsher held essentially to her story in the face of Sedgwick's display of concern, but his questions, if not her answers, had the effect of placing a hint of doubt in the minds of the jury about Willsher's motivation in testifying, her accuracy and her interpretation of events.

It was Friday afternoon, after nearly five days of trial, when Cartwright told Chief Justice McRuer that with Willsher's evidence he had concluded the case for the crown. McRuer asked Sedgwick whether he intended to call evidence on behalf of the defence. Friday afternoon, Sedgwick knew, wasn't a smart time to open a defence; the jury would have all weekend to forget his opening points. Besides, he wanted a couple of days to review the situation with his client. He asked McRuer for an adjournment until the following Monday. McRuer granted it on condition that, no later than noon on Sunday, Sedgwick would advise Cartwright whether or not he planned to put a witness in the box. If Sedgwick called no witnesses, then Cartwright would be obliged to begin his jury address on Monday. If Sedgwick elected to summon evidence, Cartwright had to prepare himself for cross-examination. Sedgwick agreed to the condition. Court adjourned.

"I spent the next day and a half woodshedding my client," Sedgwick later said. "I went over the story Eric would give if he testified. He'd tell me certain things he wanted to say, and sometimes I would have to warn him. 'Very well,' I'd say, 'you may like to put it that way, but I must warn you that it is probably not wise to use those words.' I didn't *coach* him. I never did such a thing with my clients. I *guided* him as to what would be most appropriate to his defence."

In fact, Sedgwick had little doubt from the beginning that he would call Adams to the witness-box.

"He was the only witness who would do me any good," Sedgwick said. "He was the one person who knew anything. And anyway, in a criminal defence I was always in favour of summoning the accused to the box. If he doesn't testify, the jury wonders what he's hiding. I never believed in calling peripheral evidence. I believed in calling the man himself. The key to making these choices, the key to being a good counsel, is judgment. I once said to John Robinette, 'John, you know a great deal of law and I don't, but one thing we possess in common is good judgment.' What I meant is that John and I know when to call a man and when not to call him, when to cross-examine the other side's witness and when to leave him alone. That is judgment, and it is a rare commodity in our courts."

Promptly at noon on Sunday, Sedgwick phoned Cartwright and told him he'd be placing Adams on the stand. For good measure, he phoned the same news to Chief Justice McRuer.

"Next day," Sedgwick said, "Eric Adams got into the witness-box and he performed like a lion."

Under Sedgwick's shrewd probing, Adams told his story for the first time. He wasn't defensive, nor was he outraged. His memory, which had so disastrously failed him before the Taschereau-Kellock Commission, was now apparently intact. He — and Sedgwick — steered away from evasion. He was straightforward. And he radiated a sense of certainty in his own innocence.

He was an Ottawa bureaucrat, he said, and the very nature of the jobs he held for the civil service meant that he moved in many professional and social circles. He met men and women from all levels of government. Perhaps Kathleen Willsher was at a meeting or cocktail party he attended, but so was Norman Robertson. So were many Ottawa mandarins. Did their presence in the same room with Willsher make them parties to a spy conspiracy? The answer, Adams implied in reply to Sedgwick's questions, was of course negative. Robertson and the rest weren't spies, and neither was he.

Adams conceded in his testimony that Willsher had been in his home on a couple of occasions. Perfectly innocent, he said. Perhaps Willsher perceived meetings at the Adams house as somehow linked to a cell of communists. But they were nothing of the sort. You see, Adams said, he and a few other economists began work in 1943, informally and after hours, on an outline for a history of Canada interpreted exclusively in economic terms. They met monthly at one another's homes over the following year and a half, and at one or two meetings, held in Adams' house, a government economist named Laxton brought along a woman named Agatha Chapman, who was a co-worker in the civil service. Chapman, who was later charged in the spy rings, was a friend of Willsher's, and it was she who introduced Willsher into the Adams home as a guest at the discussions. Perhaps Willsher and Chapman had something to hide, but for Adams, the gatherings were entirely innocuous affairs.

He had equally ready explanations for his other connections with Willsher. Really, his manner in the witness-box conveyed, is the crown *serious* about these silly matters? Of course Willsher had been in his apartment in Montreal one late-spring evening in 1945. She had phoned Adams and his wife out of the blue, saying she was briefly in town from Ottawa, and on the basis of their earlier acquaintance with her, the Adamses acted the decent hosts and invited her to dinner. Later in the evening, Adams drove Willsher to her Ottawa train. Nothing to it except playing the good host.

And, yes, Adams had in his possession a couple of pages of notes dealing with Lord Keynes' discussions in Ottawa in November 1944. The notes were in Adams' own handwriting and had been seized by the RCMP from his Montreal apartment. Heavens, Adams said, word of Keynes' views came to him in the normal course of his work, not from Willsher, and he made the notes, using government stationery, to keep himself up to date on current economic thinking. Nothing in the least sinister about the damned memo, Adams insisted, which was a point that Sedgwick took pains to emphasize. "If Adams were preparing an improper document," he wrote as a reminder to himself in his confidential brief, "would he logically place a memo of it on the office pad?"

In the same way, Adams explained away the mystery of the twenty-five-dollar payment to Willsher. Was it to cover her expenses to Montreal on an occasion when she delivered secrets from the High Commissioner's Office to Adams? Certainly not. Willsher, it seems, was on the executive of the Fellowship For a Christian Social Order, an organization as innocent as its name. Fellowship duties sometimes sent Willsher on missions outside Ottawa, and one such trip took her to a conference in Montreal. The Fellowship, alas, was chronically short of funds, and many of Willsher's expenses, when she didn't absorb them herself, were paid by friends and supporters of the Fellowship. Adams counted himself among the latter group, and the famous twenty-five dollars, the money which Willsher had received from Adams, the cash which the crown claimed to be in furtherance of the spy conspiracy, *that* twenty-five dollars — Adams was unequivocal about his facts — came as recompense from Adams to Willsher to cover a journey on behalf of nothing more threatening than the Fellowship For a Christian Social Order.

So much for Willsher.

Sedgwick ticked off the names of the other indicted and un-indicted conspirators. Was Adams acquainted with them? Not the Russians, he answered. Never encountered Colonel Zabotin or any of the gang from the Russian Embassy. What of the other Canadian civil servants who had been charged? David Gordon Lunan? Harold Gerson? Dr. Raymond Boyer? No, no, Adams swore as Sedgwick ran down the list. Agatha Chapman? Yes, Adams had met her, both at work and at the discussions to plan the economic history of Canada. But the acquaintance was fleeting. He had known Frederic Poland, another accused spy, because Poland had been an admirer of his wife's at McGill, and he knew Israel Halperin, also accused, because Halperin's wife and Mrs. Adams had met through their mutual association with an Ottawa nursery school. Could any connection be more harmless? Yes, he had once chatted with James Benning, another civil servant implicated in the spy ring, when the two men happened to be skiing at Camp Fortune on the same day. And he had become friendly with Fred Rose in the late 1930s through his interest in politics in Montreal where Rose was a well-known Member of Parliament. All wonderfully natural, Adams said as he shrugged his innocence from the witness-box.

What, Sedgwick asked, of "Ernst"?

The name, Adams answered, was unknown to him in any context.

Sedgwick consulted the list of documents that Ernst was alleged to have passed to the Russians, the list that was among the papers smuggled out of the Russian Embassy by Gouzenko, the list dated January 5, 1945, and prepared for Moscow by Colonel Zabotin. "Invention of Waterproofing," Sedgwick read from the list. Was Adams aware of such an invention when he was employed by the Inventions Board in Ottawa? Impossible, Adams answered. He had worked for the Main Examining Committee of the Inventions Board rather than for the Board itself and had no access to the information that Zabotin had credited to Ernst. Sedgwick quoted other documents that, according to Zabotin, had originated with Ernst. Adams denied that he'd so much as laid eyes on such documents. They belonged to a category, he swore, that was beyond his range of interest and accessibility.

"By the way, Mr. Adams," Sedgwick said suddenly, looking up from another of the Gouzenko papers, "are you Jewish?"

No.

Sedgwick drew Adams' attention to the page torn out of Colonel Zabotin's notebook that had been pieced together from three torn scraps. It was the page that described Ernst's contributions to the spy ring and characterized him as a "good worker." Sedgwick pointed to the words at the beginning of the page: "Ernst — Jew."

Yes, Adams said, he'd wondered about Ernst's religion. When the RCMP was interrogating him not long after his arrest, an inspector named Anthony asked Adams if he were Jewish. No, Adams said, but why do you ask? "I didn't think you were," Anthony said, "but my records said you are."

What of the books in Adams' library, Sedgwick asked, satisfied that he had thrown enough doubt on the Adams-Ernst connection, the so-called "communist" books?

He owned two thousand books, Adams answered, and of that great number, the RCMP had taken away a mere one hundred, the works of Marx and Lenin and Engels and other socialist authors. But, Adams insisted, all the books were useful to him simply as research and background for his work as an economist. And, for what it was worth, Adams pointed out, his library included two copies of *Mein Kampf*, one in English and one in German. The RCMP had left them behind.

And the left-wing newspapers and journals that Adams kept at home in back copies?

Oh well, Adams said, the *Canadian Tribune*, *National Affairs*, and others were quite harmless. The Bank of Canada, where Adams had done government work, subscribed to them.

Sedgwick built a climate of innocence, leading his client relentlessly through the accusations, maintaining a low-key atmosphere in the courtroom, asking the jury to appreciate as civilized men that these matters were explainable in terms that the crown, well-meaning but not in possession of all the facts, had had the misfortune to overlook.

Had Adams, Sedgwick asked, kept the oath he swore when he went to work for the civil service, the oath that bound him under the Official Secrets Act not to reveal any of his country's confidential matters to a foreign power?

Yes, Adams answered, calm and firm and unhesitating. Yes, he had observed the oath in letter and in spirit. Anyway, he went on, he was never in possession of information that would be especially valuable to Russia or any other foreign power.

Sedgwick sat down.

"On cross-examination," he said later, "Jack Cartwright couldn't budge my man. Eric stuck to his story in every particular and Jack couldn't trap him. He was a tower of strength in the witness-box."

With Adams' testimony, Sedgwick rested his case, and since he had called evidence, he was compelled to go first in addressing the jury. He spoke for over an hour. "That was a long address for me," he later explained. "I don't like to bore a jury with too much material. But in the Adams case I had a great number of points to cover." First, Sedgwick touched on the danger that Adams had faced in the apparently incriminating findings that had come out of the Taschereau-Kellock Commission and the RCMP investigation. He quoted from *Alice in Wonderland*. " 'Let the jury consider their verdict,' the King said. 'No, no,' said the Queen. 'Sentence first, verdict afterwards.' "

That, Sedgwick said, is not our system.

And again: " 'Give your evidence,' said the King, 'and don't be nervous or I'll have you executed on the spot.' "

Nor that.

Then Sedgwick underlined for the jury his major arguments: that Gouzenko could offer the court only information that arrived in his files from outside sources; that Willsher's testimony was demonstrably suspect; and that Adams had successfully explained away the evidence against him. The crown, Sedgwick concluded before he gave way to Cartwright, had not proved its case.

Cartwright took forty minutes to address the jury, coming down hard on the impact of Gouzenko's testimony and of Willsher's. The evidence of Gouzenko alone was enough to convict Adams, Cartwright argued, and he asked the jury to record a conviction. It was the end of the afternoon.

The next morning, October 26, 1946, the last day of the trial, Chief Justice McRuer wheeled around his chair to face the jury-box. "What Mr. Cartwright has told you is well and good," he said in effect, beginning his instructions to the jury, "but now I will tell you the *whole* story." He differed from Cartwright on one specific. Gouzenko's testimony was not sufficient on its own to convict Adams. No, the jury must find corroboration in the testimony of one of Adam's fellow conspirators. That corroboration, he said, was providentially offered in the evidence of Kathleen Willsher. It seemed to Sedgwick at the time that McRuer concentrated on the crown's case. As he listened to the Chief Justice, Sedgwick came to the view that McRuer was pointing out the crown's strengths and accentuating its persuasiveness. The Chief Justice went on at length, three hours in all. That proved to be a burden in time to one juryman. He fell asleep. McRuer, noting that he'd lost one-twelfth of his audience, called a short adjournment to allow the unhappy man to recover his wits. After the ten-minute break, McRuer continued his remarks until he was satisfied that no element of the Adams case remained unexamined. Content, he sent the jury away to consider its verdict.

"Mr. Sedgwick," the Chief Justice said when the jury-box was emptied, "do you have any comment on my instructions to the jury?"

Sedgwick hesitated for a moment. As he told the tale of the trial in later years, he was convinced the Chief Justice had not sufficiently put the defence's case to the jury. He thought McRuer had leaned to the crown's side and not allowed enough weight to the evidence that may have pointed to Adams' innocence.

"It's an old defence counsel's ploy," Sedgwick said later, "to object to a judge's summation on the grounds that he's slighted our side. I thought the Adams case gave me an opening to raise that objection, and I may say I was very sly about it."

Sedgwick stood up slowly from his chair in response to the Chief Justice's question, and affecting a manner that was just a trifle weary and wounded, immaculately understated, he spoke of his quibbles with the jury instructions.

"I tried to get across the impression," Sedgwick later recollected, "that his lordship may not have adequately impressed on the jury that there was a presumption of innocence in favour of the accused."

No man with as much experience on the bench as McRuer would have overlooked so basic an element in a justice's jury instructions, but Sedgwick pressed his point.

"Well, Mr. Sedgwick," the Chief Justice finally said, "do you wish to have the jury recalled?"

"Yes," Sedgwick said.

The jury returned, and once again, for a few minutes, the twelve jurymen listened to the words of James McRuer. But this time, as Sedgwick told the story in later years, it was a point or two in favour of Eric Adams that demanded most of their attention. No one dozed off, and at the end of the fresh instructions, with new information in their heads, they returned to their deliberations.

"Oh, it was glorious," Sedgwick said years later. "What you must remember about a jury is that they are not permitted to take notes. And nobody can possibly retain everything from a trial in his head. So the jury has to rely on the addresses of the crown and of the defence counsel and ultimately on the cooling words of the presiding judge. That's what they mainly remember. Well, in the Adams case, what I perceived as Jim McRuer's clear slant in the crown's direction opened the door for me, and the result was that the last words ringing in the ears of the jury as they left the courtroom for the final time were to the good of my man."

The jury was out for only ninety minutes longer than it had taken McRuer to deliver his original summation. It was gone for a mere four and a half hours, and when it returned, it presented to the stilled and wondering audience in the courtroom a unanimous verdict.

The jury was out for only ninety minutes longer than it had taken McRuer to deliver his original summation. It was gone for a mere four and a half hours, and when it returned, it presented to the stilled and wondering audience in the courtroom a unanimous verdict.

Not guilty.

Eric Adams, as reserved and contained as he'd been through the trial, immediately left the court for his home and family in Montreal. Sedgwick left for a few drinks at the Château Laurier. In a hall of the hotel he ran into Chief Justice McRuer.

"Joe," McRuer said, "I congratulate you."

"M'lord, I thank you," Sedgwick said. "And may I also say that I am grateful to you."

"Why is that?"

"M'lord," Sedgwick said, "I believe that if you had left things alone after Jack Cartwright sat down, my man would undoubtedly have been convicted."

McRuer nodded and turned away.

In the years after the Adams trial, its principals moved to fates that were almost predictably inevitable. J. R. Cartwright, a winner in most things in life except his prosecution of Adams, was invited to sit on the Supreme Court of Canada in 1949. The court was expanding from seven judges to nine, and for reasons of tradition, politics, and cultural balance, the two new members had to be a French-speaking Quebecker and an English-Canadian lawyer from Ontario. Gérard Fauteux accepted the Quebec appointment. He had served as a counsel to the Taschereau-Kellock Commission, a relentless adversary whom Eric Adams regarded as his most diabolical tormentor. Cartwright was the choice from Ontario, but before he accepted, he called on Joe Sedgwick. It seemed that a year or two earlier, Cartwright had promised his Toronto firm, Smith, Rae, Greer & Cartwright, that he would stay with it for another five years. He was the firm's senior counsel and couldn't abandon it without an expert in litigation. Would Sedgwick, Cartwright asked, give up his one-man practice and join the firm in Cartwright's place? Sedgwick agreed, taking a drop in earnings in the process but enabling Cartwright to move to the Supreme Court, where he remained until 1970. At the farewell dinner on his retirement from the court, it was Sedgwick, so at home before an audience he considered august, who gave the farewell speech.

"The motto of your old school, Upper Canada College," he said in his grand voice, plummy and orotund, "was borrowed, I believe, from Lord Nelson's arms. 'Palmam qui meruit ferat.' My lord, you have brought honour to that old school, and like that greatest of sailors, you bear the palm that your merit has earned."

Igor Gouzenko was another alumnus of the Adams trial who heard a Sedgwick address in later years. After his defection, Gouzenko displayed a wide range of talents. He painted pictures in an attractive, realistic style and he wrote two successful books. The first, an autobiography called *This Was My Choice*, earned him $150,000, and the second, a novel based on the life of Maxim Gorky, *Fall of a Titan*, won him the 1954 Governor General's Medal for fiction. During these years, Gouzenko and his family, protected by the RCMP, lived a difficult undercover existence, and it was on one of his rare excursions into the outer world that Gouzenko encountered Joe Sedgwick.

The occasion was a libel action. A dozen years after the Adams trial, Gouzenko felt that Blair Fraser, the Ottawa correspondent for *Maclean's* magazine, had libelled him in an article that looked into Gouzenko's career in the post-defection years. The matter came to trial, and it was none other than Sedgwick who argued the case for *Maclean's*. This time, his arguments to the jury weren't persuasive enough, and the trial ended with a verdict in Gouzenko's favour.

Kathleen Willsher served her term in prison, then vanished, leaving behind a mystery that persisted into the 1980s. The puzzle arose out of the identity of "Elli." That was the code name used by Colonel Zabotin for one of the most prized spies in his Ottawa ring, a spy who was somehow plugged into the British High Commissioner's Office. The Taschereau-Kellock Commission concluded that Willsher was Elli, and this view was adopted by most students of the Gouzenko affair. Montgomery Hyde, in his apparently definitive book *The Atom Bomb Spies*, took it for granted that Elli and Willsher were one, and so did Phillip Knightley, a British journalist specializing in espionage, when he re-analysed the Ottawa episode for the *Sunday Times* in mid-1981.

But other experts lined up on the opposite side. An English author named Chapman Pincher was one. In his 1981 book *Their Trade Is Treachery*, he arrived at a more shocking identity for Elli. It was Sir Roger Hollis, who headed MI5 from 1956 to 1965. MI5, the British intelligence network, dispatched Hollis to Ottawa in 1945 for a debriefing of Gouzenko on revelations that Russians had placed agents inside the highest British institutions, including MI5. According to Pincher, Hollis took steps to ensure that the elusive Elli was never uncovered. Why? Because Hollis *was* Elli.

"The records showed," Pincher wrote, "that Hollis had reported the minimum amount of information from Gouzenko, who later complained that no proper notice had been taken of his Elli disclosure and that he had obviously made a big mistake in reporting the MI5 penetration to MI5 itself."

If Gouzenko complained that no notice was taken of Elli, then Elli could not be Willsher, who had plenty of notice taken of her — she went to prison. Sir Roger Hollis couldn't respond to the 1981 claims that he was Elli. Hollis died in 1973. Willsher has never responded either. But in the fall of 1981, another possibility surfaced when previously secret testimony given before the Taschereau-Kellock Commission was finally made public. In it, during Gouzenko's testimony, he raised in passing the notion, never followed up in his questioning, that there might exist two Ellis. Willsher was one, and, in Gouzenko's words, "there is also a cover name Elli and I understand that he or she, I do not know which, has been identified as an agent in England."

For Joe Sedgwick's part, no matter what the confusions and puzzles, he had arrived at one firm conclusion of his own about Elli's identity back in 1946 during his preparation of Eric Adams' defence. He compared a list of the secret documents that Elli passed to Colonel Zabotin with a list of documents that would — and wouldn't — have come to Willsher's hand. The lists didn't match.

"This would indicate," Sedgwick wrote on page 23 of his brief for the Adams case, "that 'Elli' is not Willsher — at least in this instance and probably not at all."

Agatha Chapman, Frederic Poland, Israel Halperin, and James Benning were four of the accused spies whom Adams admitted that he had met, sometimes socially, sometimes in the course of his civil-service duties. Chapman, Poland, and Halperin were acquitted of spying charges at their trials. Benning was convicted, but his conviction was overturned on appeal. He, too, went free. Two of the several others who were charged pleaded guilty; Willsher was one of the two. Eight others pleaded not guilty but were convicted at trial and lost their appeals. Their penalties ranged from a five-hundred-dollar fine for a civil servant named John Soboloff to six years in penitentiary for Fred Rose and for another long-time member of the Communist and Labor-Progressive parties, Sam Carr.

As for Eric Adams, after the trial he settled again in Montreal, where he set up his own engineering consulting firm. He maintained his interest in events behind the Iron Curtain, and in 1951 he took his wife and two young daughters to live in Prague, Czechoslovakia. He disappeared from Western view, but some time, many years later, he must have returned to Canada, because in the late 1960s Sedgwick spotted him on King Street in downtown Toronto. The two men nodded from across the years, spoke briefly, and passed on.

"Eric was never a friend of mine," Sedgwick said much later.

"But I knew him enough to recognize that he was a brilliant man. Clever, educated, well-spoken, excellent at engineering and economics. The charges against him, the accusations of spying, ruined all of that. They ended his career, and the one thing I remember from the short meeting on King Street is how he looked."

Sedgwick paused.

"Very shabby indeed."

Joe Sedgwick did not laugh.

CHAPTER 4

A SENSE OF OUTRAGE

THE NEW PENTHOUSE CABARET wasn't the sort of place where Tom Braidwood would have hung his hat. Braidwood is, among other descriptives, straight. The Penthouse was bent. Braidwood is respectable. The Penthouse was low-down and low-life. Braidwood is fresh air and open waters. The Penthouse was smoke and gloom and grit. Braidwood's world encompasses membership in the West Vancouver Yacht Club and a senior partnership in the general law firm — Braidwood, Nuttall, MacKenzie, Brewer, Greyell & Company — that occupies the swank top floors of the Standard Building in downtown Vancouver. The world of the Penthouse over on Seymour Street accommodated strippers, pimps, and hookers and their johns. The two, Braidwood and the Penthouse, were as different as the Establishment can be from the renegade, and yet when the crunch came, when Vancouver's police and city council and British Columbia's Liquor Board descended in force on the club in the mid-1970s, it was Tom Braidwood who rallied to the Penthouse's cause. He was just slightly outraged at the barely legal means that police and politicians adopted to drive the Penthouse's proprietors from business, and he rode to the rescue.

The Penthouse was Joe Philliponi's baby. Philliponi was born on January 1, 1913, in Reggio Calabria in the southern tip of Italy — traditional Mafia territory, if anyone wanted to make an issue of his origins — and he arrived in Vancouver in 1921. From early manhood, he and his younger brothers Ross and Mickey worked the nightclub business. Joe ran the Palomar Supper Club.

He was a leader in organizing the Cabaret Owners Association, an outfit that lobbied successfully to liberalize B.C.'s liquor laws. And he opened the Penthouse, a club that by the 1970s was a high-flying, booming enterprise. It served drinks and dinner to about six hundred patrons each night. It offered two shows an evening — singers, dancers, comedians, strippers — and it acquired a reputation as a place where, for sixty or seventy bucks, gents who craved a hot time could purchase briefly a woman's sexual favours. The police estimated that as many as fifty or sixty prostitutes plied their trade at the Penthouse on any given night. Joe Philliponi recognized the presence of these working girls on his premises and enforced club rules to control their commerce. He barred open soliciting, prevented approaches by single women to single men, even forbade table-hopping by the women. For the cops, Joe's methods didn't measure up. They wanted the Penthouse shut out of operation. They were looking for Joe Philliponi's scalp.

The official assault on the Penthouse got under way in the spring of 1975, and it was a complex orchestration of undercover operatives, electronic surveillance, a policewoman masquerading as a hooker, a couple of cops pretending to be her customers, and one tireless officer who, from the middle of June to the middle of December, spent three or four evenings a week in the Penthouse documenting its traffic in prostitutes. The officer's name was Norman Elliott; he was a detective on the vice squad, and Joe Philliponi knew he was a cop. Joe bought him drinks. One gaudy night, Elliott downed twelve of them. Joe thought Elliott was gathering evidence against black pimps who were hovering around the girls. Elliott, like the dozens of other officers on the great Penthouse case, was gathering evidence against someone else — Joe — and by December 18, 1975, the vice squad figured they had Philliponi dead to rights.

On that day, thirty policemen equipped with search warrants raided the Penthouse. Four days later, the police laid charges of conspiring to live on the avails of prostitution against Joe, his two brothers, his niece, the Penthouse's former doorman and former cashier, its hostess, and its master of ceremonies. There was more to come. A day after the charges were laid, all in the short space of eight hours, a city building inspector, a fire marshal, a health inspector, a man from the Social Services Department, and a representative of the federal income tax office arrived with requests to examine the Penthouse's books and premises. Was their simultaneous visit a stupendous coincidence? Not likely. And yet even more lay ahead. A group of officers from the vice squad met with Vic Woodland, the general manager of the province's Liquor Administration Branch, and on December 26, Joe Philliponi opened a message from the Telex office advising him that the Liquor Administration Branch was "not prepared to consider application for a licence for the Penthouse for the year 1976." Four days later, December 30, two men from the office of the Chief Licence Inspector and Business Tax Collector dropped by the Penthouse with a letter for Joe from their boss. "This is to inform you," the letter read, "that in view of a report I have received from the Police Department concerning the charges against certain people in your Company, I will not be issuing a licence for your restaurant/cabaret for the year 1976. You must therefore cease operation as of January 1, 1976." The Penthouse produced a blow-out celebration for its patrons on New Year's Eve, but after the last drink was served at two a.m. on January 1, 1976, after the last hooker took home the last john, the club doused its lights forever.

The police case against Philliponi and the others — "they did conspire together . . . to live on the avails of prostitution of other persons by allowing for their own pecuniary gain the premises known as the New Penthouse Cabaret to be used by common prostitutes . . ." — was tricky. No one suggested that "the pecuniary gain" stemmed from direct payments made by prostitutes from their earnings to Philliponi and his employees. But, the police contended, the Penthouse people were indirectly enriched by the hookers in at least three ways. One source of enrichment came in admission fees to the club; patrons paid $2.95 to the cashier at the entrance to the Penthouse, and when a hooker left the club with a man she'd picked up inside, gratified him in a nearby hotel, and returned to the club, she paid another $2.95 admission fee, a process that she might repeat three or four times an evening if she continued to turn tricks. A second source came in extra payments that prostitutes were required to make by apparently established custom to Penthouse employees, a regular two dollars per entrance to the doorman, another two to the cashier, and a tip of varying amounts to the hostess who showed the girls to the tables inside the club. And a third source of money lay in a special service that the Philliponi brothers were alleged to offer to johns who were short of funds to pay for sexual favours. The Philliponis allowed the johns to draw cash on Mastercharge cards or American Express or Chargex; the item was marked down to "Merchandise" and a surcharge of twenty per cent was added for the service. This, together with the other money transactions, amounted to a case of living on the avails of prostitution. Or so the police declared.

Joe Philliponi reeled under the blizzard of charges and accusations. He appealed the cancellation of his liquor licence to the three-person B.C. Liquor Board, and after a hearing on January 8, 1976, he was turned away, his appeal rejected and his business in limbo. Somebody, Philliponi decided, was out to get him. But who? Jack Wasserman had an answer. Wasserman was a veteran newspaperman, a specialist on the Vancouver entertainment scene, a smooth operator who knew the clubs and knew the cops. He told Philliponi that a Vancouver police inspector named Lake was the mastermind behind the anti-Philliponi moves. Lake had persuaded Vic Woodland to take away Joe's liquor licence. And it was Lake who engineered the long undercover operation against the Penthouse.

"You know what it is, Joe?" Wasserman said to Philliponi. "It's a conspiracy, and you're the target."

"I gotta get the facts out," Philliponi said. "If the people on the Liquor Board know the whole situation, they'll treat me fair."

Wasserman shrugged.

It happened that Philliponi was on friendly terms, or so he thought, with one of the three members of the Liquor Board. She was Pia Tofini, and on March 29, 1976, he phoned Mrs. Tofini and asked to get together with her on the following evening. He was going to tell her his side of the whole sorry tale. He felt confident in approaching Tofini. After all, hadn't he known her late husband for several years? Cesare Tofini had been the editor of the local Italian newspaper, *L'Eco D'Italia*, and Philliponi annually placed Christmas ads in the paper. The Philliponis and the Tofinis broke bread and drank wine in the Italian custom at a dinner in Belcara Park in the summer of 1973. "Here's my wife, Pia," Cesare Tofini said to Joe at the time. "Just appointed to the Liquor Board. If you want something done, she'll see to it." When Mr. Tofini died not long after, his wife took over the newspaper, and, following the usual practice, she called Philliponi in November 1975, a few weeks before the police raid, as it turned out, to solicit his yearly Christmas ad. Of course, Philliponi said, and he sent along his cheque for thirty dollars. Philliponi had no hesitation in ringing Pia Tofini about setting the record straight on his troubles with the police and the liquor people. She'd understand.

What Philliponi didn't know was that Pia's current boyfriend was a policeman, and when she met with Philliponi in his office at the Penthouse on the night of March 30, she was wearing a body pack that transmitted the conversation to a police truck down the street from the club. Her boyfriend and a couple of other officers were monitoring and recording every word that Joe Philliponi spoke. A few days later, after police had reviewed the taped conversation, they laid another charge against Philliponi: ". . . that he unlawfully and corruptly did offer certain valuable consideration and did unlawfully and corruptly give certain valuable consideration to Pia Tofini, the holder of a Judicial office, in respect of something to be done by her in her official capacity for himself. . . ." The "valuable consideration," the bribe that Philliponi was alleged to have presented to Tofini, consisted of a bottle of Scotch, a bottle of gin, and a cake that Joe's old mother had baked especially for Pia.

It took a year and a half for the various Philliponi cases to wind their way to conclusions, and, in the end, Joe Philliponi stood convicted. The avails trial lasted sixty-one days before a County Court judge. The bribery trial took nine days before another County Court judge. And in both, the judges pronounced Joe and his co-accused guilty as charged. Philliponi appealed each conviction, and it was at this crucial point, in preparing for the British Columbia Court of Appeal, that Tom Braidwood swung into action. He had not acted for Philliponi at the avails trial, but he had been the counsel on the bribery case. And he was determined to redeem both Philliponi setbacks.

"The point about Joe Philliponi," Braidwood says today, "is that he had always been a sore spot for the Vancouver police and the rest of the city authorities. So when the morals crackdown came, he was made the scapegoat."

Braidwood has small capacity for what he regards as injustice. Perhaps the attitude owes its origins to his background. He came by his success the hard way, the son of a butcher who earned his way up each step on the legal ladder. One good break arrived through his father's friendship with Angelo Branca, a gifted and famous Vancouver litigation lawyer. When Braidwood graduated from law school, he joined Branca's small firm, and so did David Nuttall, the son of another old Branca pal, RCMP Corporal Ernest Nuttall. Together, the two young men, both burners of the midnight oil, helped push the firm in size and distinction. When Branca left for the bench in 1963, the growth continued, and Braidwood flourished. He lives a good and honest life today, an earnest, low-key lawyer and a plain family man. He sails his forty-four-foot sloop and he treats himself and his wife to the luxury of two-month travelling holidays each summer. But at the same time, amid the pleasures, he has retained a sense of proportion about the ways in which the legal system fails to measure up. He speaks out against Canada's wire-tap laws and against the crown's practice of paying its witnesses in cash for their evidence. And when the Philliponi case came along, he got his dander up at police tactics which he considered at best high-handed. Maybe some of his yacht-club set questioned the propriety of acting for people like Joe Philliponi — it was hardly the done thing — but Braidwood waded without pause into the battle.

"I just shrugged off the nasty remarks," he said at the time. "You see, I have a family as well. I guess you could say I fight for the right kind of world for them."

First came the appeal on Philliponi's conviction for living on the avails of prostitution.

Braidwood began by taking a swing at the "facts" gathered by the police. Consider, he said to the three-man Court of Appeal that heard the Philliponi appeal, the ramshackle quality of Leslie Schulze's evidence. Schulze was the policewoman who played the role of a hooker at the Penthouse through two months of undercover activity, and at the avails trials she testified about the repeated admission fees that prostitutes paid at the door to the club and about the bonus sums they handed out to the doorman, the cashier, and the hostess. The testimony was entirely damning, but Braidwood invited the appeal court judges to look behind Schulze's words.

Schulze was, to begin with, a police officer of astonishingly limited experience. She had been sworn in on March 23, 1975, as a duty driver in charge of picking up police bulletins and delivering mail. A mere two months later she was pressed into service as a secret operative. But how ably did she perform, a fledgling in a role cut out for a female James Bond? How much weight, Braidwood asked, should be given to her evidence?

And what about Wendy Rhodes, the silent member of the undercover team? Rhodes was, by police admission, Schulze's partner as a pretend prostitute, but she wasn't called as a witness at the avails trial, nor did the crown advance a reason for her failure to testify. Shouldn't an adverse inference be drawn from the absence of a witness whose evidence would apparently rank in importance with Schulze's? Or didn't Rhodes' version of events match up with Schulze's?

Then Braidwood homed in on a peculiarity in Schulze's evidence. Whenever Schulze testified at the trial as to conversations she had with the Philliponi brothers, repeating her memory of words spoken by her on one side and by the Philliponis on the other, the evidence came across as damaging to the Philliponi case. But whenever the Schulze evidence derived from tapes that recorded the conversations verbatim by means of the body pack that Schulze occasionally wore under her clothing, it turned out to be far more favourable to the defence. Braidwood cited one specific example, a tape of a conversation between Schulze and Ross Philliponi on May 30, 1975. The tape, Braidwood pointed out, had been concealed from the defence by the crown and only came to light when Joe Philliponi and his trial lawyer dropped by police headquarters to read transcripts of other tapes and an officer mistakenly included in the batch a transcript of the May 30 tape.

"No wonder the crown tried to keep the tape secret," Braidwood says. "Ross's answers to Schulze's prodding about the way the club was run couldn't have been better if I'd written them myself."

Braidwood read the tape for the Court of Appeal:

SCHULZE: "Hey Ross, can I have a word with you?"

PHILLIPONI: "Ya, sure."

SCHULZE: "Listen, I'm um not sure what goes on, but the other night I, uh . . . well, not the other night. I've been in San Francisco. Last week, I had a couple of tricks that didn't turn out to be tricks, and I came back here, and I had to pay the full money. If I don't turn the trick, do I have to pay the money?"

PHILLIPONI: "Oh ya, once you go out there, we don't give a goddamn whether you do or not. Once you go out, you have to buy another ticket. Ya."

SCHULZE: "No, I mean, well, no, you know, Joe wasn't too sure about it. He said to check with you."

PHILLIPONI: "Ya, once you go out there, that's it."

SCHULZE: "Well, even if I'm gone for ten minutes?"

PHILLIPONI: "Sure, once you go out there, that's it. We don't give a damn whether you have a trick or not, once you go out there."

SCHULZE: "Yah."

PHILLIPONI: "We don't ask for no cut off your trick, right? Right."

SCHULZE: "Well, you know . . ."

PHILLIPONI: "That's it."

SCHULZE: "Well, I have to pay this girl at the door and . . ."

PHILLIPONI: "Well, you just buy . . ."

SCHULZE: ". . . the guy . . ."

PHILLIPONI: "No, you don't have to pay the guy. Who told you you hafta pay the guy?"

SCHULZE: "Well, they *take* the money."

PHILLIPONI: "Well, he'll take it if you give it to him, sure, they're gonna take it."

SCHULZE: "Well, he's taken it from me, you know."

PHILLIPONI: "Well, he don't hafta take it. You're not forced to give it to him."

SCHULZE: "Like . . ."

PHILLIPONI: "If you don't give it to him, he's still gonna let you up if you have a ticket."

SCHULZE: "Ya, well, I just thought that that was . . ."

PHILLIPONI: "If that's what you thought, that's ah . . ."

SCHULZE: "Your policy."

PHILLIPONI: "I dunno, there's no policy."

SCHULZE: "No."

PHILLIPONI: "Just make sure you buy a ticket when you come back, okay?"

SCHULZE: "Yah."

PHILLIPONI: "Right."

SCHULZE: "And what's the chances, do you know anybody I can get associated with who can . . . like, I'm new here."

PHILLIPONI: "No, I can't help you out there. You're a customer up here. You just sit down like a customer. That's all you are as far as we're concerned, okay?"

SCHULZE: "Okay."

PHILLIPONI: "Right."

The points that emerged from this exchange, Braidwood argued, were legion on the defence's side. The policy of requiring the Penthouse's patrons to pay an admission fee at the door had nothing to do with their status as prostitutes. "Once you go out," Ross Philliponi had said, "that's it"; you pay again. Prostitutes paid a repeat fee to return to the club, but so did other Penthouse customers. Nor did payment hinge on the certainty that a prostitute had earned money from a john during her absence. "We don't give a damn whether you have a trick or not," Ross said, "Once you go out there."

As to the extra fees that hookers were alleged to pay to the doorman and the cashier, two dollars to each at every entry, Braidwood contended that in the taped conversation Ross seemed to register only a hazy understanding of the practice: "You don't have to pay the guy. Who told you you hafta pay the guy?" In fact, Braidwood went on, other evidence at the trial established that once Joe Philliponi learned of the payments — learning of them, in a nice piece of irony, partly through Policewoman Schulze's nagging inquiries — he fired the doorman and the cashier and circulated an unequivocal notice to Penthouse employees that read in part: "It has been brought to the attention of the management that certain employees are *demanding* gratuities and tips and in some cases a specified amount. . . . We cannot impress too strongly the seriousness of this illegal practice, and this will serve as notice that anyone in any capacity making such demands or not charging according to our published list will be automatically dismissed without notice." So much, Braidwood concluded, for that supposed source of enrichment.

In even swifter fashion, he waved away the significance in the prostitutes' tipping of the Penthouse hostess. Such tips, he argued, represented a normal transaction in a nightclub. Many patrons might pass a dollar bill or a handful of coins to a hostess when they were ushered to their tables. It wasn't a custom exclusive to prostitutes or exclusive to the Penthouse. Besides, Braidwood went on, a tip to the hostess didn't constitute a benefit to his client, Joe Philliponi. Neither did the payments to the doorman and the cashier. The money went into the employees' pockets. Not Philliponi's. Was he enriched by the cash that prostitutes might spread among the Penthouse staff? The answer, Braidwood said, was patently negative, and it followed as night follows day that, at least as far as these tips and payments were concerned, Philliponi could hardly be said to profit from the prostitutes' avails.

Braidwood turned to the credit-card arrangement, the alleged practice at the Penthouse of allowing johns who were short of cash to draw funds at a twenty-per-cent charge on Chargex or American Express or Mastercharge. The crown's evidence, he said, was "vague and uncertain." Only four instances of such transactions had been raised at the trial, and all four were instigated by undercover policemen who approached Joe or Ross Philliponi with their complaints of money shortages. Even accepting their testimony, the crown had entered no evidence to demonstrate that the Philliponis wouldn't give their patrons cash against credit cards for purposes other than paying hookers. The arrangement, in short, hadn't been shown to relate exclusively to encouraging the Penthouse's customers to make deals with prostitutes. Just consider, Braidwood said, a line that one of the undercover policemen attributed in his testimony to Joe Philliponi during one of the credit-card transactions. "What you do with your money," Joe said to the cop as he handed him $72.45, "is your own business."

None of the facts that the crown offered as evidence, according to Braidwood's interpretation of them for the Court of Appeal, was sturdy enough to support a conviction of Joe Philliponi. But hold on, Braidwood continued, there's more. The crown's case, he said, falls apart in *law* as well as in fact. He turned to the section of the Criminal Code under which Philliponi and the others were charged, Section 195(1) "Every one who . . . (j) lives wholly or in part on the avails of prostitution of another person . . . is guilty of an indictable offence and is liable to imprisonment for ten years." That was the offence which the judge was called on to deal with at the Philliponi trial, Section 195(1)(j). There was another offence, a quite separate offence, under Section 195(1)(h), which read: "Every one who . . . for the purpose of gain, exercises control, direction or influence over the movements of a female person in such manner as to show he is aiding, abetting or compelling her to engage in or carry on prostitution with any person or generally . . . is guilty of an indictable offence and is liable to imprisonment for ten years." This was a different offence — and *not* one under which Joe Philliponi and the others were charged.

Here were two separate and distinct offences, two that the Criminal Code was at pains to set apart, and yet, Braidwood argued, the judge at the trial had irretrievably confused the two to the detriment of Philliponi and his fellow-accused. Braidwood put his finger on a concluding sentence in the trial judge's written judgment, a sentence that immediately preceded his verdict of guilty as charged. "The conspiracy charged and proven," the judge wrote, "is an agreement to obtain pecuniary gain by exercising control, direction and influence over the movement of prostitutes who use the Penthouse premises for the purpose of soliciting their customers which aided those prostitutes in engaging in or carrying on prostitution."

No, no, Braidwood argued. The words were wrong. "Control" and "direction" and "influence" were the words of Section 195(1)(h) of the Criminal Code, the section that was *not* at issue in the trial. The judge, he said, had somehow stepped away from the section that *was* at issue, Section 195(1)(j), with devastating consequences.

"The result," Braidwood wrote on page 164 of the Statement of Fact and Law that he presented to the Court of Appeal, "is that the accused were found guilty of an offence for which they were not charged and, similarly, that the accused were not found guilty of the offence for which they were charged."

On that nice point, Braidwood rested his case.

The Court of Appeal mulled over the argument — and, in the end, the court's three judges bought it in whole. On behalf of the other two members of the court, Mr. Justice Robertson wrote the judgment, nineteen pages long, and he agreed with Braidwood that, yes, the trial judge had mixed and merged the two sections of the Criminal Code. "With respect," he wrote, "the learned judge lost sight of the offence which the accused were charged with having conspired to commit." Robertson shook his head over the mess and quoted Braidwood's line from page 164 of his Statement — that the trial judge had convicted Philliponi and the others of a crime they weren't charged with and hadn't convicted them of the crime they were charged with. On this ground alone, Robertson wrote, the appeal might be allowed, but he elected to go further and decide whether the evidence indeed proved the charge against the accused. The answer? No, Robertson held, no in every instance. Not on the evidence of the admission fees, not on the evidence of the payments to the doorman, cashier, and hostess, not on the evidence of the credit-card arrangement. And, with those words, he let Philliponi off the hook. Appeal allowed, conviction quashed, and verdict of acquittal directed.

The decision squared just about perfectly with Braidwood's pitch to the court, but one of its members, Mr. Justice McFarlane, couldn't let the opportunity pass without weighing in with one small, preachy footnote. He agreed with Mr. Justice Robertson's judgment, he wrote, but, perhaps disturbed at the seamy evidence that had been read out in court, "I wish to add that it is no part of the judge's function to pass moral judgment on people and we shall not presume to do so in this case. We wish, however, to make it clear the decision of the court is simply that the evidence adduced does not prove the appellants guilty of the specific offence charged against them."

Well, all right, Braidwood conceded, his client might not be exclusively on the side of the angels. Joe Philliponi worked the cabaret business, hardly an industry noted for its Rotary Club morality. But he had also operated a legitimate and profitable enterprise at the Penthouse. And he wasn't the sort of entrepreneur who would risk his future over a bribe worth fifteen dollars, the price of two bottles of booze and a cake, which was, alas, the very charge that Joe still stood convicted of.

On the bribery case — the appeal against Philliponi's conviction of "offering" and "giving" Pia Tofini "valuable consideration" in return for her possible favours at the B.C. Liquor Board — Braidwood was again confronted with facts that waffled and law that showed soft spots. But at least the issues were narrow and not much in dispute. Both crown and defence agreed that Philliponi had invited Tofini to chat about his problems with the Penthouse's liquor licence and that at the end of the discussion Joe had sent Pia on her way with a package containing the two bottles of liquor and the freshly baked cake. That left one basic area of contention: did the encounter amount to the offering and giving of a bribe?

At the trial, Tofini had been the crown's principal witness, and her interpretation of the meeting with Philliponi suggested shady dealings. "I understood from Mr. Joseph Philliponi," she testified, "that he wanted me to do something through the board." And had Joe slipped her a gift when she left the meeting? Of course, Tofini told the court, and she referred to a transcript of the taped conversation that she had with Philliponi as she was leaving in her car.

TOFINI: "Bye, bye Joe. What are you carrying there?"

PHILLIPONI: "Hey."

TOFINI: "Say, what are you carrying there?"

PHILLIPONI: "Oh, it's just a little package for you."

The gift of the cake and the bottles was nothing new in Philliponi's way of doing business. As the evidence at the trial demonstrated, he'd been spreading largesse among Liquor Board employees for years. And those two elements — the meeting with Tofini and the ongoing history of under-the-counter presents — were enough to persuade the trial judge that Philliponi had committed a crime.

"Joseph made frequent gifts to Liquor Control Board inspectors," the judge wrote in his reasons for judgment. "In cross-examination, Joseph admitted that he knew the gifts might cause someone to do him a favor in their line of duty. . . . I am satisfied beyond a reasonable doubt that it was precisely for this type of favoritism that Joseph gave Mrs. Tofini the two bottles of liquor as she left his place after the conversation on March 30, 1976. Based upon his habitual practice, it came as second nature for him to try and create some small sense of obligation in Mrs. Tofini as a person who could perform a useful service for himself and his family. . . ."

Guilty, the judge concluded, as charged.

Not guilty, Braidwood argued to the Court of Appeal. Never mind Philliponi's past practices, he said, but examine his state of mind at the meeting with Tofini. Braidwood plunged into Philliponi's worries and anxieties. Joe was a man convinced of his innocence of the avails charge, convinced that the vice squad had marked him as a target, convinced that he wasn't getting a fair shake, convinced that the Liquor Board had turned down his appeal on the basis of incomplete information and of hearsay evidence. Joe was frantic — but not stupid.

Braidwood put his finger on Philliponi's testimony at the trial, the testimony that touched on his motives for seeking out Tofini.

One example: "To tell you truthfully," Philliponi had said to the court, "in the back of my head I was very cunningly trying to find out about this alleged conspiracy as was reported to me, but I knew I had to do it very diplomatically, and I could not come straight out with it, and I was fishing to the best of my ability for that purpose."

Again: "I've got to suffer all of this agitation of my place being closed down just because of incompetence on the part of the board or conspiracy or whatever occurred, and I'm trying to find out but badly. I'm not trying to bribe her in any way, shape or form. A straight bribe? I can think of a lot of ways to bribe but not that way. I could have come around and given her $10,000. The money could have been in the cake."

And again: "I was sitting thinking to myself, here I have a pretty worthy cause or worthy reason, and unless she is going to push that worthy reason which she has got to believe, well, that is surely the thing. It was just to see that justice was done."

And yet again: "I gave her the gift for Easter, and that was for her kids, the cake, and she said she liked Scotch and gin. She never drank anything in the place that night, so I gave her a bottle of Scotch and gin. That is what she drank, and the cake she liked for her family. I didn't give her the cake. My mother sent her the cake, and that's what started the whole thing. If it wasn't for that cake, she wouldn't even have got the bottles."

A cake for *Easter*?

To be sure, Braidwood argued. The tapes of the conversation recorded through Tofini's body pack indicated as much. What Tofini testified as hearing Joe say on the tapes, "Oh, it's just a little package for you," was in fact, on closer listening "Oh, it's just a little bag for you for Easter."

Braidwood analysed Philliponi's past relationship with the Tofini family, the friendship with Pia's late husband, the annual Christmas ads purchased on the Tofinis' solicitation for their newspaper, the sharing of bread and wine at the 1973 picnic in Belcara Park. Why, Braidwood pushed on, evidence at the trial established that before Christmas 1973, Philliponi had sent Mrs. Tofini two bottles of the Beaujolais which she had remarked on with pleasure at the picnic, two bottles of Beaujolais and two boxes of chocolates, gifts that Pia accepted gladly.

Thus, Braidwood argued, two currents ran through the case: one was an ongoing relationship between Philliponi and Pia Tofini, a friendship that allowed for gifts offered and accepted, and the second was Philliponi's concern that justice had been denied him by the Liquor Board. So it was natural, given the past dealings with Tofini, that Philliponi might tender her an Easter gift. So it was understandable that he would press his case to her for a fair review of his standing at the Liquor Board. And, against this background, there was one element missing in Philliponi's conversation with Tofini on the night of March 30, an element crucial to the crown's case.

What was it?

"Corruption," Braidwood said to the Court of Appeal.

In order to make a case that Philliponi had bribed Tofini, it had to be demonstrated that he *corruptly* offered her valuable consideration. All the previous reported cases on the point, Braidwood said, all the cases that dealt with bribery, required that the accused person display a dose of this ingredient, corruption, in his efforts at seducing an official person. There lay the key — a corrupt intent. Granted, it was a matter of fine lines. It was the difference between, say, lobbying and corrupting. One was a matter of merely pressing a point and the other of offering material gain in return for a favour. Philliponi hadn't crossed the line, not in the way he'd gone about unloading his troubles, along with his liquor and cake, on Pia Tofini. And it was the one requisite item — a sense of corrupting — that was lacking in both the crown's case and the trial judge's decision.

"I respectfully submit," Braidwood said to the Court of Appeal, "that the learned judge erred in that he never even considered whether or not the intent and actions of Joe Philliponi were corrupt."

Enough, enough, the Court of Appeal, said, nodding in brisk agreement with Braidwood's argument. No corruption, the court held, and therefore no conviction. The appeal was allowed, and once again justice had come to Joe Philliponi, as in the avails trial, on appeal, the second time around.

But Philliponi's troubles weren't quite over. The Vancouver City Council got into the act by passing a by-law directed specifically at Philliponi and forbidding him a liquor licence for the new club he intended to open. Braidwood took action by way of a Writ of Certiorari, a measure that moves the records of one body to a superior court. In this case, it was from the city council to the B.C. Supreme Court, and when Mr. Justice Verchere of that court looked at the by-law, he threw it out as lacking in natural justice. Joe Philliponi came away a final winner.

But there was also a loser in the long and expensive hounding of Philliponi and the Penthouse. The loser was the City of Vancouver. The first hint of problems came at the avails trial when Detective Norman Elliott of the vice squad underwent cross-examination by Philliponi's counsel. Elliott was the detective who spent so many nights hanging around the Penthouse during the police undercover operation. After charges were laid against the Philliponis, he had moved on to other vice-squad duties around the city. And what, he was asked, had he observed of the trade in prostitution in Vancouver?

"Since the Penthouse closed," Elliott answered, "I have seen the ladies who used to frequent the Penthouse in such classier hotels as the Devonshire and the Bayshore Inn."

That was the problem.

"The prostitutes used to be confined to the Penthouse," Braidwood says. "Now they've spread around to the better areas of downtown Vancouver. As soon as the club went out of business, the women moved into the streets very openly, and the nuisance has become far worse for the police and everybody else than it ever was in the days of the Penthouse."

And the irony of the situation is compounded by Joe Philliponi's reappearance on the cabaret scene.

"Joe's back in business," Braidwood says. "He prides himself in running a nightclub that features nude and semi-nude dancers."

Braidwood adds a bemused addendum: "Not that it's anything obscene by the standards of today's morality."

Still, Philliponi's new club has something in common with the old Penthouse — it isn't the sort of place where Tom Braidwood would hang his hat.

CHAPTER 5

THE MINEFIELD

LOOKED AT IN ONE WAY, Don Bitter has spent the last thirty years searching out the essentials in life. Now, in his early fifties, he's got them whittled down to a precious few: his two sons, his golf game, his work with Alcoholics Anonymous, his collection of jazz records, his skills over a hot stove, and his criminal law practice in Kitchener, Ontario. Among the items more or less jettisoned along the way are a heavy drinking habit, severe attacks of angst, and marriage ("I've got ex-wives who think I'm a great guy but can't stand to cohabit with me"). He's emerged a cool, wry, funny gent, and sometimes it amazes him that he's survived.

"Everybody who gets involved in my area of the profession ends up with a strange personal life," Bitter said one bright and zingy Saturday morning in autumn. He sat at his kitchen table as he talked, mainlining cups of dark, aromatic coffee, and in the background his two teenaged boys, Jason and Clark, who live with him, watched television, checked out their sports equipment, and kibitzed around.

"All kinds of things can happen in criminal law that might tip a guy over the edge," Bitter said. "Just little things that make you think the world's a crazy place and you don't know whether you're the keeper or one of the inmates."

Then he told the story of his sometime client, Albert Hazzard.

"Hazzard's a black guy," Bitter began, "and people are always calling him a nigger. Or maybe he fantasizes people call him a nigger. That may be his problem. Anyway, he went into his apartment building one day, and a guy was fixing the door to one of the suites, down on his knees tightening a screw. The guy calls Hazzard a nigger. Or Hazzard fantasized it. Whichever it was, Hazzard pulled out a knife that had a blade about fourteen inches long and he grabbed the guy around the neck and held this fourteen-inch blade to his throat.

" 'I'm gonna slit your throat from ear to ear,' he said to the guy, who was practically paralysed he was so scared.

" 'In case you didn't get that,' Hazzard said, 'I'm gonna repeat it.'

"The thing about Hazzard is that he's always involved in legal situations that are absolutely terrible. He never leaves any room for the smallest doubt about the laws he's about to break.

" 'I'm gonna slit your throat from ear to ear,' he says to the guy a second time.

"Well, he didn't slit any throats, but the guy eventually called the cops, and Hazzard is charged with possession of an offensive weapon, to wit a knife with a fourteen-inch blade. We go to court and Hazzard's got a record as long as both his arms and all of it is for violent stuff. I negotiated with the crown attorney, and we ended up pleading guilty to a slightly reduced charge. Not that it really mattered, because those terrible facts about the knife and the threats and everything were read out in court anyway. I mean, a rose is a rose is a rose.

"So I knew Hazzard was bound to get some time in jail, but I stood up and made my pitch to the judge, nothing especially stirring, just putting the best light I could on this awful situation. I sat down, and right away the judge gives his sentence.

" 'There'll be a fine of one hundred dollars,' he said.

"*What*? I was stunned. That had to be the most ridiculous sentence I'd ever heard, turning loose a guy with Hazzard's record on a case as bad as that. I couldn't figure what possessed the judge. All I knew right then was that I felt scared to leave the courtroom. I sat at the counsel table and I turned to the lawyer sitting beside me.

" 'There's gonna be a lynch mob outside,' I said to him. 'Not for Hazzard. For *me*. People'll think *I'm* the one responsible for putting that guy back on the streets.'

"So I sat there till the air cleared a little, and I thought, Christ, it's always a little crazy in this business, but this time the justice system has completely snapped."

Bitter poured himself another hit of his killer coffee.

"Hazzard, strange as he was, had a certain amount of persuasive charm about him," he continued. "And that shows you one of the pitfalls in practising criminal law. Y'see, the demi-monde is actually kind of irresistible, and the rounders who live in it can be very attractive people, personable and interesting and colourful. They don't act in any conventional way. No matter how much money they've got, they're always looking for an edge, and that kind of mentality gets to be fascinating to the criminal lawyers who act for them. The trouble is that a lot of lawyers get *too* close to clients like that, and if you start to run with them, it can be lethal. At the best, you end up drinking with them, hanging out in their joints, ruining your health and your marriage, and at the worst, you might find yourself in the jug charged with the same offences as the rounders. I've seen so many lawyers go down the tube in one way or another. Sad, really sad and swift."

Bitter launched into a quick rundown on his own career. "I got off to a fast start in Toronto as a junior with a sensational criminal lawyer named Walton C. Rose. The number of bandits who came through his door was unbelievable, and inside a couple of years I was handling some of the livelier stuff, acting for people whose names were on the top of the bad-guy list of practically every cop in town. I could see how easy it was to get caught up in the glamour of the street life, and after a few more years I decided to move along. I went over to the other side of the business and practised as an assistant crown attorney in Kitchener and Parry Sound and Sault Ste. Marie. The Soo was a graveyard for crowns, and I developed a problem with the booze. I stepped on a few toes in that town, too, and at Christmas one year I had to move my family out of the house because some idiot laid a bomb threat on it. This, I said, I don't need. So I went back to private practice on my own in Kitchener, and the last dozen years have gone down about as smooth as I could ask for."

Bitter went for one last zap of heavy-duty coffee and, sipping it, he mustered a summing-up of his life and essence and survival as a criminal lawyer. "I drifted around in my time. I won my share but I've never really distinguished myself. I suppose all I've done over the years is avoided stepping on mines. That's what criminal law is — a minefield. I've seen dozens of lawyers blow themselves up. Liquor gets one guy, women another, rubbing shoulders with the rounders wipes out a few more. So far I've picked my way past all the live mines, and that in itself isn't such a bad accomplishment."

CHAPTER 6

THE COURTLY COUNSEL
FROM WINNIPEG

AS HE'LL LET YOU KNOW HIMSELF, Harry Walsh has a tendency
to dominate his surroundings. At a party, over the dinner table,
or in a courtroom, it's Walsh who catches the eye and the ear. He
has the looks appropriate to a Roman senator: he's short, but his
figure is upright with just a hint of stately paunch, and his head
is noble, with long silver sideburns sweeping majestically over his
ears. His voice tone is soothing, his delivery insistent, his choice
of language correct in a deliciously traditional style, and those
attributes equip him ideally for two roles: litigation lawyer — he
is, in his late sixties, the dean of Winnipeg's counsel — and
raconteur.He doesn't shirk either.

"Dorothy Christie's case seemed at first glance to be hopeless,"
he begins a recollection one autumn morning as he sits in his
office in a building at the corner of Portage and Main. "She was a
petite and comely woman of some twenty-four years of age, and
she was married to a big, husky, handsome fellow who was a year
or two older than she. The marriage was only of about six months'
duration, but it was already going badly for Dorothy. Indeed,
her husband, who was nicknamed Bunny, had bragged to her
that he had recently slept with two other women. Nevertheless
they continued to live together in a boarding-house in one room
that served the function of living-room, kitchen, and bedroom.
They were of modest means, and their one extravagance was
Bunny's motorcycle. He belonged to a club of fellow motorcycle
addicts — nothing evil or illegal about them, nothing that suggested
Satan's Choice or the Hell's Angels — and on many occasions the

husbands and wives of the club would ride into the country to enjoy the fresh air. That was what Mr. and Mrs. Christie were doing on the Friday in June 1957 that ended in Mr. Christie's death and a charge of murder against Dorothy Christie.

"Now, during the weeks prior to the tragedy, Dorothy was bothered by headaches and insomnia. She had a prescription for pills from her doctor to alleviate the dual complaint, and on the evening when she and her husband returned from this particular Friday outing, she took one pill before she retired for the night in the same bed with her husband in the room that was bolted shut from the inside. Dorothy awoke at about seven o'clock the following morning and snuggled up to her husband. He didn't move. She sat up and looked at him. There was a small hole in his temple from which blood was trickling. Even to Dorothy's untutored eye, it was clear that he was dead, and lying beside him, in between the body and Dorothy, was the husband's twenty-two-calibre rifle.

"Dorothy looked around the room. The door remained bolted, the windows were down, and there was no evidence of an intruder. In the agony of the moment, Dorothy realized that it could only have been she who shot her husband, and yet she had no memory of the act. She telephoned to her husband's brother. 'I have shot Bunny,' she told him, 'and I'm going to shoot myself.' Then she picked up the rifle, and though she hadn't any knowledge of firearms, though she had never before in her life so much as fired a gun, she somehow managed to manoeuvre the rifle into position and shoot herself in the abdomen.

"Christie's brother had meanwhile called the police and directed them to the boarding-house, and when they arrived, they broke down the door and rushed Dorothy to the hospital. Eventually she recovered and gave the police a simple statement in which she said that she must be the killer but that she loved her husband despite their differences and could never do harm to him. She was charged with murder, and when her family retained me to act on her behalf, I recognized that in all the curious and damning facts of the case there was only one possible defence. That was a defence of automatism. I would argue that Dorothy was in such a state of mind, a sleepwalker's state if you will, that she could form no intent to commit murder. Intent in those days, back in 1957 before amendment of the Criminal Code, was an integral part of the definition of murder under the Code, and without the presence of intent to kill, there could be no murder.

"The trouble with such a defence, automatism, is that it is one which engenders suspicions in the minds of a jury. It sounds like something a lawyer might put up in desperation to save a hopeless case. And indeed there was virtually no precedent that I could find of automatism being raised as a defence in earlier capital cases. There were no Canadian cases on the subject and not much solace in the few English cases. But I was determined, and I had facts on which to base my argument. There were the sleeping pills. It turned out that Dorothy Christie had renewed her prescription on the day before the killing. It was for twelve sleeping pills, but on the morning after the crime, police found the pill vial on the floor of the room, and it was empty. Although the only pill that Dorothy remembered having taken from the vial was the one on the fatal Friday evening, it seemed that she must have ingested eleven more pills at some point during the late-night or early-morning hours. She could not remember, but she must have done so. And when I interviewed her doctor and her pharmacist and a chemist who analysed the type of pill that Dorothy took, I became convinced that the consumption of so many pills would have reduced her to a legitimate state of automatism.

"The matter came on for trial, and the crown attorney put his case to the jury based on the very cut-and-dried events that seemed so persuasively to point to Dorothy's guilt. Then it was my turn. I called the doctor and the pharmacist and the chemist to the witness-stand, and then I called Dorothy. As a general rule, defence counsel are reluctant in a murder case to use the accused person as a witness even when he or she is perfectly innocent. One never knows whether the poor accused, out of sheer nervousness, might blunder into an injudicious answer. But with Dorothy I had no choice. She was the only person who could testify as to certain facts in her favour. She was the only person who could swear, for instance, that she did not flush the sleeping pills down the toilet or otherwise dispose of them. So I called her, and she made an excellent witness.

"The courtroom in the Winnipeg Courthouse in which the trial was being held was then and is now a formidable place. The ceiling is high and of stained glass, the walls and prisoner's dock and witness-stand are of marble, the well of the courtroom is very large, and the judge's bench towers over everything. Behind the judge, on the wall, are three words in giant type, 'Truth. Justice. Mercy.' I imagine an accused person looks at the words and wonders, 'Why mercy? I'd just like to be acquitted.' In those surroundings, Dorothy Christie, so tiny and pretty and distressed, struck a very appealing figure for the jury, which was all male. And when she answered my questions on examination-in-chief, she spoke honestly and forthrightly and said that, yes, it must have been she who shot her husband. As she talked, her voice had a monotonous quality, as if, even there in court, she remained in a kind of trance, and I trusted that the jury took note of her strange and distraught condition.

"I finished my questioning, and the crown rose to cross-examine Dorothy. He took her through a few unimportant preliminary points. Then he reached the obvious and expected highlight of his cross-examination, namely the rifle. What about the rifle? Hadn't it been around the Christie living-quarters for some months? Didn't she see her husband handle it? Had she really not ever held the gun herself? The crown began to press Dorothy for answers, and he was most insistent.

"As he talked, the crown walked around from behind his table, which was about seventy feet from the witness-stand in this large and imposing courtroom. He picked up from the table exhibit number six in the case, the rifle itself, and he made his way very deliberately on the long route that took him behind the counsel tables and past the jury-box toward the witness-stand. He had reached a point directly opposite the middle of the jury-box when Dorothy, seeing him with the rifle in his hands, the terrible murder weapon, and knowing that he was going to press more questions about it, broke into a shuddering shriek and began to sob in a most pitiful manner. The crown counsel stopped in his tracks, holding the rifle, and at that moment one of the jurymen looked at him and said something that was quite audible over the sound of poor Dorothy's sobbing.

"'You son of a bitch,' he said to the crown counsel. 'You son of a bitch.'

"It was an electrifying moment. There had been a question on the crown counsel's lips, but it went unasked. He looked up at the judge in a silent inquiry. The judge said nothing, and the crown turned and walked quickly back to his table. Dorothy had by then recovered, and the crown continued with a few more questions. He was, however, clearly shaken by the events, and his line of cross-examination had lost much of its thrust. Soon he finished and sat down.

"A little later, when I made my address to the jury, I found them most receptive to my argument of automatism. 'If the mind does not know what the hands do,' I said to them, 'there is no crime,' and I could almost feel them reaching out to me in agreement. Indeed, when they retired to consider their verdict, they were back in the courtroom within a mere thirty minutes. Not guilty, they said, and at that announcement the courtroom, which was packed, broke into applause and cheers as if the spectators were at a sporting event. Dorothy Christie walked away not to the gallows but to freedom. And I felt very content. It was the first time that a defence of automatism had succeeded in a British Commonwealth court.

"And" — Walsh pauses to let the drama sink a notch deeper — "I was, of course, most grateful to the jury member who spoke so frankly to the crown counsel."

Violence in the family. Wife shoots husband, son guns down father, husband kills wife's lover. Walsh has defended in dozens of such grim trials. "Killing is rarely an instance of planning and deliberation," he says in his courtly way. "Rather, it is usually the result of emotions running amuck, and so often that occurs within the family unit." Perhaps Walsh's own background opens him to a special relationship with cases that begin in family grief. He grew up in Winnipeg's rough North End, and when he was fifteen his father died, leaving the widow and mother to raise six children on a small income. To pay his way through the University of Manitoba, Walsh sold newspapers at the corner of Portage and Main, outside the very building that now houses his office. His first wife, the mother of his two children, lived in sickness for a dozen years and died a young woman. Walsh survived, and throughout his practice, over forty years at the bar and over one hundred murder cases, he has identified with families and their distress.

"A case in the summer of 1962 up in the town of Selkirk, about twenty-five miles north of Winnipeg," he launches another reminiscence. "A fellow named Thomas Baty was accused of murdering another chap of the town, Rudy Bendl. Both men were in their early thirties, both worked at the Selkirk Mental Institution, and both owned small spreads of farming land. Baty was married and had three young children. Bendl, on the other hand, was a bachelor and had something of a reputation as a Lothario in the community. He was alleged to have had relations with many local women, some of them married, and among his married partners was Baty's wife, Zelda. That, according to the crown's case, was the motive for Thomas Baty's killing of Rudy Bendl.

"The affair between Bendl and Zelda Baty dated back several months before the night of the crime, but as so frequently happens in these matters, Thomas Baty was the last person in town to learn of his wife's trysts. It was the wife herself who told him about her relationship with Bendl one night in the middle of July after she had drunk several glasses of wine. Her tongue was loosened and she said that Bendl wished to marry her and to take her and the three children to live in Australia. Baty was devastated. In the two weeks that followed, he was unable to eat or sleep and he grew weak and gaunt. To make the situation more painful, he was compelled to work at the Mental Institution alongside Rudy Bendl, and now that the affair was out in the open, now that Zelda Baty had moved from her husband's house to live with her mother, Bendl felt free to taunt Baty, bragging about his escapades with Zelda. On a couple of occasions, the two men fell into fisticuffs, and each time, Bendl knocked Baty to the ground. Baty was clearly being driven to the very brink of emotion.

"On the day of the killing, the first Saturday in August, Baty wept in front of his brother and complained bitterly that he could not stand the idea of Bendl taking his children to a place as far off as Australia. This was what was upsetting him, the fear of loss of his children, and that Saturday, after midnight, he decided to act in the manner he thought any red-blooded Canadian would in the circumstances. He would confront Bendl and warn him off. He drove to the Mental Institution, parked his stationwagon, and went up to Bendl's room. He carried with him a double-barrelled shotgun which he kept in the stationwagon to shoot badgers on his farm property. He pounded on Bendl's door, waking him up and also waking the man in the next room, and there followed a short, loud discussion between Baty and Bendl. The next sound that the man in the neighbouring room heard was the blast of a shotgun. When he made his way into the hall, Thomas Baty was emerging from Rudy Bendl's room, and inside Bendl lay dead.

"At the trial, I elected to base my defence of Baty on a contention that the killing was accidental. I set the stage by eliciting testimony from the police ballistics expert that Bendl's body showed powder marks and signs of gases from the barrel of the shotgun. This established that the gun had been fired from very close range and in circumstances, I would argue, that indicated a struggle had taken place. Then I summoned Baty to the witness-stand. As in the Dorothy Christie case, he was the only witness who could testify to certain crucial events. I led him through the preliminary matters, establishing his feelings over the revelation of his wife's affair with Bendl, the threatened loss of his children, and finally I brought him to the night of the shooting.

" 'Why,' I asked, 'did you carry a gun when you called on Rudy Bendl?'

" 'Well,' Baty answered, 'he'd already given me a couple of beatings. I needed it to frighten him away from me.'

"That was a good, sensible explanation, so I moved on to the next logical question.

" 'Did you,' I asked, 'have any intention of shooting Bendl?'

" 'No,' he answered, 'I just didn't want any trouble. I just wanted my kids. I told him Zelda was a young woman and could have many more children and why did he have to have *my* children?'

"Baty was a most passionate witness. He wept on the stand, and there were several people in the courtroom, friends and relatives of his, who were also weeping.

" 'What happened in Rudy Bendl's room?' I asked.

" 'He tried to grab the gun,' Baty said, 'and it went off.'

" 'Did you intend to shoot him?' I asked again.

" 'I didn't mean to shoot Rudy Bendl,' Baty said from the witness-box. 'What good would it do me? I've lost my kids, my wife, my job. Now I'm sitting in prison next to that execution room.'

"Well, this was very powerful testimony, but everything depended on the way in which the jury reacted to it. Would they accept Baty's version of the shooting? It was my feeling in the Selkirk courtroom that they would. A jury doesn't apply the principles of law with surgical precision, not the way a judge sitting alone on a case is more likely to. People on a jury understand life as it is lived in the community more acutely than a judge does. That has been my experience of juries. They are composed of people who are out in the world, and they accept the emotions that affect a man like Thomas Baty. At least, that was how I was reading the jury in Selkirk.

"The jury was out of the courtroom not more than forty minutes and returned with a verdict of not guilty. It was an extremely popular decision in Selkirk. Everybody in the community seemed to think that Baty had acted properly in challenging Bendl, the interloper in his family, and if there was an accident that ended in death, it was too bad for Bendl, but Baty should not have to suffer more than he already had.

"And he did not" — Walsh smiles and shakes his head in mild disbelief — "because, as I understand it, after all the turmoil, Thomas Baty's wife Zelda rejoined him with their children in the family household. It is strange what passions these cases let loose."

Walsh leads the way out of his office building. It's the Childs Building, ancient and endearing, and the only stone structure left among the glass and steel towers at Winnipeg's principal intersection. Walsh's firm — Walsh, Micay and Company — has occupied the seventh floor of Childs ever since Harry Walsh and Archie Micay were called to the bar in 1937 in a class of eleven men and one woman (she, Walsh proudly points out, was Ruth Vogel, who served as executive assistant to Stuart Garson when he was Premier of Manitoba and Minister of Justice in Ottawa under Lester Pearson). Walsh and Micay articled with Edward James McMurray, Solicitor General in a Mackenzie King government and for decades Winnipeg's wizard of the criminal courts. Walsh caught some of his relish for litigation from McMurray, and in the long years since McMurray's retirement and death, he has assumed his old mentor's starring role in the courts.

Now Walsh is steering through the noon-hour crowds to lunch in the Winnipeg Inn across the intersection from the Childs Building. This is Walsh territory. The maître d' in the plush Velvet Glove Room bows him to his favourite table, the one directly opposite the fireplace, and Walsh orders without consulting the menu. Over mushroom soup and grilled pickerel, he recalls the Zimmerman case. Another family in distress.

"They lived on a farm outside the town of Ashern, seventy miles from Winnipeg up near Lake Manitoba," Walsh begins. "The father, John Zimmerman, was a man in his middle forties and he was an autocrat around the house. More than that, he was cruel. He used to beat his wife. Mabel was her name, and drunk or sober, he would beat her and abuse their three children. It later came out at the trial that on one occasion when the younger daughter, Barbara, was two years old, John Zimmerman seized her and shook her and threw her to the floor, all the while screaming at her, 'Talk, talk!' It seemed that poor little Barbara had not yet spoken a word and was so traumatized by her father that she did not begin to talk until she was four years old. That was the father's pattern of behaviour, one of violence and irrationality, and in retrospect, it was small wonder that one of the members of the family finally killed him.

"On the day of the killing in January 1968, the father arose at four in the morning. That was his custom. He was unable to sleep more than a very few hours each night, and when he was awake, he demanded that the others also be out of their beds. This particular morning, matters seemed to be coming to a head. The father was as usual angry at his wife for no apparent reason. He was dissatisfied with a job he had at the creamery in Ashern. And he was venting rage at his son, Keith, a lad of twenty-two. The father blamed Keith for the death of some of the farm's calves earlier in the winter, and he argued with the boy over Keith's expressed feelings that it was time he left the farm and made his own way in the world. By eight o'clock when John Zimmerman departed for the creamery, some four hours after the family had risen, he had worked himself into a towering temper.

"'I'll see that you suffer,' he said to his wife as he went out, according to the later word of the wife and son. 'I'll make you suffer if I have to kill you. You better think fast because you don't have much time to think any more.'

"Mabel Zimmerman and Keith Zimmerman fretted over the father's parting statement all through the rest of the day.

"'If you leave home,' the mother said to her son, 'I know he'll kill me tonight.'

"Late afternoon came. It was dark, in the deep of Manitoba winter, and the family was in a terrible state of fear as they awaited the father's return. They heard his car, a little Volkswagen, coming down the driveway to the farmhouse. Suddenly Keith must have decided to act. He told his mother to lock herself and Barbara in a room — the third child, another daughter, was away from home that night — and he rushed down to the basement and came back with a rifle. He ran out the back door, not pausing to put on a coat against the bitter cold. His father had pulled the car into the garage about fifty feet from the house. The garage doors were open, and John Zimmerman hadn't yet moved out from behind the steering wheel. Keith fired through the back window of the car and hit his father in the shoulder. John Zimmerman got out of the car. Keith fired again and caught the father in the chest. The father pitched to the ground, and Keith rushed over to him and shot once again into his body as the father lay fallen.

"Keith returned immediately to the house. 'Mum,' he said, 'I had to shoot Dad.' Then he said something strange but significant. 'You'll sleep tonight, Mum,' he said.

"Mabel Zimmerman telephoned to the local RCMP detachment, and the officers arrived immediately. Keith sat at the kitchen table in a shattered state. His mother poured him cups of coffee, which seemed to bring him around, and a little later when the RCMP officers took him and the murder weapon to the station, he gave them a statement that was frank and open and forthright. Indeed, the statement later contributed in an instrumental way to my case for Keith.

" 'All I could think of,' he said to the RCMP, 'was just to stop Dad from coming in the house.'

"The defence I mounted at Keith's trial for the murder of his father was an extension of the principle of self-defence, which is rarely resorted to in a capital case. Usually, of course, self-defence arises where you yourself are attacked. The law says you may resist and defend your person provided you do not use more force than is necessary under the circumstances. In the Zimmerman case, Keith was acting not in his own defence but in the defence of a third party, his mother. That is a quite different matter. Still, I had many of the elements for my argument — the long history of the dead man's brutality to his wife, the threats that he had uttered on the morning of his death, the fear that young Keith felt for his mother's life. What I lacked was a weapon that I could place in or near the father's hands. It was all very well for him to have threatened the wife's life, but how was he going to act on the threat? What weapon, apart possibly from his bare hands, would he employ? If there was such a weapon, then I could be more persuasive and convincing in arguing that Keith felt an immediate danger to his mother's safety, so immediate that he was compelled to act as drastically as he did in order to save her life. But there appeared to be no weapon.

"Then I made an extraordinary and fortuitous discovery. I was looking through the photographs that the police had taken at the scene of the crime within an hour or two of the killing. One photo showed a view into the garage. The car was parked, and the door on the driver's side stood open. Through the window of the open door, I could make out the top of an object that was leaning against the back wall of the garage. I looked at the object more closely. Was it what I thought it was? I got a magnifying glass and studied the object in the photo for several minutes before I was completely satisfied. It *was* what I suspected. It was the barrel of a rifle, and that rifle, leaning against the garage door, would have stood within easy reach of the father as he stepped from his car. I had my weapon.

"It was very curious about the rifle. By the time I discovered it in the photograph — this was several weeks after the killing — it had gone missing from the garage. I questioned Mrs. Zimmerman, and she said the garage had been cleared out and she could recall no rifle. I believed her. She was an honest person, as was Keith. What was even more curious was that the RCMP had absolutely no notion of the rifle's existence. They had apparently missed it at the scene of the crime, and they hadn't spotted it in the photograph. The first news they had of the rifle came at the trial when I cross-examined the chief investigating officer. I showed him the photograph. Could he identify the object against the garage wall? No, he said, he couldn't be certain. Would he look at it through a magnifying glass? He would, and when he looked, he registered complete astonishment. He was forced to admit that the object was certainly a rifle, that he had entirely missed it in the investigation, and that the rifle must have been standing in its place when John Zimmerman parked his car a few feet away from the weapon on the night of the killing. I thanked the officer most sincerely.

"Well, the jury sat up and took deep interest in that piece of testimony, and when I addressed them, reminding them of the sense of terror that prevailed in the Zimmerman household, of Keith's statement to the RCMP in which he expressed the necessity he felt to act on his mother's behalf, and of the presence of the rifle so close to the father's hand, I was certain that I had them with me. They felt compassion for the Zimmerman boy's predicament, and they were searching for a means to express those feelings. I believe the rifle showed them the way. It must have been difficult for them — they were at their deliberations for five hours — but ultimately they came back with a verdict that acknowledged my argument of self-defence.

"They acquitted Keith Zimmerman."

Walsh finishes his meal and orders coffee.

"A year or two later," he continues, "I received a letter post-marked in the Ashern area. It was from young Keith. He wrote that he was working at a good job, and he enclosed something he wanted me to have — an invitation to his wedding."

Walsh sips his coffee.

"In my profession," he says, "a man learns to appreciate a happy ending."

CHAPTER 7

A PERSON'S GOOD NAME

JULIAN PORTER DEALS IN WORDS. Angry words. Mean words. Clever and malicious words. Words strung into sentences and paragraphs that, intentionally or not, sting and hurt and insult. Words that turn up, giving offence, in books and on radio and in magazines. The words constitute Porter's professional territory. He's a Toronto counsel who specializes in libel and slander.

When Jim Coutts, the former principal secretary to Pierre Trudeau, claimed that Allan Fotheringham, the newspaper and magazine columnist, had libelled him, Porter acted for Fotheringham. He took the defence when movie producer Garth Drabinsky decided that *Maclean's* magazine had dipped his name in the mud. He performed similar services for the *Canadian Jewish News* when Peter Ustinov took umbrage at the newspaper. He has sued the *Toronto Star* and the *Globe and Mail* on behalf of various complaining clients, and he was retained by the plaintiff in perhaps the most sensational libel action of the late 1970s, Leslie James Bennett versus Ian Adams. Bennett was a retired RCMP officer who had headed up the Mounties' intelligence service, and Adams was the author of a novel called *S: Portrait of a Spy* that told the tale of a KGB agent who infiltrated the RCMP and rose to the top post in its intelligence division. Bennett figured that Adams had based the fiction, with a libellous twist or two, on his own career. He sued.

"I did some of my best work on that one," Porter says of the Bennett-Adams case. "I took Bennett as a client because I thought it was the most monstrous libel I'd come across, accusing a man of betraying his country, and when I got into the action, I was tough and I was nasty and I was persistent and I didn't give a damn about the costs. For the time and effort I put into the case, I could have billed $70,000, but Bennett had no money and I knew from the start that my fee would be $2,000. Hell, my out-of-pocket disbursements came to $3,000. So the position I took with the other side was that this was my free case and I was ready to ride it to the highest court in the land and really ram it to them. In the end, after examination for discovery and a lot of preliminary motions, we settled out of court, $30,000 for Bennett, and I knew that he was a client who'd got the best conceivable service. It was a case that made me very happy to be a lawyer."

The specialty — libel — suits Porter. He loves words. His life is awash in them. He reads three or four books a week, mysteries and art books and political biographies, novels and books about show business. His wife is a book publisher. Anna Porter is so beautiful that Irving Layton wrote a poem about her and so brainy that she ranks near the top of Canadian publishing. She was at one time second in command at McClelland and Stewart of Canada, and later president of Seal Books, a paperback company owned jointly by McClelland and Stewart and Bantam Books of the United States, and today she is co-proprietor of another publishing outfit. Manuscripts, galley proofs, page proofs, finished books — they're the furniture of the Porter household.

Maybe, in Julian Porter's personal order of priorities, the spoken word is even more precious than the written word. He revels in his voice, in lectures and toasts and after-dinner speeches, in comic turns and impersonations. Invite Porter to say a few words and he'll assume the floor for a performance calculated to every dramatic pause and laugh line. He's on most prominent Torontonians' list of crowd favourites. When Robert Macaulay, a Toronto developers' lawyer and former Ontario cabinet minister, turned sixty, the speakers at the $150-per-plate dinner held in his honour at the Toronto Four Seasons Hotel were Ontario Premier Bill Davis, Pierre Berton, Mr. Justice Charles Dubin of the Ontario Court of Appeal, and Porter. When Barbara and Murray Frum exhibited their large and valuable collection of African art at the Art Gallery of Ontario, it was Porter who delivered the speech that opened the show. And when Trevor Eyton's daughter was married — Eyton is president of Brascan Limited — Porter ambled to the microphone after the completion of the traditional speeches at the reception, played the role of a wedding drunk, and built the routine into a series of snappy one-liners. It brought the house down.

Porter immerses himself in a busy list of chores beyond his profession, and invariably they're jobs that include a built-in performance factor. He's a past president of the Canadian National Exhibition, a member of the Stratford Festival Board of Governors, and chairman of the Toronto Transit Commission. Such posts come with their burdens in paper-work and boardroom manipulations — two areas that Porter handles adroitly — but they're also public positions that run to press conferences, presentation ceremonies, and celebratory dinners. Porter gives these occasions the light touch, dispensing the requisite information and kudos and at the same time laying on the comic phrase that turns up later in newspaper reports and audience memories.

He looks right in the limelight, a man at home with out-front roles. He's in his mid-forties, husky and strong and blocky in the manner of a football lineman, which he once was on a University of Toronto team that won the intercollegiate championship. His face is handsome or distinguished depending on the way the light happens to hit it. One of "Toronto's Ten Dreamiest Dudes" is how the *Toronto Star* labelled him in October 1980. His is a look that's cut out for television and head tables.

In a sense Porter grew up with the impulse to act and speak on public and legal occasions. His father, Dana, was a lawyer who entered politics and held four cabinet posts, including attorney general, in the Ontario Tory governments of the 1940s and 1950s before he finished his career as Chief Justice of the Ontario Supreme Court. Porter picked up his father's beat. Before he was twenty, he was writing political speeches for Robert Macaulay, and later he campaigned for Senator Wallace McCutcheon, his first wife's father, when McCutcheon took a shot at succeeding John Diefenbaker as head of the Conservative Party. The senator lost to Robert Stanfield, and a year later Porter plunged himself into the federal election, a Liberal sweep for Pierre Trudeau as it happened, as Stanfield's advertising manager.

"There's a reason I take on those outside jobs, the CNE and the TTC and the rest," Porter says. "It has nothing to do with money, because some of the jobs, the CNE for one, are unpaid. It has to do with keeping alive. I see so many lawyers who work in their narrow fields of law and by the time they're fifty-five they're bored out of their minds. I put a day and a half a week into public-service stuff, and that cuts two ways — it gives me a more interesting range of experience than most of my contemporaries have and it keeps alive my love for the law."

Porter had his eye on litigation from the start, and for his first ten years in law, as student and lawyer, he worked in the litigation department of an old Toronto firm, Fasken and Calvin, under an especially gifted and eccentric counsel, the late Walter Williston. "Walter was a peculiar-looking fellow," Porter says. "He reminded me of Elsa Lanchester playing the Bride of Frankenstein. Coke-bottle glasses, belly stuck out, booze and pepperoni on his breath, a mumble for a voice. But he was a prodigious worker, a master at cross-examination, and he knew more law than almost anybody. He taught me as much of it as I could take in." And it was Williston who, willy-nilly, introduced Porter to libel.

"I had a desk outside Williston's office," Porter says. "It was in what used to be a clothes closet, just big enough for a table and chair and me, but the one advantage was its position. From where I sat, I could see everybody who went in to consult Williston, and when it was somebody interesting, I'd duck behind them and sit in on the discussion. One day I looked up and there were three guys from the Montreal Canadiens hockey club coming down the hall, Toe Blake, Frank Selke, and Jean Beliveau. I joined them, and it turned out to be pretty intriguing. Blake was the Canadiens coach at the time, and after a game in Montreal that his team lost, he told reporters that the way Eddie Powers, the referee, handled the game, it was as if he had a bet on the outcome. Powers sued, and Williston sent me out to learn the law of libel. That's what I did, poking around in the library at Osgoode Hall for six weeks to get an education on one subject."

The case was settled with a small payment to Powers, but Porter was hooked on libel, and when he left Williston a few years later to head out on his own, eventually forming the small firm of Porter and Posluns, he packed the specialty with him. He practises a wide range of litigation law today, taking drug cases, handling hearings for the Ontario College of Physicians and Surgeons, and defending in conspiracy charges (Porter acted for one of the accused, McNamara Construction Company, in the famous Hamilton dredging case of the late 1970s, the most costly trial in Canadian legal history, in which, over the course of fifteen months to the tune of seven million dollars, eleven executives of nine dredging companies were tried for conspiring to rig bids on government contracts; McNamara Construction was convicted and fined two million dollars). Porter is prepared to step into almost every variety of litigation. "The only people I won't act for are Scientologists," he says. "I've acted for Nazis and Communists. Not Scientologists. Those people never blink — they're *trained* not to blink — and that unnerves me." But generalist that he may be, he's never lost his fascination with one specialty — libel law.

"I've always thought that the most important thing a person owns is his reputation," he says. "That gives a libel case an extra spin for me, knowing that I'm protecting something so fundamental. The point about libel actions, though, from the plaintiff's side, is that ninety per cent of people who want to sue for libel shouldn't bother. And I tell them so. They don't have the temperament to stand up to the ordeal. I tell them that if they sue, the libel they're complaining about is going to be repeated many more times during the examination for discovery and at the trial. That's hard to take for most people. I tell them that they and their reputation are going to be put under severe cross-examination by the lawyer on the other side. Maybe they could stand up to rough treatment when the only thing at stake is their money. But they can't when it's their good name that may suffer."

Technically, Porter says, a libel action is utterly unique among lawsuits. It means a mandatory jury trial, a rare event in civil cases in recent years, and the approach to the jury that the plaintiff's counsel must take sets it apart from all other jury trials.

"In a criminal trial," Porter says, "the issue is so obviously serious — I mean, you may be talking about murder — that often your best bet as counsel is to lighten up the atmosphere for the jury. Do a song and dance. Make them smile a little. But in a libel action the issue is not obviously serious to most ordinary people. The jury isn't dealing with a dead body. All it is, they think, is words, just words, and what do words really matter? So you have to keep raising the point that when a person dies, the only thing he leaves behind is his name. You must underline the seriousness of protecting a reputation. And when you address the jury, you've got to give them a tear in your eye and a choke in your throat. You've got to play King Lear, just lose yourself and go over the edge and make sure the jury is watching you go over the edge. Otherwise, the importance of your client's reputation will mean nothing to them."

And the psychology in a libel action is delicate and tangled on both sides, plaintiff's and defendant's. "Suppose I'm acting for a plaintiff and he's suing somebody who's accused him in public of being an incompetent accountant," Porter says by way of illustration. "That's a very damaging statement to a professional man. All right, my guy *isn't* an incompetent accountant, but he *is* a philanderer. Do I go to court and risk exposing to the jury that my guy's a rotten person who cheats on his wife? That's got nothing to do with his abilities as an accountant but the jury may get wind of the philandering, take a dislike to the guy, and award him next to nothing in damages. That sort of situation is a constant threat in libel actions."

And on the defendant's side: "Maybe he's pleading truth as a defence. He's called the plaintiff an incompetent accountant and he's going to prove it's true. Well, where's he going to get the independent witnesses to say in court that the accountant's lousy with numbers? People don't mind saying hard things about a person in the privacy of a cocktail bar, but they shy away from repeating them in court. Truth is a perfect defence. It's establishing it that's tough."

What gives a libel case one more dimension, making it the chess game of litigation, marked by moves and counter-moves, ploys and checkmates, is the immediacy of the battle. In Porter's experience, a libel case has often put him in the risky business of pulling chestnuts out of fires. There was, for example, the swift and nervy action that events — and his knowledge of libel — forced on him during the last twelve days of October 1981.

On Monday, October 19, the *Toronto Star* carried an advance excerpt from the prologue of Peter Newman's book *The Acquisitors*. In the excerpt, Newman sketched the occasionally bizarre ways in which Canada's rich spend their money, and he cited as one among many illustrations the case of Carol Rapp. She is the wife of a wealthy Toronto businessman, and, so Newman wrote in a one-sentence anecdote, she once ordered new sets of chauffeur uniforms in a bright-blue shade that matched the colour on the bottom of her swimming pool. Mrs. Rapp read the *Star*'s excerpt and picked up the telephone. The story was untrue, she told the man whom she rang, a formidable counsel named Aubrey Golden; it ridiculed and trivialized her. A couple of days later, on Thursday the twenty-second, Golden served a notice of Mrs. Rapp's intention to sue for libel on the *Star*, Newman, and *The Acquisitors'* publisher, McClelland and Stewart. Late the following afternoon, just as Porter was packing his car to drive to the family cottage, McClelland and Stewart's president, Jack McClelland, called and retained him to act for the company and for Newman. At that stage, the matter struck Porter as something he could put on hold for a few days.

"If I'd been acting for the *Star*," he says, "I would've been more immediately concerned, because with a newspaper, if an apology's called for, you want to get it into the very next edition. But with a book, you've got more time to sort through the situation. So I worked at it a little over the weekend at the cottage and I didn't worry about speed."

Worry and urgency set in for Porter at 8:45 on Monday morning when Golden reached him by phone in his office at the Toronto Transit Commission.

"Here's our position, Julian," Golden said. "Unless your people do something right away to stop the book's distribution, we're on our way to court to ask for an interim injunction that'll keep it out of the stores."

Golden paused while Porter took in the news.

"And if you're thinking of arguing in court that the story about my client is true," Golden went on, "let me give you a tip."

"What's that?"

"I've got the hat to the chauffeur's uniform sitting here on my desk," Golden said. "It's black."

Even as Porter was speaking to Golden, McClelland and Stewart were shipping 48,000 copies of *The Acquisitors* to stores across Canada in time for the book's official publication date on Saturday of that week. *The Acquisitors*, priced at $24.95, was counted on as the publishing house's major Christmas seller, and an injunction would mean a heavy — perhaps crippling — loss of sales. Porter called Jack McClelland and warned him of Golden's talk of the injunction. McClelland repeated what Porter already knew, that it was too late and too expensive to recall the books. Porter hung up and drove forty miles to Hamilton, where he was representing a client that morning at the preliminary hearing on a drug charge.

At four o'clock in the afternoon, back in Toronto, Porter heard from Golden that the threatened proceedings were now in the works, and before dark, Porter accepted service of an application for the injunction. It was to be heard by a judge of the Ontario Supreme Court in chambers at Osgoode Hall on Wednesday afternoon. The heat was on, and from nine o'clock until midnight, Porter and his partner, Donald Posluns, plotted a strategy to resist the injunction and to defend against the allegations of libel.

Porter spoke to the man who had passed to Newman the tale of Mrs. Rapp and the bright-blue uniforms. He was Michael Levine, a Toronto lawyer who has cornered a large section of the business in Canada in entertainment law and who had arranged for Newman the lucrative deal that sold the advance excerpts from *The Acquisitors* to the *Star* and thirty other Canadian newspapers.

"Sure, the story's true," Levine told Porter. "It came from my father. He's in the clothing business and he knew Carol years ago when the whole incident happened."

"Okay," Porter said, "we'll need an affidavit from your father spelling the thing out."

"My father's in Florida," Levine said.

"In that case," Porter said, "we'll take an affidavit from you. We'll just put down the facts the way you heard them from your father. It's second best, it's hearsay, but the thing about these applications for interim injunctions is we're allowed to file something that's hearsay when the original witness isn't available."

Porter and Posluns sketched out the wording of Levine's affidavit. A secretary would type it in the morning, and after Levine signed it, it would be served on Golden in the afternoon. Porter wouldn't be around until late in the day. He had to wind up the drug preliminary in Hamilton.

Two pieces of news waited for Porter in his office on Tuesday afternoon. Neither was welcome. The *Star* was running a correction of the Rapp excerpt in all editions of the day's paper. "The *Star* has now learned," the notice read in part, "that the incident described did not occur." But the *Star*'s correction was small potatoes compared to the other piece of news. Michael Levine, Porter discovered, had experienced second thoughts and changed the wording of his affidavit. Now, instead of saying that Mrs. Rapp had ordered the uniform in a shade to match the bottom of her swimming pool, the affidavit called the colour similar to that of "a domestic accessory or a car or a swimming pool."

"That's vastly different," Porter said on the phone to Jack McClelland. "Comparing the colour to a domestic accessory or a car *or* a swimming pool doesn't have the same sting as the wording in the book. But we're pleading the truth of the story, so we've got to go with it."

At 2:30 on Wednesday afternoon, the lawyers gathered before

Mr. Justice David Griffiths in one of the small courtrooms in Osgoode Hall. Golden spoke first. He's a forceful, articulate man who looks like a younger version of the actor Jose Ferrer and has much of Ferrer's theatrical flair. And he came out in court firing all his guns. He ticked off Porter for filing an affidavit from Michael Levine rather than from Levine's father, the original source of the story. He quoted from an affidavit by Mrs. Rapp which called the story "totally untrue and without any basis in fact." Mrs. Rapp and her husband, Golden read from the affidavit, were "deeply concerned about our reputation for good taste and discretion."

"A libel contained in what is likely to become one of Canada's best-selling books," Golden told Griffiths, all cool understatement, "is undoubtedly of great concern."

The immediate remedy, Golden finished, was an injunction to keep the books from distribution.

As Porter rose to reply, Golden hit him with another surprise. He handed Porter an affidavit that dealt with Michael Levine's father, the man who set the story of the uniform in circulation, the man who was supposed to be in Florida. Mr. Levine, so the affidavit said, had been in Toronto all week. He left for Florida only that very day, at noon, a mere two and a half hours before the hearing began.

"The way I felt right then," Porter says, "is the way you feel in a hockey game where you know the score is going to be against you and it could be 11–0 or 4–0. You're sure to lose, but you have to get in there and fight because 4–0 is a hell of a lot more respectable than 11–0."

At least Porter was confident that the law was on his side. In libel actions where the defendant is pleading truth as a defence, as Porter was, the plaintiff is not entitled to an injunction. That dictum had been most recently stated by the Ontario Supreme Court in a 1970s libel action, Canada Metals Company versus the Canadian Broadcasting Corporation. Porter referred to the case and swung to the attack, speaking in a firm, confident voice and, in his own description, "laying on a little histrionics." He insisted that the anecdote in the Newman book was true, that he would prove it was true if the issue came to a jury trial, and that the jury might well accept it as true. Who could say what a jury would decide? For that matter, who knew what would be revealed in the pleadings and arguments in the libel case? It wasn't up to Griffiths to decide such matters at that stage of the proceedings. The decisions must be left to the jury somewhere down the line, somewhere in the future. An injunction, if it were issued at such an early point in the action, would constitute premature judgment on the case.

Porter made his pitch, but he had a terrible feeling that Griffiths wasn't entirely persuaded. The judge and Golden took turns jumping on his arguments. Golden pointed out that McClelland and Stewart had continued to ship books across Canada after the company had received notice of the impending libel action. Wasn't this a sign that the defendants were reckless in spreading the alleged libel? Golden emphasized the point, and Griffiths joined in with stern questions for Porter. What about the failure to file an affidavit from Levine senior? Wasn't that improper? Porter paused during the bombardment and looked up at the courtroom ceiling, his arms spread apart. Not good, his posture announced, not good at all.

Mr. Justice Griffiths ended the hearing at four o'clock, advising counsel that he would hand down his decision at 9:15 on Saturday morning. Porter left the courtroom and arranged to meet Ron Rolls, a counsel with whom he'd worked years earlier under Walter Williston at Fasken and Calvin.

"Right now," Porter told Rolls, "I'm convinced we're in deep trouble. Griffiths is going to issue that injunction. I'm frightened — I really am — and maybe the best thing I can do is sit down with somebody like you who's got a little wisdom and get myself together again."

Porter came away from his conversation with Rolls, a cool and rational review of the whole messy Rapp business, in a fresh and balanced mood. As he thought through the case, he made a 180-degree turn in attitude and strategy. He wasn't going to plead truth as a defence to Mrs. Rapp's suit, and he had a persuasive reason for his change of mind: there *wasn't* any truth in the story, he concluded, and even if there were, the memories of the witnesses who might testify to it had grown too frail to rely on.

The decision freed Porter to get on with the practical business of preparing for the worst on Friday — a decision by Griffiths to place an injunction on the sale of *The Acquisitors*. He and Jack McClelland made complex arrangements for word to go out by telephone, telex, telegram, and night letter to all booksellers advising them to hold the book from public sale until they received further instructions from McClelland and Stewart. That, Porter knew, ought to demonstrate to Griffiths the defendants' good faith. Next, the two men put their minds to the root problem. How would they deal with the short passage on page seventeen of the book that mentioned Mrs. Rapp and the infamous uniforms? Now that they had eliminated truth as an eventual defence, they must somehow expunge the offensive material in a way that would satisfy both Griffiths and Mrs. Rapp.

"Black felt pen," McClelland said spontaneously during one session with Porter. "We tell the stores to take a black felt pen and ink out Rapp's name. It only appears twice in the damn book, page seventeen and the index."

"I like it," Porter said and tucked away the idea until Friday morning.

On Thursday night, Porter, McClelland, and Newman gathered again, but this time the occasion was social. The scene was the Porter home, a large brick house in the comfortably upper-middle-class Moore Park section of Toronto, where the Porters, McClelland and his wife, and another couple, *Saturday Night* editor Robert Fulford and Geraldine Sherman, a senior producer at CBC radio, were throwing a party for their friend Doris Anderson to celebrate the publication by McClelland and Stewart of her new novel, *Rough Layout*. It was a crowded, convivial party, and it took in an almost definitive representation from the city's journalistic and literary communities. The guests drank, laughed, gossiped, and zeroed in on the juiciest drama of the week, Rapp versus *The Acquisitors*. Newman shrugged at everyone's questions. McClelland unloaded one-liners ("What if I go into court tomorrow wearing a toga? I'll say it was dyed to match the colour of my bathtub"). And Porter, normally the life of any party, was uncharacteristically subdued.

"I'd never met Carol Rapp, but I knew that a lot of the people at the party were friends of the lady's," he says. "And I knew that everything I said would get back to her in a flash. So I was very guarded in my conversations. I let everybody know that I was concerned, that I was a decent fellow who felt badly that we were all in this jackpot together. I was sending out the message that we wanted to fix the trouble with as little fuss as possible. It was the kind of strange situation that isn't supposed to come up in a lawsuit."

Porter performed with consummate tact at the party, but he saved his most convincing show for the next morning.

"Do you have anything further to add to last day's argument, Mr. Porter?" Mr. Justice Griffiths asked after he settled on the bench in court at 9:15 a.m. Golden, as he'd earlier advised Porter, was away on a short holiday, and his junior appeared for Mrs. Rapp. Newman and McClelland sat at the back of the courtroom, and lying in front of Griffiths was the fateful order that he intended to read aloud.

"No, m'lord," Porter answered, his voice smooth and creamy. "I've made all my submissions, but after you've issued your order, I have some suggestions to make that I think will ensure as far as it's possible that the order will be respected in other parts of the country. This is an Ontario order, m'lord, and there may be some doubt as to its effect in the rest of the provinces."

For a moment Griffiths mulled over the implications in Porter's words.

"I had to be very careful about the way I approached those opening remarks," Porter remembers. "If I had more arguments to make on Aubrey's motion, I would've been obliged to tell him so he could be in court to reply. I was trying to get at something different — make yards with Griffiths without talking about the substance of the motion for injunction."

Griffiths had mulled enough. "Well, Mr. Porter," he said, "why don't you give us your suggestions now."

Porter proceeded to walk briskly through the door that Griffiths had opened for him. He hunched over the lectern in front of him. His manner, in contrast to his arm-waving display on Wednesday, was, as he later characterized it, "the way the great Arthur Martin used to handle criminal juries, kind of wringing your hands and speaking softly and asking everybody to be reasonable."

"We have here, m'lord, a question of psychology," he began. "What's the right way to handle the booksellers so that we get the best results for Mrs. Rapp and the publisher and the other parties before this court?"

He reviewed in quick order the steps that McClelland and Stewart had taken since Wednesday's hearing to keep *The Acquisitors* off book counters. All the stores, Porter assured Griffiths, were waiting for instructions later that day when the court's order was known. But, Porter went on, let's see about satisfying Mrs. Rapp's complaint. Let's consider the ways of shielding her good name at this stage.

"We could call the books back from the stores," he said, shaking his head slightly in sorrow. "But that would be very costly to the defendants. Besides, some stores will obey our instructions to return the books and some stores will not. Your lordship's order, if that were the case, would be flouted."

Porter produced another possibility. "We could paste a sticker over Mrs. Rapp's name in the book," he said. "That's been done before." And he held up an earlier Newman book, *The Canadian Establishment, Volume One,* showing Griffiths how, on page seventy-four, a small section of type had been pasted over an offending paragraph. "But," Porter warned, "how can we monitor this sort of process? How can we be sure that the bookstore owner in Saskatoon will take the time to go through the mucky business of gluing in the stickers? I can assure you, m'lord, that McClelland and Stewart will do a paste-over job on Mrs. Rapp's name in the 72,000 copies of the book that haven't yet been shipped out to booksellers. But the immediate problem is with the books that are already in stores in all parts of the country."

Porter had set the stage for the black felt pen. He took one from his pocket and waved it at Griffiths.

"We'll cross out Mrs. Rapp's name, m'lord," he said. "It's the simplest solution. Nothing complicated, nothing mucky. McClelland and Stewart will send immediate instructions to every single person and store and outlet that's handling the book. We'll tell them to run thick lines of black ink through Mrs. Rapp's name. Mrs. Rapp will vanish from *The Acquisitors.*"

Porter looked, all in a single expression, calm and reassuring and composed — and just a trifle beseeching.

"This," he told Griffiths, "is the best chance that the court order has of being respected."

Porter had been speaking for less than ten minutes — a few minutes in which he staked his case on what seemed to him in his less optimistic moments a long shot — and when he finished, Griffiths announced a short adjournment.

"I'll have to think about it," he said as he retired to his private chambers.

Griffiths was gone for fifteen minutes.

"What we thought, Newman and McClelland and I," Porter said later, "was that Griffiths changed his mind while he was out. We thought he reworked the order he'd already written. But who's to know?"

Back in the courtroom, Griffiths announced his decision. "In general," he read from the order in front of him, "on balance of convenience, the injunction should not issue." Porter and his clients were part way home. But "the defendants will use their best efforts to black out the name of the plaintiff by black felt pen. . . ." Griffiths had gone for Porter's argument, and his clients were in clear sight of home.

Porter and McClelland spent much of the rest of the day dispatching details of the court order to bookstores across Canada. The word went out. Take a black felt pen to Carol Rapp's name. Page seventeen and the index. Don't let a book out of the store until the inking job is done.

"In some ways, this was the most tense period of all," Porter says. "We sent instructions, and then over the weekend we made follow-ups so we knew the order was being carried out. The other side, Golden's office, was monitoring every move we made. We couldn't afford to slip up."

At the same time, Porter was devoting himself to the wording of an apology to Mrs. Rapp, something that would persuade her to wind down the libel action. "It couldn't be half-assed," Porter says. "It had to speak sincerely to the Rapps." Porter drafted a version. Golden reworked it. The apology shunted back and forth until the Rapps were satisfied. "The reference to Carol Rapp in the book *The Acquisitors* was entirely without foundation," the finished apology read in part. ". . . Neither she nor her husband represent the behavior described in the Prologue of the book. . . ." The apology was published at McClelland and Stewart's expense in the *Globe and Mail*, the *Star*, and *Books in Canada*. Mrs. Rapp was content and the libel action came to a halt.

"A few days after the Friday hearing before Mr. Justice Griffiths," Porter says, "I went to the opening of an exhibition at an art gallery. This was a big affair. Lots of people. And during the evening a woman came up to me and introduced herself and her husband. She was an attractive blonde woman. Most friendly. A charming woman. She was Carol Rapp. I felt speechless."

For once in his life, Julian Porter had run out of words.

CHAPTER 8

THE ELEGANT CONJURER

THE ONLY ITEM OUT of sync in Bert Oliver's office was the bottle of Maalox on the desk. Otherwise he represented the last word in sang-froid and elegance. His face wore a look that was sleek, astute, and kindly, the expression of a diplomat. Indeed, he *is* a diplomat of sorts, Consul General since 1954 of the Republic of Liberia for Western Canada. He spoke in a plummy voice with an accent that would blend seamlessly into the genteel chatter of a Buckingham Palace drawing-room. He comes by the vocal tones honestly: his education began at the Dean Close School in Cheltenham, England, and continued through the London School of Economics; his military career embraced six years with the Royal Norfolk Regiment and the British Army's Intelligence Corps; and his adventures at the bar were launched at the Law Society's School of Law in London. Everything about Oliver seemed of a piece — including the 1962 Bentley parked in the driveway of his home in Vancouver's plush Shaughnessy Heights district — except the Maalox. That, a concoction for soothing the stomach, speaks of stress, hard work, and tight squeezes. And no wonder — Bert Oliver, sixty years old and the senior partner in a small firm, has been practising criminal law from the day of his arrival in Vancouver in 1952, and he has rightly earned a reputation, based on brains and long nights at the office, as perhaps the city's foremost criminal advocate.

"Basically, of course, the sort of law I practise is all wrong," he said in his office, enunciating in his characteristic fashion, deliberate and ironic. "In a well-run legal firm, conveyancing and corporate work are your bread and butter, litigation is the jam. I've been living off the jam for thirty-five years."

In those years he has evolved a handy and humane set of principles that define his relationship with the clients who walk through the office door. "In a criminal practice, you get nice people and nasty people as you do in a corporate practice. The corporate firms have their robber barons for clients, but these are simply people who manage, barely, to keep within the law. In firms like mine, we have some charming clients who are charged with murder and some obnoxious ones who are charged with impaired driving. Criminal clients are people like everyone else. They have merely committed the unforgivable sin of being caught. Or so the crown alleges."

Murderers, among these clients, are different from the others for reasons that have little to do with long-term evil. "Murder is a crime that is rarely committed by criminals," Oliver said. "It may be the most serious offence in the Criminal Code, but for most people charged with it, it is the only occasion in their lives when they've faced a charge. Of all the murder cases I've taken over the years, there was only one man who had a criminal record of any consequence. All the rest were of such a sort as Geno Casagrande."

But before Oliver delved into his memories of Casagrande, he offered a check-list of cases he has handled in his courtroom career. About thirty murder defences. A notorious 1968 Satan's Angels case in which he acted, unsuccessfully, for the leader of a motorcycle gang who kidnapped a young hippie and subjected him to a series of perverse cruelties. A string of narcotics conspiracy charges ("Everyone has heard of the famous French Connection," he said, all smiles and irony. "Well, I acted in the less famous but equally complex Czechoslovakian Connection"). A number of prosecutions for municipal corruption and stock fraud ("White-collar crime became the offence of the moment in the 1970s"). And a wide range of other cases that covered the territory from rape to careless driving.

"Part of the fascination of practice as a trial counsel," Oliver said, "is the variety, not just in the cases themselves but in the many disciplines that become involved. If one is defending in a drug case, for example, then one must master the intricacies of spectographic analysis of narcotic substances. I'm attracted to things of that sort. I have a curious mind."

Oliver also possesses a resourceful mind, and it went on display most conspicuously in the trial of Geno Casagrande.

"Casagrande was a little Italian chap who came from the earthquake country north of Venice," Oliver began. "He arrived in British Columbia at the start of the 1950s, in about the same year as I got here. I could identify with him in that regard. When I was practising law in London, I knew the Agent General for British Columbia in England. At the time, I believed B.C. to be a crown colony on the east coast of South America. Nevertheless, on my friend's suggestion I came out to have a look and liked the place. Mr. Casagrande probably reached this province with even scantier knowledge than I.

"In any event, Geno fell deeply and passionately in love with a Vancouver prostitute. He decided that he was going to reform her and take her back to Italy. He obtained a job in a logging camp in the bush and stayed there for most of the following three years. He didn't smoke or drink during that period, he kept every penny he earned, and he mailed off his savings at regular intervals to the prostitute. Once in a great while he'd emerge from the bush to visit her in Vancouver. The situation seemed to him to be optimistic.

"Finally, after three years, he left the logging camp for good. He took a temporary room in a Vancouver boarding-house and went to visit his lady-friend. 'My darling,' he said, 'We now have enough money saved up. Next week we'll be married and I'll take you home to mama in Italy. You won't have to work in such a deplorable manner any longer. You will become a respectable Italian housewife.'

"'You must be mad,' the prostitute said. 'My boyfriend comes out of the penitentiary next month, and we're going to set up housekeeping on the money you've been sending me.'

"At this news, Casagrande became understandably upset. He took out a knife and killed the prostitute on the spot. The police charged him with murder.

"Provocation appeared to be my only possible defence. The prostitute's terrible words, her deceit, had provoked Casagrande to his blind act. If this defence were accepted, it would at least enable a jury to convict on the lesser charge of manslaughter and not send Casagrande to the gallows. But provocation is unacceptable as a defence unless the accused acts on the spur of the moment. He can't carry a butcher knife from one end of Vancouver to the other in the unlikely event that he is going to be provoked and forced to use it. And that appeared to be the situation with Casagrande, because the landlady at his boarding-house was prepared to testify that the knife in question came from her own kitchen.

"The trial was called before Mr. Justice Manson, now deceased, who was renowned for his irascibility and for his relish in sentencing convicted murderers to be put to death. I had difficulty with him from the beginning of the case. I asked his lordship to grant me an adjournment in order to have Casagrande examined by a psychiatrist. Poor Geno had been badly wounded when he fought in the Italian army during the Second World War. I suspected he was suffering from brain damage, and I wanted a psychiatric opinion. Manson refused. So I had Casagrande brought to court on a stretcher, and that is how he remained for the entire trial. At first he lay on the floor of the dock. But Manson complained that he couldn't see the prisoner. The court attendants placed Casagrande's stretcher across the top of the dock. That was too bizarre. We compromised by propping the stretcher alongside the dock. That was also bizarre but acceptable.

"The landlady was the key to the crown's case. Her testimony would lead to the inevitable conclusion that Casagrande deliberately took the knife with him when he left the boarding-house to call on the prostitute and that it wasn't simply a knife he habitually carried with him and pulled out spontaneously under the provoking circumstances created by the prostitute. The landlady made an impressive witness, as so many untruthful people do. I am not accusing her of a calculated lie, but I think she was representative of a dilemma one finds in our system. Again and again, in many trials I have heard a judge say to the court how impressed he was with a certain witness and how he has watched the accused and has found him a halting and evasive witness. But what the judge has neglected to point out is that normally the accused is a person who has never been in a court before and is scared witless. A policeman, to take the opposite extreme, is a professional witness who has spent years polishing his skills in the witness-box. I'm far from saying that every policeman is an accomplished liar and every accused is a fine upstanding lady or gentleman. All I am saying is that it is a mistake to judge credibility on first impressions. And yet what else do we have to go on? This is a weakness in our system of justice.

"The landlady in the Casagrande case was like other witnesses in other cases in that she did not, no doubt, set out deliberately to deceive. But, also like other witnesses in other cases, once she had convinced herself that something was so, that the knife which killed the prostitute came from her kitchen, then she would not yield in her view of the facts, and she was bound to be a difficult subject for my cross-examination. When the crown questioned her and showed her the knife that Casagrande had used in the stabbing, she said, yes, she'd recognize it anywhere, that long blade ground thin with sharpening over the years and that distinctive brown handle with the three silver studs in it. Yes, she said, it was undoubtedly her butcher knife. So it was tagged as an exhibit in the trial and placed in a long manila envelope.

"Shortly after, it came time for my cross-examination. I approached the landlady with a long manila envelope in my hand and removed from it a butcher knife with a tag dangling from the handle. She examined it. Oh yes, she said, it was undoubtedly her knife. I thanked her.

"'My lord,' I said to Manson, 'may I enter this envelope and this knife as an exibit?'

"'If you'd been paying any attention,' he said, 'you'd have noticed that the knife was entered as an exhibit in that envelope by the crown an hour ago.'

"'No, my lord,' I said. 'That was *another* manila envelope and *another* knife. This knife, as you see, has one brass stud on the handle rather than three silver studs. It is yet a second knife that the witness has now identified as hers.'

"Manson was furious. He didn't care at all for the method I had used in casting doubt on the landlady's identification of the knife. He was determined that Casagrande would be convicted, and when the trial reached the stage for him to instruct the jury, he took an inordinate length of time in his instruction, and he devoted by far the majority of it to the crown's case. At one point in his charge he left the bench and walked up and down in front of the jury-box for thirty minutes shaking his fingers at the jurymen, who were so intimidated that they hardly hesitated in finding Casagrande guilty as charged of murder.

"I appealed the conviction, and the Court of Appeal, with five justices sitting, took the opportunity of the hearing to chide me for the trick I had managed with the knife and the landlady. I pointed out to their lordships that the last time such a device had been resorted to at trial occurred fifty years earlier when the great English barrister Sir Edward Marshall Hall had successfully cast doubt on a witness's identification of a murder weapon by producing a second similar weapon, a pistol in that instance. I'm not certain whether their lordships were as impressed as I was.

"In any event, the Court of Appeal had no doubt that a retrial should be ordered, and in their judgment they criticized Manson and, incidentally, myself. The judgment was brief and to the point."

Oliver reached for a case-book, Volume Thirty of *Canadian Criminal Cases*, 1958, and read from page 76.

"'We all think there must be a new trial in this case,' Chief Justice DesBrisay of the Appeal Court wrote. 'It was not enough for the learned judge to say over and over again that the facts are for the jury if he has so dealt with them beforehand as to belittle their significance for the defence, and leave them heavily in favor of the crown. As we see it, that is what happened here. It is not without significance that the judge's charge occupied five and three-quarters hours and the addresses of each counsel something over an hour. The case presented no difficulty, yet it was conducted in an atmosphere of irritation, due in part, perhaps, to accused counsel's vehemence in pressing his points after ruling by the learned judge.'"

Oliver put aside the case-book.

"I thought I was done with Mr. Justice Manson. Alas, I was not. It happened that the Chief Justice of the trial division of the B.C. Supreme Court had just retired, and Manson, as the senior judge, was temporarily the acting Chief Justice. As such, he assigned himself to hear the retrial of the Casagrande case. I asked that he disqualify himself on the grounds of prejudice. He refused, and ultimately it fell to a delegation of his fellow justices to wait upon him and suggest that he remove himself from the case in the interests of justice being seen to be done as well as being done. They were successful.

"Manson remained on the bench only a year or two longer. He was already seventy-five years old, and Parliament passed legislation requiring judges of the Supreme Court to retire at age seventy-five. It was said at the time that the legislation came into effect specifically to speed the well-deserved retirement of Mr. Justice Manson. For myself, I'm not convinced it's necessary that judges end their careers so early. I recall that Mr. Justice Humphrey was still stitting in England when I practised in London, and he was ancient enough to have been junior counsel at the trial of Oscar Wilde. But in the case of Manson, it was not a moment too soon for him to step down.

"The second Casagrande trial lacked the drama of the first, but the results were more satisfying. The judge permitted me to introduce evidence of provocation, and before the case went to the jury, the crown and I were able to agree that Casagrande would plead guilty to the lesser charge of manslaughter. So he was sentenced to prison for a short visit."

Oliver leaned back in his chair.

"Like so many of my clients," he said, "Geno Casagrande was nothing more dreadful than an ordinary citizen who found himself in unfortunate conflict with the law."

Oliver smiled seraphically and more than ever, in that instant of self-satisfaction, the box of Maalox looked out of sync in his office.

CHAPTER 9

A HOUSEHOLD NAME

THE MAN WHO INTRODUCED John Robinette as the guest speaker at the school alumni banquet on the rainy night of October 22, 1981, described him to the audience as a "household word." That night, Robinette was a month short of his seventy-fifth birthday, and of all the lawyers in the country, of all the counsel who had been practising in Canadian courtrooms over the previous half-century, he was the only man whose name had become the stuff of headlines. Perhaps Arthur Martin approached him in fame in the early years of his practice, and maybe Eddie Greenspan had edged close in publicity in recent years. But for most Canadians, Robinette remained our Louis Nizer, our Clarence Darrow, a lawyer for the courtroom and a lawyer for the news stories. His name began to circulate in the press and among the people in the mid-1940s when he took Evelyn Dick's trial. She was a glamorous woman from Hamilton, Ontario, who was charged with murdering her husband under the seamiest circumstances, and Robinette won an acquittal for her in the face of apparently overwhelming evidence of her guilt. His reputation was secured. He defended sixteen more Canadians accused of murder before he began to shift away from criminal law in the mid-1950s and into civil litigation and appeal work before the provincial Courts of Appeal and the Supreme Court of Canada. He acted for big business: E. P. Taylor's breweries and K. C. Irving's newspapers were clients, both in anti-combines cases. And he acted for concerned citizens: he appeared, successfully in both cases, for groups who opposed the extension of a four-lane expressway into downtown Toronto and the construction of an international airport near Pickering, Ontario. He made himself the ranking expert in constitutional cases, and when Pierre Trudeau arrived in Ottawa, Robinette became the federal government's favourite counsel. In court challenges, he spoke in defence of the Anti-Inflation Act, of the Official Languages Act, and ultimately, in the spring of 1981, of the government's constitutional resolution. The last case would have made Robinette a household name. Except that he already was one.

Now, on the wet night in October, he was rising to speak to the alumni banquet at the Royal York Hotel in Toronto. The heavy rain had briefly threatened to delay his afternoon flight from Ottawa, where, appearing on behalf of Gulf Canada before the Restrictive Trade Practices Commission, he had used uncharacteristically harsh and slangy language in describing accusations that the major oil companies had cheated Canadians of $12.1 billion over a fifteen-year period. "The rip-off charge should be taken for what it really is," he told the commission. "A cheap publicity trick." Then he hurried to the airport. He would never want to miss the banquet, an annual gathering of graduates from one of the institutions that had shaped his life. It was the University of Toronto Schools, a small and exclusive elementary and high school for brainy students which Robinette had attended from 1914 to 1923. He drank a Scotch and water with old classmates during the pre-banquet cocktail hour, then took his place at the head table, and when speech time arrived he rose to the introduction, a tall, bulky, deliberate man, the look of the grand and traditional Ontario Wasp about him, his face bracketed in a series of deep vertical lines and his voice identified by a fine, light, mellow resonance.

His speech came as a surprise. He did not talk of the courtroom or the constitution. He didn't mention his cases or his views on the economy or the price of oil or the Canadian political future or any of the other matters that his arguments before judges and commissioners have surely affected. Instead, by his own choice, he spoke of the nine years of his youth when he attended one school. Robinette, it soon became clear, almost seventy-five years old, had the intellectual and emotional foundations of one man — himself — on his mind.

He mentioned "the beauty of Latin." He remembered a mathematics teacher who could, freehand, draw an exact circle on the blackboard. "I saw," Robinette said, "that there is something very satisfying about perfection." His voice broke at one point in the speech when he recalled an event from 1917. "The war was going badly," he said, "and some of the senior boys from the school enlisted. The headmaster, Bull Crawford, called a special assembly to say goodbye to them. They were handsome and they were valiant and some of them did not come back." In the same couple of sentences Robinette had evoked both another age and a set of values that he continued to embrace. He moved on. He celebrated the drop kick, an intricate and antique football manoeuvre, a form of kicking performed by one man — an individual art — that has been replaced in modern football by the place kick. And he praised in all forms the generalist over the specialist, the man who trains and educates himself to move confidently in a whole range of disciplines rather than the man who hews to a single form. "I prefer," Robinette said, "the generalist."

There was plenty that was sober about Robinette's speech and nothing at all that was flamboyant. That balance describes him as a man and as a counsel. He is not a courtroom counsel on the same colourful order as the great Americans, not an F. Lee Bailey or a Melvin Belli. He is an Upper Canadian of the truest sort, proper and substantial and grave. He grew up that way. His father died when he was thirteen, and the event changed his perspective. "That life's a serious business," Robinette has said, "came to me a little earlier than if my father had lived." It wasn't that Robinette senior's death left the family in a perilous financial situation. The father, Thomas Cowper Robinette, had been almost as prosperous and famous a counsel in his own day as the son became in his, and the family — there were four boys, all of whom grew up to practise law — continued to live in a large house in a solid Toronto neighbourhood. It was just that the father's death gave young Robinette a lasting whiff of life's grim responsibility.

"John's always struck me as a curious fella on the social side," Senator David Walker says of Robinette; until his retirement, Walker was himself a leader of the Ontario civil-litigation bar and Robinette's friend and courtroom rival for almost fifty years. "I remember one time when we were together in London, England, for a lawyers' conference, and John and I had to take a taxi to our hotel. All along the ride, he'd be saying to me, 'Now, Dave, that's Buckingham Palace and there's Westminster and here comes the National Gallery.' Hell, I'd been in London a dozen times. I knew what everything was. But that was John's way of being social. He's a thoughtful fella, but his knack of handling people is on the far side of formal."

From the beginning, Robinette was a scholar. He won the gold medal in political science at the University of Toronto and the gold medal in law at Osgoode Hall Law School. After his call to the bar in 1929, he stayed on at Osgoode as a lecturer. "He taught my class a course in real property," David Walker remembers. "He was the best teacher we had, and the thing that amazed most of us was that he'd graduated only a couple of years ahead of us and he was younger than most of our fellas and here he was so damned smart." Typically, since Robinette has never been a man to resist an intellectual challenge, the courses he taught at Osgoode lay on the chancery side of law — property, mortgages, and trusts, subjects that are almost entirely alien to the litigation lawyer. He remained at Osgoode through the early years of the Depression, earning extra income by editing the reports of cases in the various courts for distribution among the legal profession, until he entered private practice with the Toronto firm of Lawson, Stratton, Green and Ongley. Earl Lawson, a prominent lawyer and politician of the day, had been a partner of T. C. Robinette and was pleased to offer space to the bright young son of his old friend. Robinette's early work was on the academic side, writing opinions on exquisite legal points for his old Osgoode students who were now in private practice and remembered that their former lecturer seemed to know more law than anyone. He took a few criminal cases and began to appear before the Ontario Court of Appeal. If he had a reputation, it was exclusively among the fraternity of litigation lawyers. Then came the call from the Barton Street Jail in Hamilton. Evelyn Dick was on the line.

"I never knew what made her get in touch with me," Robinette says today. "I was just a young fellow, just a pretty good technical lawyer. All I can imagine is that someone must have told her I'd done some effective appeal work. That's the sort of lawyer she needed at the time because she'd already been convicted at the first trial for murdering her husband and sentenced to hang. I took the appeal. I won her a new trial and stayed on to act for her at it, and I guess I saved her life. The trial was intellectually stimulating, which is rare among criminal cases. Much of it turned on the alleged confessions she'd made, and when I was able to raise some doubts about their admissibility as evidence, the jury acquitted her."

The Canadian press and public battened on Evelyn Dick's trial as they have on few others in the twentieth century, and the rush of publicity carried Robinette into a permanent spot in the popular imagination as the wizard of Canada's courtrooms.

"There was a reporter at the *Toronto Star* named Al Tate," Robinette recalls, "and he could take down a verbatim report of a trial. Every day of the Dick case, he'd scribble away, and the *Star* would run three or four pages of questions and answers. That was the way it went, so much linage and so many photographs in every newspaper. When the trial ended, the front page of the *Star* carried a double red headline, 'Evelyn Acquitted.' Nobody needed to be told what that meant. I've never seen a case for such sensation, and overnight I went from being an academic lawyer to being a criminal lawyer."

Criminal law wasn't substantial enough to sustain Robinette's perpetual interest. "It's good training," he says, "because you learn to be careful in your examinations of witnesses and your cross-examinations. You can't risk getting bad answers. But criminal cases run to type, and it's only one out of ten that raises a fresh legal point. Besides, I prefer to be a generalist, not a specialist in one type of case." Robinette acted in several dozen criminal matters, including those sixteen more murder trials, but by the late 1950s his fascination with a wider range of contentious issues had reasserted itself. "The kind of cases that sound a terrible bore to the outsider," he says, "are the ones that most excite me." Constitutional cases, for example. In one such case, he took the side of the Cigol petroleum company in western Canada, in attacking the Province of Saskatchewan's oil-taxation legislation. The courts, absorbing Robinette's arguments, declared the oil-tax structure constitutionally invalid and sent Saskatchewan's legislature back to the drawing-board. "They'll have to get it right the second time," Robinette said. To him, getting it right the first time is the whole point.

The explanations for Robinette's enduring excellence as a courtroom lawyer, at trial and on appeal, in criminal cases and in civil, border on law-school cliché. "You win by preparation and drudgery," he says. "You do research and you read law." And, true enough, more than other leading counsel, Robinette has always relished legal scholarship. He prefers to prepare his own case law rather than follow the practice of most counsel of delegating the research chores to juniors. For years he carried his independence to lengths that fellow counsel considered to be slightly bizarre. "You'd see him arrive in court on his own," another senior counsel says of Robinette. "No junior, nobody to take notes for him in court. Other counsel, *lesser* counsel, would be surrounded by assistants, and there was John with an ordinary pencil and a lot of lined paper jotting down his own notes on the arguments. It was as astonishing to me as if I saw Wayne Gretzky arrive at an arena carrying his own stick and skates."

There remain other reasons for Robinette's success. There is his unmatched knack for getting to the essence of a case, shaking off what he calls "the red herrings, the irrelevant and the window-dressing" and concentrating on the "one or two salient points that a court will base its decision on." There is his courtroom presence; "he's the Louis St. Laurent of lawyers," a Toronto advocate named Rod Heather says, "unwavering and believable and comforting and steady as a rock, all of which are traits that judges traditionally relate to." And then there's something more. Robinette is, after all, the man who has brought a touch of genius to the practice of litigation law. There must be something more, and David Walker has no doubt put his finger on it. "In court and in himself," he says of Robinette, "John has gone beyond hate and competition and ego."

This ability of Robinette's — a gift for plugging into the judicial process without letting self get in the way — probably says as much about a fundamental change over the last forty years in the ways in which lawyers and judges conduct litigation as it does about Robinette. For at least the first third of this century, a trial in a Canadian courtroom was a piece of theatre, and counsel and judges assumed their assigned roles. Judges were apt to be rude and arrogant. They butted into the action in front of them with comments and jokes and by-play. They performed. So did counsel. A trial was the occasion for them to trot out their theatrical turns. They worked the house, relying as much — or more — on their oratorical flourishes as on the law that was available to them. They emoted. T. C. Robinette himself provided a definitive example of the early-twentieth-century counsel in full flight; his style is described in a 1926 book, *Not Guilty and Other Trials*, in rich detail: "His opening syllables arrested the attention of usually immovable magistrates. Courts hung on his accents. He touched men in their most vulnerable parts. It is not mere rhetoric to say that tears flowed copiously and hearts melted noticeably during the passionate appeals which he repeatedly made to those bodies of men known as petit juries."

When young John Robinette first came to the law, the court-room ways of counsel like his father remained the standard. Robinette observed and studied them. The revered W. N. Tilley was the leader of the civil bar in Toronto, and Robinette remembers him as a counsel who "used the bludgeon. He assumed the court knew nothing about the facts and even less about the law and proceeded from there." Arthur Slaght was the star of the Toronto criminal bar, "the most eloquent man I ever heard," Robinette says of him. "He made wonderfully colourful jury addresses, and he had a trick he always used. He'd have the accused man's wife or mother sit in the front row of the courtroom, and at the end of the address he'd indicate the woman and ask the jury in a very hushed, quivering voice to send the accused back to his dear little wife or mother as the case might be." Colourful stuff all right, but Robinette recognized that the forensic approach of Slaght and the others, reaching back to his own father, belonged to a courtroom age that was swiftly vanishing.

"The emotional way of handling a case," he says, "was fine for its time, but by the years I was getting started, it became clear that if a counsel gave a dramatic sort of address, the jury would laugh his case out of court."

Sophistication had arrived in the courtroom. No more melting hearts in the jury-box. No more performing judges on the bench. No theatrics from counsel. No high-flown oratory. No displays of lawyerly conceit. Robinette's natural inclinations, his manner and personality so free of ego, equipped him ideally for the changing courtroom. He seemed the steadiest of counsel, the man who could relate the law to judge and jury with minimum fuss and maximum comprehension. "He has the great knack for fastening on the real point of the case," says former Ontario Chief Justice George Gale in describing Robinette's strength. "He stays with it. And he expresses himself more succinctly than other counsel." To be sure, Robinette maintains his small share of ploys in court — when opposing counsel are presenting arguments contrary to his, he has a disconcerting habit of shaking his head in sorrowful disagreement — but in all ways he remains the purest of counsel. Other courtroom lawyers may boast similar abilities to pick up on the one crucial point in a case, to shape the law to fit the point, and to persuade judge or jury of the justice in their arguments. But no counsel matches Robinette in his peculiar talent for conveying a personal reading of the law in an unhindered line from his mind to the minds of the judgment-makers on the bench or in the jury-box. In court, Robinette turns invisible. All that remains is the law — in his version.

In the catalogue of Robinette's courtroom appearances, there is nothing typical about the Steve Suchan trial. It was a murder case, and Robinette lost it. His client died on the gallows of Don Jail in Toronto. For a rare occasion in his career, Robinette was devastated by the results of his advocacy. And yet it was the Suchan case that, without any hesitation at all, Robinette was pleased to recall and analyse during a conversation in his office on a bright late-autumn afternoon in 1981. As ever, ego wasn't something that intruded on a good legal discussion.

Robinette's office is on the forty-seventh floor of the Toronto-Dominion Bank Tower, one of the three floors occupied by McCarthy & McCarthy, the firm with which Robinette has been associated as counsel for more than thirty years. The office is medium-sized and neutral. It speaks of a man whose life is orderly, consistent, and compartmentalized, three attributes that, as it happens, nicely sum up Robinette. He has lived in the same large stone house in the Forest Hill section of Toronto for twenty-eight years and has spent his summers in Southampton on Lake Huron for fifty-five years. He has a couple of diversions that he single-mindedly devotes himself to, travel and reading. He embarks with his wife on frequent and regular journeys outside Canada, and his reading takes him far beyond the law. "He has an amazing broadness of mind," Bernie Chernos, a fellow counsel, says of Robinette. "You want to talk about the stories of Willa Cather, okay, he's read her. He's the most civilized man I've ever met."

Steve Suchan would seem at first impression a client that the civilized Robinette wouldn't relate to except as the bearer of an intriguing legal problem. Suchan was a bank robber by profession and a murderer by happenstance, but, large as his failings were, Robinette liked him. "He was a kindly sort of fellow," Robinette said, remembering Suchan during the conversation in his office. "At the trial, when it was his life that was at stake, he worried more about the way I was taking things than he did about himself. He had some culture to him. He was a good violinist and played in some orchestras around Toronto. There was a lot that recommended him to me." But Suchan had another side. "His basic trouble was his laziness. He got in with these other fellows, hold-up people, and he thought, gee, this looks like an easy way to make money. It was too bad he didn't stick to the violin."

The "other fellows" whom Suchan hooked up with were known around Toronto in the early 1950s as the Boyd Gang, perhaps the slickest bunch of villains in the city's history. Edwin Alonzo Boyd was the brains of the outfit, and from time to time he'd recruit assistants for his meticulously planned and executed bank stick-ups. Hence, "the Boyd Gang." Boyd was so cool and ingenious that when the police at last nabbed him and locked him and two of his occasional henchmen, Leonard Jackson and Willie "The Clown" Jackson (no relation), in the Don Jail under close surveillance pending trial on a long list of hold-up charges, he engineered a successful escape. The breakout wasn't a matter of guns and violence but of a hacksaw smuggled into the jail and a rope fashioned out of prison bed-sheets. The three patiently hacked through a barred window, lowered themselves forty feet into an exercise yard, and scaled a sixteen-foot outer wall. They scurried to a nearby apartment where, by pre-arrangement, Suchan arrived in a car and drove them deeper into hiding in the Toronto underworld. It was Sunday, November 4, 1951, and the Boyd Gang was back in business.

Suchan, in his mid-twenties, was the youngest member of the operation. But he was eager, daring, and skilled at the risky game of robbing banks. He took extra assurance, and a measure of pride, from his constant companion, a .455 Smith and Wesson revolver. He acquired the gun in a trade for his violin. Suchan carried it when he teamed up with Boyd and the two Jacksons in a hold-up shortly after the Don Jail escape. The take was $46,207.13, the largest amount robbed from a Toronto bank to that date. Citizens were outraged at the gang's audacity, the police were embarrassed, and the robbers were laughing.

By late winter of 1952, however, a pair of Toronto policemen thought they had sniffed out two of the gang. The officers were Sergeant of Detectives Edmund Tong and Sergeant Roy Perry, and partly through diligent sleuthing, partly through a piece of good fortune, they came into possession of the description and licence number of a car that they suspected Suchan and Leonard Jackson were using to get around the city. At midday on Thursday, March 6, they spotted the car on a busy west-end street. Suchan was at the wheel and Jackson in the front passenger seat, though at first Tong and Perry weren't certain of their identity. The two policemen tailed the car for a few blocks until it stopped for a traffic light. "Pull over to the curb, boys," Tong called to the pair from the passenger side of the policeman's car. Suchan did as he was instructed. The police car stopped to the rear and the right of the Suchan-Jackson car, and Tong stepped out, his hands empty of any weapon. He had approached to within three or four feet of Suchan's door when Suchan rolled down his window, turned in the seat, and fired his Smith and Wesson. He caught Tong in the left chest. He continued to shoot, hitting Perry, who had begun to move from behind the steering-wheel, in the right arm. Jackson, a pistol in his hand, stepped from his side of the car. "Christ, it's a cruiser!" he shouted at Suchan. "Get out of here!" The two roared away in their car and spent the day and night travelling by car, taxi, and bus to Montreal, where each kept an apartment under a fake name. Their freedom was brief. Montreal police arrested both men within a few days in two separate raids, each accompanied by a hail of bullets, and returned them, wounded, to Toronto. When Edmund Tong died in hospital on March 23, Suchan and Jackson were charged jointly with murder.

Robinette's interest in the adventure was no more intimate than the average newspaper reader's until one night a few weeks after the murder charge was laid when he was labouring over a brief late in his office at McCarthy & McCarthy. "There was a cleaning lady on the floor," he remembers. "She was a hard-working, decent, quiet woman, and she came to me, just the two of us alone at night in the empty offices, and she said her son was in trouble. Would I help him? 'What's his name?' I asked. 'Steve Suchan,' she said. 'Isn't he charged with murder?' She nodded. Well, she was such a nice woman that I couldn't say anything except that I'd help her."

Leonard Jackson had his own lawyer. He was Arthur Maloney, in only his ninth year of practice but a man destined to blossom into a brilliant defence counsel. Maloney is sweet-talking and loquacious, as Irish as a glass of Bushmill's Whiskey (a drink he wouldn't turn away). He's a fervent Catholic, and his sense of religion, a mix of hard-line righteousness and genial kindliness, suggests he'd have made a swell priest, part thundering Jesuit and part Bing Crosby in *Going My Way*. He channelled his drive to serve into other areas besides the law; he sat as a Conservative M.P. for five years, helped to found the Canadian Society for the Abolition of the Death Penalty, and acted as Ontario's first ombudsman from 1975 to 1978. When the call came to represent such an apparent loser as Leonard Jackson, he accepted. The call came from an unexpected direction.

"I was on my way into the Great Hall at Osgoode for my lunch one day," he remembers, "and Chief Justice James McRuer stopped me. 'I've just come from court over in City Hall,' he said. 'This fellow Jackson was before me and he doesn't have a lawyer. May I appoint you to act?' Well, it was the last thing I wanted. I'd never handled a major murder trial. But you don't say no to a chief justice, especially McRuer. And besides it was my chance to sit beside John Robinette."

Maloney had already experienced a strange brush with the case. On the night of March 5 that year, he was taking a late dinner in the dining-room of the Metropole Hotel, a comfortably down-at-the-heel Toronto landmark of the day, and as he was eating, two policemen whom he knew from his courtroom appearances wandered in for a beverage.

"What are you boys up to?" Maloney asked.

"Plenty," one of the officers said. "Some time in the next twenty-four hours we're gonna pick up a couple of thugs."

The two policemen were Tong and Perry.

The case against Suchan and Jackson was in the hands of a tough, veteran crown counsel named Bill Gibson. "He wasn't much in the administration line of things," Robinette says of Gibson. "But in court ability he was one of the best two or three crowns we've had in Ontario during all of my years."

It was clear to Gibson and everyone else in the case that only one man could have fired the single bullet that killed Tong. Suchan seemed almost certainly the correct candidate for that role, though there might be some lingering possibility that Jackson, too, had fired his gun. Whoever pulled the trigger on the fatal shot, Gibson intended to establish that both men were guilty of murder because they had conspired together to use violence in resisting the arrest of Jackson, who was at the time a fugitive from justice. Or perhaps he could prove another conspiracy — one to carry

143

out *any* unlawful purpose by violence and to assist each other in the purpose. If a conspiracy had been formed, then the Criminal Code said that both men were parties to the actions that one or the other carried out in furtherance of the conspiracy. If one man killed Tong, in short, both men in the conspiracy were equally guilty of murder.

The defence to Gibson's case had to be, by necessity, narrow and legalistic. "The best we could hope for," Robinette says, "was manslaughter. After all, someone was dead." Suchan's story, which Robinette would use as the basis of his case, was that, shortly before Tong and Perry pulled him over, his car and another had nearly collided. He thought it was the men from this car who were shouting at him to park at the curb, and he wanted to avoid any confrontation which might lead to the discovery that he was driving Jackson, a fugitive. He didn't recognize Tong as a policeman or Tong's car as a police cruiser, and he fired his gun only to disable the other car's engine and help him make his own geta-way. His intention wasn't to shoot Tong. He didn't *see* Tong when he turned in his seat to fire. The facts, as Suchan declared them, made him guilty of manslaughter at worst. Jackson's defence was more direct. He hadn't fired his own pistol and he wasn't aware that Suchan was carrying a gun. He hadn't made a pact with Suchan to resist arrest by violence; he was himself prepared to take violent action to avoid his own apprehension — he would even have shot at the police — but he didn't expect or intend to get assistance from Suchan. Hence, there was no conspiracy to resist arrest, and the event that followed, Tong's death, couldn't be tied in to a joint act by the two men.

"What we wanted the jury to do," Maloney says, "was come to the conclusion that Jackson hadn't shot his gun and Suchan didn't mean to kill Tong, and then give them both manslaughter."

But before Robinette and Maloney had their day in court, they temporarily lost their clients. So did the police. Suchan and Jackson had been locked away with their old associates in crime, Edwin Boyd and Willie Jackson, who had also been recaptured. The four occupied the Don Jail's death row, a group of cells isolated from the rest of the prison population. Escape-proof, the Don's officials figured. Not escape-proof, however, to Boyd, whose de-vious mind concocted another break-out scheme. This time, his agencies were a key modelled from a scrap of metal and a hack-saw once again smuggled in from the outside. On September 8, the four lit out, over the wall and through the wilderness that filled a valley running north from the jail.

The daring escape sent a shiver of memory through Robinette. "In 1918, my father acted for a man named Frank McCullough," he says. "This fellow was convicted of murder and sentenced to hang. While he was waiting for his execution, McCullough escaped. It was from the same cell that my client Suchan was occupying in 1952. McCullough's escape was the great sensation of 1918, just the way Suchan and the others became the great sensation of 1952. Eventually, McCullough was caught."

So were the Boyd Gang, nabbed after a massive manhunt in a farmer's barn several miles north of the jail on September 16, eight days from the date of their escape. The murder trial had already been scheduled to start on September 22, a mere week away, and Robinette, arguing that he'd had too little time to prepare his defence, applied for an adjournment to Chief Justice McRuer, who had designated himself to hear the case.

"You should have asked for an adjournment earlier than this," McRuer said. "Back on September 8."

"At that time," Robinette said, "I wasn't sure there would be a trial."

McRuer turned him down.

"The Chief Justice was a stern man," Robinette says. "He could make things hot for defence counsel."

On September 22, Bill Gibson began marshalling for McRuer and the jury the crown's case against Suchan and Jackson in swift and orderly fashion. The parade of witnesses, forty-three in all, included the wounded Sergeant Perry, the shopkeeper who exchanged Suchan's violin for the Smith and Wesson, and an expert from the RCMP's Crime Detection Laboratory who swore that the fatal bullet came from the Suchan gun, and their testimony shaped an argument for the accused men's guilt that seemed relentless and inevitable. Two pieces of evidence struck Robinette as especially damning. One established that two of Suchan's bullets went through the police cruiser's windshield. "If you're trying to put a car's engine out of commission," Robinette says, "you don't shoot into the windshield. Bill Gibson kept hammering that point to the jury." The other critical piece of evidence was physical — a dressmaker's dummy from the basement of the house where Suchan and Jackson had been hiding out. The two used the dummy for target practice on the day before Tong was killed. "We argued with McRuer that the dummy should be kept from the jury," Robinette says. "If they got a look at it, we knew they'd form the unmistakable impression that Suchan and Jackson were pretty deadly shots and weren't likely to miss anything they aimed at. The dummy has bullet holes in it — through the heart and through the head." Robinette and Maloney took the position that the dummy was, as evidence, irrelevant and inflammatory. McRuer rejected their arguments, and the dummy was carried into the courtroom. "That just about finished us," Robinette remembers. "The jury looked at the dummy and went into a kind of stunned state. I was pretty shocked myself."

When Gibson finished the crown's case, Robinette and Maloney called one witness each, Suchan for Robinette and Jackson for Maloney. Suchan's testimony was consistent and credible, and following Robinette's deft examination-in-chief, he stuck to his story that he hadn't intended to shoot Tong and that his purpose in firing was to protect his own position, not Jackson's. The latter piece of testimony paved the way for Robinette to counter the crown's contention that Suchan and Jackson had entered into a common purpose to resist arrest. No joint act, Robinette would argue, no conspiracy, and therefore no double conviction for murder. Towards the end of Suchan's testimony, Robinette led him to tell the jury that in Montreal when the local police fired at him and wounded him during the shoot-out capture at his apartment, he hadn't shot back. The point Robinette hoped to demonstrate was that Suchan wasn't normally given to shooting policemen, that his gunning of Tong was a single, unplanned, accidental fluke.

"In fact I think there was another reason why Suchan didn't shoot at the Montreal police," Robinette says. "He was one of those fellows who may have been weak in spirit. When he got into the shooting in Toronto, it was because Jackson was beside him. He wanted to impress Jackson. But he would never have shot at the Montreal police. He was alone at the time, and there was no one to impress."

Suchan stepped from the witness-box, and Jackson took his place. He responded to Maloney's examination-in-chief with the story that Maloney expected, telling the court that Suchan's shooting of Tong came to him as a terrible surprise, an event that had been neither planned nor expected. But when Bill Gibson began to cross-examine Jackson, his story developed holes. He conceded that, by riding with Suchan in the car, he was, as a fugitive, looking to Suchan for protection. He knew he could count on Suchan in a show-down with the police. When McRuer got into the act, following up Gibson's cross-examination of Jackson with his own clarifying questions, Jackson grew belligerent. He abandoned most of the story that Maloney had led him through.

"I was shattered," Maloney remembers. "I listened to Jackson and I knew he'd thrown in the sponge. He virtually admitted that he knew Suchan was carrying a gun, that it was loaded, and that he knew Suchan would use it to shoot anybody who tried to stop the pair of them."

Jackson finished his self-damning testimony.

"I asked later what made him say the things he had on the stand," Maloney says. "He looked at me and he said, 'If those bastards, that judge and that prosecutor, want me this bad, hell, I'm gonna give myself to them.' Then he thought it over, and he said to me, 'I let you down, didn't I?' I answered him back. 'You didn't let me down,' I said. 'You let yourself down.'"

It was time for counsel's addresses to the jury. Robinette went first. He offered the jury his theory in Suchan's defence, that the shooting was accidental and that Suchan was guilty of no more than manslaughter. Robinette spoke for thirty-five minutes in his measured, steady manner, and then, toward the end of the address, referring to the shooting in the Montreal capture, to the wounds that Suchan received from the police bullets, Robinette conjured up the image of Suchan lying in his own blood on the apartment floor. "Something intervened," he said. "He could have died there, but he didn't." It was a rare excursion into melodramatics for Robinette, a suggestion that a greater force had somehow saved Suchan, and it was a line that, to Robinette's chagrin, Bill Gibson wouldn't let him forget.

Maloney followed with his address — "Leonard Jackson will not walk from this courtroom a free man," he said, "but he does not deserve to die" — and then it was Gibson's turn. "I've been working on this case for months and months and months," he began. "Today for the first time, I've heard it said that the case involved divine intervention. . . ."

"That was a spectacular opening," Robinette says today. "I've never fogotten those words of Bill's. They just got the jury riveted and they made a kind of mock of the reference I'd put in about a higher power. Bill followed that same blunt approach all the way through his address, and the jury seemed to go for it. Bill was bound he'd get a murder conviction."

He got it. McRuer briefly instructed the jury after Gibson's address, and the jury left the courtroom to arrive at a decision. They were out for a mere one hour and forty-five minutes and returned with the same verdict for both Suchan and Jackson.

"Guilty of murder as charged."

For the first time in the trial, McRuer's emotions surfaced. His voice grew soft and trembling.

"You shall be taken to the place from where you came," he said in turn to both Suchan and Jackson, "and there kept in close detention until the sixteenth of December, 1952, and thence you shall be taken to the place of execution, and there be hanged by the neck until you are dead. May God have mercy on your soul."

Robinette turned to Maloney as the two men sat side by side at the defence table.

"My God," he said, "I've never heard those words before."

Robinette and Maloney rushed to appeal the case, asking for a new trial on the grounds that the evidence had not shown there was a common intention on the part of Suchan and Jackson to resist arrest and that McRuer had erred in allowing the dress-maker's dummy to be entered as evidence. On November 12 they presented their arguments before five justices of the Ontario Court of Appeal. The judges listened, retired to consult together, and returned in fifteen minutes. Appeal dismissed.

Robinette and Maloney travelled to Ottawa on December 5 and applied to a justice of the Supreme Court of Canada sitting alone for leave to appeal the case to the whole court.

"It was Mr. Justice James Estey who heard us," Robinette says, "and he gave us all the time in the world. I think what bothered him about the case was that McRuer had made us go on with the trial so quickly after the jail escape without an adjournment. We played this point up with Estey, and I'm sure he was disturbed enough to take our arguments more seriously than he might have."

Estey announced that he'd reserve his judgment for a few days.

"That was unusual," Robinette says. "On applications for leave, the judges normally come ahead with a fast answer, and they never bother with written reasons."

Estey took a week to ponder the case, and he produced four-teen pages of judgment. It added up to a close analysis of all that law that Robinette and Maloney had cited to him, but its conclusion was the same as the two lawyers had heard from the Ontario Appeal Court. Leave to appeal, Estey held, was denied. The date was December 12, four days to execution date.

Suchan and Jackson, alone on the Don's death row (Boyd and Willie Jackson, convicted of bank robbery, were serving time in a penitentiary), found religion. It was Arthur Maloney's doing. Suchan's mother, a Catholic, had approached him as a co-religionist, regretful that her son had left the Church and asking if Maloney could coax him back. Maloney recruited Father John Kelly, a Catholic priest who later became president of St. Michael's College in Toronto, and in daily visits to Suchan, Kelly brought him around to his old Catholicism. Jackson followed. He was Jewish, but the conversations between Father Kelly and Suchan so intrigued him that he asked the priest to baptize him into the Catholic faith. Jackson took to his new religion with such zeal that, as his final meal before the execution, he demanded to be served the same food that Christ ate at the Last Supper. Father Kelly pointed out that the communion which Suchan and Jackson would take on the morning of the execution was a re-enactment of the Last Supper. That satisfied Jackson, and he switched his order to the same meal that Suchan had chosen — fried chicken, apple pie with ice cream, and a fat cigar.

Robinette visited Suchan for the last time at five o'clock on the afternoon of December 15. Suchan had written a letter to his mother. It was in Slovak, but Suchan translated it for Robinette, reading aloud to him in the cell on death row.

"Straight from my heart, I love you, Momma," the letter ended. "And my small brother, a million times. Please forgive me, Momma, for bringing you so much sorrow."

Robinette left the jail.

"When he read the letter to me," Robinette says, "it tore me apart."

A few hours later, shortly after midnight on December 15 and early on the morning of December 16, Suchan and Jackson were hanged.

"Arthur said something to me about the hanging," Robinette remembered almost twenty-nine years after the execution, sitting on the late-autumn day in 1981 in his office at McCarthy & McCarthy, smoking his pipe and thinking back. "Arthur said, 'Y'know, John, you never had a man executed. Well, you'll be a better person for it.'"

Robinette tapped the ashes out of his pipe.

"I guess Arthur was right," he said. "You lose a case like that, lose the man, and you probably learn to have more sympathy with people. Maybe it all makes you a little more human."

In these last fifty years, Robinette might have accepted other roles in Canadian life. He might have become the leader of the Ontario Liberal Party. The Grits wanted him for the job in the late 1940s, and a few years later, when Lester Pearson was prime minister, the post of federal Minister of Justice was Robinette's almost for the asking. But Robinette, though he is a forever Liberal, turned his back on both positions. "I was never really interested in politics," he says, "because it would invade your privacy." In 1953 he accepted an appointment to the Ontario Court of Appeal — a job that, in the minds of many lawyers, would have inevitably led him one more step up the judicial ladder to the Supreme Court of Canada — but at the eleventh hour, shortly before he was to be sworn in, Robinette resigned from the appointment. His lifetime role, he recognized, was not to be on the bench but to be facing it. He wasn't destined to decide cases. He was meant to argue them.

And as an advocate, his influence on the legal profession has probably been more pronounced and specific than that of any other counsel in this century. "He's a model for the rest of us," an experienced Toronto counsel named Mike Temple says. "That's the first way you measure what he's done." Temple has gone against Robinette in several land-development cases — Robinette acted for ratepayer groups — and he describes Robinette as "the ideal example of the adversary who keeps you always on edge. He has this way of dealing with the weak points in his case right up front, and that tends to take some of the steam out of your own case before you even get to argue." And Temple sees Robinette as setting the standard for other counsel in his versatility. He performs with equal effectiveness both at trial and on appeal, a difficult double, since trial work, with its emphasis on handling witnesses and evidence, is so intrinsically different from appeal work, where the required skills are for steering sceptical judges through thickets of law, that most counsel are satisfied to specialize in one form of advocacy.

And he's helped to establish patterns for the profession in other areas. There's his willingness to take on tough cases. "If you look in the case-books," Temple says, "you'll find that several of his reported cases are ones where his clients haven't been successful. What that means is that clients and other counsel brought him cases that looked tough to start with. He probably took them because he spotted an interesting point that he thought the courts should hear about." He hasn't hesitated either to accept unpopular causes. Harold Ballard's, for example. In the early 1970s, Ballard was accused of diverting Maple Leaf Gardens' funds to his personal use. Robinette took the case. The damning facts against his client left him little room for manoeuvring, and his arguments were mainly of a technical sort. But Robinette gave judges in the different courts all the way to the Supreme Court of Canada plenty of fresh law to mull over. Eventually he lost the case and the appeals. Ballard went to prison. But Robinette, in the face of restless public opinion, had ensured Ballard's honest and complete day in court.

"There's a rectitude about the man that's corny and rare and necessary," a prominent civil-litigation specialist named Martin Wunder says. "Some lawyers are cutting corners these days. The profession is going through hard economic times just like everybody else in the country, and with that atmosphere, you look to a man like Robinette, who's not only a tremendous counsel but someone who has been visibly the soul of integrity all these years."

But Robinette's impact has also been felt outside the legal profession. It has spread in particular ways to the non-lawyering population. He has, indeed, contributed to the making of law that has affected other Canadians. As a basic truth, lawyers don't often make law. Judges make law. And elected legislatures make law. But in a few instances, under special circumstances and among gifted counsel, lawyers have a hand in the process. It happens in, at most, five per cent of a great counsel's cases. It happens when a lawyer is so correct in his reading of the changing drift of social circumstances, so intuitive in his recognition of the need for new law, and so persuasive in his arguments to a court, that in the end, through the judgments of the court, his ideas enter into the law of the land.

"Robinette made law in the constitutional cases," Ian Scott says. Scott is himself a Toronto counsel of enormous talents, a witty, perceptive man in his late forties who appears regularly before the Supreme Court of Canada, sometimes arguing in opposition to Robinette, sometimes arguing in the same interest. He likes what he calls "Robinette's combination of humanity and playfulness." He remembers a case before the Supreme Court when he and Robinette were lined up on the same side. "My student thought of an argument for our case that nobody else had come up with," Scott says. "We took it to Mr. Robinette, and he asked if he could use it. He got so excited. The man was in his seventies by then, but he acted just like a little kid because he had this new argument, this new toy that hadn't been tried out."

Scott was in the Supreme Court in Ottawa during the week in 1976 when the court heard the Anti-Inflation Act case. It was perhaps the key to all the constitutional cases in recent years, the case that Robinette calls "a landmark in Canadian constitutional law." The federal government had passed legislation that, generally, made an attempt to control inflation in the country and, specifically, set up the Anti-Inflation Board. The provinces, various corporations, and other national groups challenged the legislation, contending that the federal government had overstepped itself and lacked the constitutional authority to legislate in such ways. Counsel for all the parties gathered before the Supreme Court of Canada to argue the issue. Scott appeared for the Ontario Public Service Employees' Union. Robinette appeared for the federal government.

"It was a classic situation," Scott says. "Right there in the courtroom we had the two men who knew more than anyone in the country about constitutional law — Robinette and Chief Justice Bora Laskin. How was it going to come out? Were the feds going to get their way? Or was their legislation going to be upset? Nothing was a sure thing when we started."

The early calculation among counsel was that the Quebec judges on the nine-man court would vote against the federal government's legislation and that at least a couple of other judges, notably Martland and Ritchie, could also swing to the province's position. Going into the case, Robinette could expect Laskin to line up on his side, along with two or three other federalist-minded judges, but his case was far from a certain winner. He could easily see the court vote against him by a five-to-four count.

Robinette based his argument on Section 91 of the British North America Act, the section that empowers the federal government to take whatever steps are necessary to preserve the country's "peace, order and good government." Traditionally, the government in Ottawa has called on the section to justify its actions in times of war and of obvious civil emergency. Robinette suggested to the court that the power under Section 91 should be extended to cover situations such as in the 1970s, when inflation has become a national emergency. He cited one small precedent in his favour. It was an 1882 decision of the Privy Council, the British judicial body which for years heard appeals from Canada's Supreme Court, and it held that the high rate of alcohol consumption in the country during the 1870s constituted a national crisis and that the government could thus pass Dominion legislation under Section 91 regulating the sale of liquor across the country. Robinette cited the case, but his argument went far beyond that homely precedent.

"It wasn't a case where you talked case law," Scott says. "It was much more difficult than that, much more complicated. It was a case where you talked to the judges about the kind of country you want to have. You talked about federal power versus provincial power. You talked about the meaning of a strong central government. It takes a particular kind of counsel to get away from case law and argue persuasively about concepts. Robinette is very good at that unique art, and he was quite beautiful in court on the Anti-Inflation Act case."

When the nine judges had heard the arguments from all counsel, they voted seven to two in favour of Robinette's position. They supported the government's anti-inflation legislation, and they extended the national concept of the "peace, order and good government" section to a different kind of peacetime situation. They altered, slightly but crucially, the workings of the Canadian constitution.

"That," Ian Scott says, "is how John Robinette helped to make some law."

CHAPTER 10

THE HOCKEY PLAYER AND THE MARINE DRIVE SOCIALIST

MIKE ROBITAILLE didn't mind when the New York Rangers hockey club took him away from home. It meant he'd escape the tension of life with his mother. The family scraped by in Midland, Ontario, in tough financial circumstances, and Geraldine Robitaille was a woman whom middle age had visited with demons. She suffered two nervous breakdowns, and when her moods were at their blackest, it was Mike who was the special target of her wrath. He was the youngest, a change-of-life baby, born nine years after the next last in line of the eleven Robitaille children, and his youth left him isolated and vulnerable. Ernie Robitaille, husband and father, was a saint, as Mike always said, patient with all the kids, but he couldn't stand up to his wife's demons. Mike was hardly sad to leave the house on the wrong side of the tracks in Midland. He was bound to be moving into a more promising world. It was the autumn of 1962 and Mike was fourteen years old.

The Rangers sent him further south in Ontario to play junior hockey in Kitchener. He and a teammate rented a tiny basement apartment where they shared a double bed behind the furnace. Mike didn't log many sleeping hours, mostly because the other boy led parades of girls and beer through the apartment. He was a sophisticate, five years older than Mike and the bragging possessor of a couple of arrests for car theft. Mike was intrigued by the hint of danger that the teammate brought into his life. He dropped out of classes at St. Jerome's College, a school in Kitchener for proper Catholic boys, and might have been headed down the fast road to trouble.

Mike had two rescuers. One was hockey. Mike recognized it as his ticket to fame and fortune. He was obsessed with the dream of climbing away from the hard and money-poor times he'd known in his parents' home, and he drove himself to make a career in hockey. His other salvation was the love of a good woman. Her name was Isabel, blonde and lovely and strong-minded, and he met her in February 1967 at St. Mary's Hospital in Kitchener, where she was a medical secretary and he was receiving treatment for a hockey injury. Isabel's family took to Mike. "They practically adopted me," he later said. The couple became engaged in May 1968 and were married at the end of the hockey season a year later, May 24, 1969. Stability entered Mike's life.

His hockey skills improved steadily. He played defence. He was a big kid, an inch short of six feet and five pounds shy of two hundred, and he had long, flat, hard muscles that looked as if they'd been layered on his body by a sculptor. His face, square and handsome in the jock style, gave off waves of determination and dedication. He played tough but, perhaps surprisingly, not dirty; in his 382 National Hockey League games, he would receive only 286 minutes in penalties, a remarkably low figure for a defenceman. His forte was the hip check. He could take a forward out with it in one brief, bruising instant, and any opposing player who carried the puck into Robitaille's zone learned to keep his head up. He also possessed an excellent right-hand shot from the point and he was gifted at moving the puck briskly out of his own end. He gave honest work in every game and qualified as somewhere above average among professional players, not a superstar but much more than a journeyman.

In 1968 the Rangers promoted him from the Kitchener juniors to Omaha in the professional Central Hockey League, where he spent two years. In his second season with Omaha, he scored fifty-eight points and was named the league's most outstanding defenceman. He played a few games for the Rangers, then went through a couple of trades, first to the Detroit Red Wings and eventually to the Buffalo Sabres, where he settled in as a solid NHL defenceman. He put in three good seasons for Buffalo until the fall of 1974 when the Sabres traded Robitaille and Gerry Meehan for Jocelyn Guevremont and Bryan McSheffrey of the Vancouver Canucks. Mike was on his way to the west coast and he was taking with him a contract that quoted impressive figures. At the end of the 1973-74 season, he had signed a three-year deal with the Sabres calling for salaries of $75,000 in 1974-75, $85,000 the next season, and $90,000 in 1976-77. The Canucks would, of course, assume the contract. Robitaille, unhappy to be moving away with Isabel and their baby daughter, Anique, from friends among the Buffalo players, nevertheless looked forward to a flourishing career with Vancouver. He was only twenty-six years old, and he was approaching his prime as a player and, maybe more important, as a money-earner.

To be sure, he was paying a price for the success he had driven himself to achieve. He suffered from anxiety attacks. They had begun when he was nineteen and they were brutal, sometimes giving him the sensation that his chest was being crushed. "You would think you were having a heart attack," he later described the feeling. "Your mind would be playing a big game on you, and you were very fearful that death or something was going to happen and everything inside was going to let loose, like your heart might fly apart." Mike fought off the attacks with Valium. Some doctors for NHL clubs freely handed out Valium capsules in the dressing-rooms, and Mike was rarely without a supply in his pocket. Some days he might take as many as eighty milligrams, almost four times the maximum dosage that a sensible doctor would allow a patient. But for Mike they seemed at those terrifying times his only defence against the fear that his heart might burst out of his chest.

The dependence on Valium contributed to a crisis for Robitaille that peaked in September 1976. He felt, as he would later say, under the gun with the new hockey season growing nearer. He had given an excellent performance during his first year with the Canucks, 1974-75, and had put in an accomplished enough season in 1975-76, though an ankle injury near the end of that year meant that it closed on a down note. (He was accustomed to enduring injuries and playing hurt: in his NHL career, he survived three shoulder separations, a broken wrist and finger, torn rib cartileges, and ripped ligaments in one knee.) But the upcoming season, 1976-77, was the last under his three-year contract, and Mike sensed pressure building inside him to produce a superior year of hockey that would yield him the upper hand in negotiating an even more lucrative deal. "I promise to give you one hundred per cent this season," he wrote to Phil Maloney, who was both coach and general manager for Vancouver, in a letter before training camp. Still, Mike was torn. He recognized that his best hockey might elude him unless he freed himself from his Valium addiction, and at the same time, in the early days of training camp, the familiar attacks of anxiety grew in such intensity that he found himself struggling against inexplicable bouts of weeping.

Early in September he consulted a Vancouver psychiatrist, Dr. Eric Termansen, who recommended that Mike check himself into a hospital long enough to shake the need for tranquillizers out of his system. Mike, desperate, told his troubles to Maloney, left training camp, and entered the Lions Gate Hospital in Vancouver as Termansen's patient. The cure was a swift success. In ten days Mike's Valium habit had vanished, replaced by a program of relaxation exercises and transcendental meditation that seemed to hold his anxiety in check. Reassurance washed over him, and he felt comforted, too, by a series of tests that the Lions Gate psychiatric staff ran on him.

"They showed I'm not neurotic," Mike told Isabel, proud that he had managed to hang on to his marbles in spite of a turbulent adolescence. "And they showed I've got a high IQ."

Not everybody was so convinced, not Phil Maloney and not Bill Hughes, the Canucks president. They weren't entirely persuaded of the soundness of Mike's health, especially of his mental health.

"I met with both Maloney and Hughes to explain Mike's situation," Dr. Termansen later recalled. "They thanked me, but I wasn't sure the message had gotten across. Maloney wanted to know whether Mike could fulfil his contract. Was he going to go freaky? Was Mike just using the emotional trouble as a way of copping out of his obligations to the team?"

Mike missed the first three games of the season, all of them on the road, but he dressed for the Canucks' home opening game on October 13. He played with such skill and élan that he was named one of the game's three stars. His confidence — and the calibre of his performance — shifted to a higher plateau. Mike was flying. And he flew for a couple of weeks until, as if fate had decided that Robitaille must be parcelled good fortune in small doses and bad luck in generous portions, he came out of a game in St. Louis with a shoulder that was throbbing and inflamed. And it was at this point that Dr. Michael Piper arrived on the scene as a crucial performer over the next four years in the drama, on and off the ice, of Mike Robitaille's life.

The Canucks had three doctors on their payroll. Michael Piper was the most active, an orthopedic surgeon from New Westminster just down the highway south of Vancouver. None of the doctors took the job for the money, a measly $2,500 per season. They got their satisfaction from the perks: a pair of season tickets in the coveted red section at the Coliseum where the Canucks played their home games, free parking in prime space, and the heady chance to mingle on the inside of big-league hockey. Piper was a fan. In his early forties, he was tall and dark, trim and fit, smartly turned out in blazers and white shirts. His career in orthopedics was escalating at a satisfactory rate, and the post with the Canucks, which he had accepted in that fall of '76, came as one more indicator of his upward progress.

When Robitaille returned to Vancouver from the St. Louis game, Dr. Piper took X-rays of his right shoulder.

"Bone chips," he told Mike. "Bunch of them floating around in there. It's such a mess you're going to need an operation. But that's some time down the road, maybe at the end of the season."

For now, Piper told Mike, he should take a short rest from hockey until the inflammation receded. Not long. Maybe a few games. Be almost as good as new. Piper cheered Mike on his way.

Mike accepted the advice — he'd been knuckling under to hockey doctors, to coaches and general managers and owners, since he was fourteen — but unease nagged at him. There was something else wrong, something besides the bone chips in the shoulder. It was this strange numbness in his right arm. It wasn't entirely new. He'd felt it a few times the season before, but thirty minutes of hot packs from Patty Dunn, the Canucks' trainer, had always cleared away the tingles. Mike asked again for the hot-pack treatment, explaining to Dunn that the numbness from last year was acting up. Dunn lathered balm on Mike's neck, right shoulder, and arm and put him under a heat lamp for twenty minutes. The numbness retreated, but somehow Mike couldn't shake his uneasiness. Maybe — he didn't articulate his worry so much as intuit it — he had a problem that was beyond the temporary relief of Patty Dunn's balm and heat lamp.

Mike recognized he had troubles of another sort when he picked up the *Vancouver Province* on November 1 and read Eric Whitehead's sports column. Whitehead was writing about the Canucks' efforts to climb higher in their NHL division, closer to eventual playoff contention, and he quoted Phil Maloney's views on the team's recent lack of success. "Of course," Maloney told Whitehead, "we were short a defenceman with Robitaille out (sore shoulder). I don't know how bad it is but I can tell you he'd better start playing. If he doesn't, I'm going to have to consider suspending him."

"You really mean what you told the papers," Robitaille said to Maloney later that day at the Coliseum.

"Damn right."

"*Suspend* me? Suspend me when all I'm doing is resting a bad shoulder?"

"Listen, Mike," Maloney said. "There was this guy who played with me in the NHL years ago. The 1950s is when I'm talking about, only six teams in the league and you had to work your butt off to stay up there. This guy had the most rotten shoulder I ever saw, but he played. He strapped up his shoulder and he played. That's what you got to do. Tough it out or I'll suspend you."

Robitaille played. What choice did he have? His career was on the line, the money, the future, the new contract, the long climb out of Midland, Ontario. He missed three games while he rested the sore shoulder. Then he played. Dr. Piper had been correct in his diagnosis of the chips inside the shoulder, but Piper raised no objections when Mike returned to hockey action. At least Piper said nothing to Mike. Maloney spoke to Mike and so did Bill Hughes, the Canucks president, and their message was clear: *play*. Mike played. He tended to labour on the ice, not flying the way he had in mid-October. But nobody could make noises about suspending him. He was playing.

Robitaille's ancient devil, anxiety, began to surface again. To hold it off, he stepped up his program of relaxation exercises and transcendental meditation. Before each game he spent ten or fifteen minutes in the team's steam room putting himself through a series of exercises. He carried a tape machine and some cassettes on road trips, and sitting on planes and buses he'd plug into his machine, soaking up the soothing message of relaxation that kept his anxiety at bay.

To his teammates, Mike's dedication to the tapes and the TM and the curious relaxing regime marked him as a mild figure of fun. They kidded him, Mike the weirdo. The Canucks management took notice, too, of Robitaille's unorthodoxies. Hockey players weren't supposed to rely on such foreign gimmicks as TM.

It smacked too much of another culture, too effeminate for a real man. "Mike Robitaille. Tape recorder. Bus. Van. Seattle," Patty Dunn wrote in his team diary in an entry for December 2, 1976. The note was a reminder to Dunn that he'd observed Mike tuned into one of his funny tapes during a team bus ride from Vancouver to connect with a plane at the Seattle airport. Dunn kept the diary as an informal record of the players' physical condition, and he thought it worth noting Robitaille's behaviour. Mike was acting strange, not like a head case exactly but like someone whose mind was working differently from the other guys'. Dunn thought so. Maloney did, too, and Bill Hughes. Piper was coming around to the same opinion. And Orland Kurtenbach was willing to go along with whatever the others thought. He had been promoted on December 22 from his coaching job at Vancouver's farm team in Tulsa to take over as coach of the Canucks in order to let Maloney concentrate on his general manager's duties, and Kurtenbach wasn't going to challenge the thinking in the front office, not on the issue of Mike Robitaille's health.

His first up-close introduction to Mike's complaints came at a Holiday Inn on Long Island, New York, on the morning of New Year's Day 1977. The Canucks had left Vancouver the previous day for a gruelling road trip, six games in eight days, beginning with a January 1 game against the New York Islanders in Nassau, Long Island. Mike woke up that morning with pain reaching down his back on either side of his spinal column and spreading over his right shoulder as far as the elbow. It felt, he later said, "like somebody took a ball peen hammer and banged away at the points around my shoulder and elbow." He'd been experiencing the old numbness, the pain and the tingles and the fuzziness on his right side, at an intensified degree ever since early December. He noticed that his skating had been growing clumsy. He fell down when no one was near him. All of this frightened him, and when he mentioned the numbness and the awkwardness and the hurts to Dunn, Patty shrugged and gave him the usual treatment, the balm and the heat lamp and the hot pack. Their curing effect was minimal, and on New Year's Day morning the pain had reached a new and excruciating level.

"I don't know if I can play tonight, Kurt," Robitaille said to Kurtenbach when he saw him in the Holiday Inn lobby.

"Get yourself some heat," Kurtenbach said after he'd heard

Robitaille's trouble. "We'll leave it till game time. Then we can talk about playing or not."

But Kurtenbach said nothing to Mike that night, and he played. He moved cautiously on the ice and took care not to run into anybody, no body checks, no skirmishes, no hitting. And back on the bench, the right arm throbbing between shifts, Mike sat with his head hung low, below his shoulders, and the right arm held flat along the boards. It was the only posture that offered comfort.

No relief came the next day when the Canucks travelled into Manhattan for a game against the Rangers at Madison Square Garden. Mike complained again to Dunn and asked to see a doctor. It wouldn't be Piper, since team doctors rarely hit the road. "After the game," Dunn said, "we'll get the guy from the Rangers." Midway through the game, Mike came to more grief. A big, tough New York forward named Nick Fotiu slammed him to the ice with a ferocious check. A shock ran through Mike's body, and his right leg turned to rubber. When he tried to skate, the leg barely responded. Mike couldn't generate any speed. No quickness. No drive. It was as if he were skating in a thick, inhibiting fog. He explained the feeling to Dunn in the dressing-room after the game. Dunn summoned the Rangers doctor, who examined Mike for a minute or two. "Pulled muscle," he diagnosed. "You pulled a muscle somewhere in your back." Dunn said he'd give Mike some heat. That always helped a pulled muscle.

The rest of the road trip was like a nightmare for Mike. He caught a cold, and each time he sneezed or coughed, pain flashed down his right side. He played badly in the January 4 game in Pittsburgh. After the January 5 game in Atlanta, another poor effort for him, the Flames team doctor gave him a five-minute examination and decided Mike had stretched a back muscle. "That," Mike later recalled, knowing his trouble amounted to more than a back muscle gone wrong, "pissed me off." In the January 7 game against Cleveland, a humiliating 8-4 loss for Vancouver, Mike couldn't muster the strength in his right arm to pass the puck. He'd shovel it ahead. Kurtenbach shook his head at the sight, and in the January 8 game in St. Louis, yet another embarrassment to Robitaille, Kurtenbach benched him during much of the last period. Mike hardly cared. The pain pounded through his right arm and leg, and on the flight home to Vancouver, he reminded Dunn to make an appointment for him to see one of the team doctors.

"I'm in trouble, Patty," he said.

On Monday morning, January 10, Dunn reached Dr. Piper. Robitaille might be a little strange, Dunn thought, the tapes and the exercises and all, but maybe this time a doctor ought to have Mike over to his office and check him out.

It would keep till Wednesday, Piper indicated on the phone to Dunn. Wednesday was the next Canucks home game, January 12, against the Minnesota North Stars.

"Somebody'll see Mike at the game," Piper said.

Mike arrived early for the Wednesday game. He took the usual massage and heat treatment from Dunn and waited for a doctor. None appeared. Mike dressed and played, and late in the third period, with barely two minutes left in the game, he found himself skating backwards alongside his defence partner, somewhere close to the Canucks blueline, waiting to check an on-rushing Minnesota forward. The North Star was a rookie, and he pulled a manoeuvre that only an inexperienced player would attempt, cutting into the centre of the ice and diving head-on between the two Vancouver defencemen. All three players smacked the ice. Two of them didn't get up. The North Star's wind was knocked out of him and he rolled on the ice in a temporary spasm. Robitaille lay beside him, writhing under the impact of an inner shock that made him feel, he would later say, "like I'd stuck my finger in an open light socket." His right leg had gone dead. He pushed himself to his feet, and with the one leg unable to hold its share of his weight, he spun around in a series of half circles. Dunn arrived on the ice and helped Mike to the dressing-room. The right leg jerked out of control. "It looked the way a fish does when you haul it out of the water," Robitaille described it. He felt sick at his stomach and he sat on his stool in the dressing-room, almost in a trance of suffering, willing a doctor to come to his aid.

Shortly after the end of the game, Dr. Piper opened the dressing-room door. He crossed the floor, passing among the players and looking straight ahead. Mike watched him silently as he went into Patty Dunn's private quarters at the back of the main room. When he's talked to Patty, Mike thought, when he's heard about my leg, he'll take care of me. He will. He'll check my back and arm and leg. He'll do something about the pain. A few minutes later, Piper reappeared from Dunn's room. He walked purposefully through the dressing-room and out the door. Robitaille stared, disbelieving, at the closed door.

"I felt so discouraged," he would later say of the moments in the dressing-room. "I'd been seeing myself as a kind of saint because I went out and played hockey when I was practically dying from the pain. But nobody cared. None of those people cared about me."

Isabel drove Mike home, and he lay awake most of the night, twisting to find a position in the bed that didn't aggravate the throb on his right side. The next day, he visited Dr. Termansen for one of his regular sessions of psychiatric therapy. Although Termansen felt that Mike's emotional problems had stabilized, he continued to see him as part of a regular ongoing program of therapeutic support, as is common with many psychiatrists and their patients. Termansen wasn't treating Mike's body, but he made a note in the Robitaille file about events of the previous night. "1-13-77. Injured in game last night. Complains of severe neck pain radiating down right leg." The talk with Termansen, just a talk, gave Mike a measure of comfort, and to his relief in the days that followed, the leg seemed to recover strength, at least enough to allow him to practise with the team. He skated gingerly, avoiding fast stops and sharp turns, and he managed to get through a home game on January 15 against Cleveland. It helped that Kurtenbach used six defencemen rather than the usual four or five. That meant Mike had longer rests between shifts on the ice, and he figured that his play didn't shame him. The leg was better, but not the neck and not the back. They buzzed and tingled and ached, and suggested to Mike the sensation of a decayed tooth that had spread through all the tissues of his body.

When Mike left home late in the afternoon of January 19 for a game against the Pittsburgh Penguins at the Coliseum, Isabel told him not to worry if he looked up into the stands to the section where she sat for the games and couldn't spot her.

"Don't be upset, Michael," she said. "Those stairs are getting too much for me. I'll probably stay in the wives' lounge for the second period."

Isabel was six months pregnant, and her condition made her one of the few people in the Coliseum that night who didn't see

Dennis Owchar of the Penguins hit her husband with a blind-side body check. Mike took a two-minute minor penalty in the second period, and as he stepped on to the ice at the end of the two minutes, the puck came loose and squirted in his direction. He was a couple of strides from a breakaway, and he pushed toward the Pittsburgh goal. The crowd roared. Mike thought the noise was a celebration of his breakaway. It wasn't. It was a collective shout of warning. Owchar, a rugged winger, was making a wide U-turn, lining up Robitaille for a check. Mike, intent on the puck, skated ahead unaware of Owchar's motion. The Pittsburgh player closed in on Robitaille at a speed of almost twenty-five miles per hour. Bodies and pads collided. The crunch echoed over the crowd noise and reached up into the press box. Mike took Owchar's shoulder in his chest and the side of his face. The hit to the face was immediately visible in a wide scrape across Robitaille's cheek, "one huge raspberry," as he later described it. The scrape didn't bother Mike, not as much as the buzzing in his right arm and leg, the shock to his body, the sense of oblivion that overwhelmed him.

"Help me," he said, lying on the ice and looking up at the player nearest him, a Pittsburgh defenceman named Don Awrey. "Please help me."

The hush in the Coliseum was so complete that the building might have been empty. People sucked in their breath and held back their fears for Robitaille. One fan spoke, a well-dressed, grey-haired gentleman sitting in a red seat three rows above ice level. "That man is seriously hurt," he said. He was Dr. Gordon Thompson, a Vancouver neurosurgeon, and he was speaking to the person in the seat next to his, Michael Piper. "You'd better get down there, Mike," Thompson said. Piper had lit a cigarette a moment before the collision on the ice. He didn't seem to Thompson to be in a hurry to leave his cigarette or his seat.

Down below, Patty Dunn skidded across the ice to Robitaille.

"I can't get anything to work," Mike said.

"Let's try and get you up," Dunn said.

Robitaille flopped over, pushing with his left arm and leg, while Dunn got a grip on his body. A Vancouver player, Chris Oddleifson, swung one of Robitaille's arms over his own shoulder and the other over Dunn's. The two supported Mike by grabbing the seat of his hockey pants and steered him toward a gate in the boards. Robitaille's legs cut grooves in the ice as they dragged behind him. The three-man procession moved in an agony of slow-motion, and the crowd, angry that Robitaille hadn't been placed on a stretcher, broke their silence to boo and jeer at Dunn.

Piper was waiting at the side of the boards by the gate. So was a stretcher. Dunn and Piper supervised Robitaille's shift on to the stretcher. Mike fell from their grip as he was manoeuvred through the tiny gate. He sprawled half on, half off the stretcher. The awkwardness of the position sent pain screaming up Robitaille's arm and leg. The minutes between the Owchar check and the stretcher seemed like an eternity.

In the dressing-room, Dunn ripped out the laces of Mike's skates and pulled off skates and stockings. His feet were bare, and Piper ran a sharp object across the soles; there was no reaction. Another doctor arrived in the dressing-room, an older man named Walter Brewster who had been Piper's predecessor as team doctor. "Something is really wrong," he said, but he deferred to Piper for diagnosis and decisions. Piper continued testing for five or six minutes. He finished and gave Mike a look that Piper intended to be reassuring.

"When you get home," he said, "treat yourself to a shot of Courvoisier and you'll be fine, Mike."

Piper left the dressing-room.

"Don't let the other fellas see you like this," Dunn said to Mike. "Don't let them think Pittsburgh's hurt you bad."

He helped Mike into his training-room off the back of the main dressing-room. Mike took two ammonia tablets to give his body a lift and sat on a table wrapped in a blanket.

No one spoke to Isabel about Mike's injury, and when she returned to her scat for the third period, she was puzzled that her husband was missing from the Canucks bench. She made her way to the Vancouver dressing-room and knocked. The door opened quickly. Piper and Dunn stood inside the entrance. Guilt flickered over Dunn's face, and he spoke swiftly and anxiously.

"We didn't take him off on a stretcher," he said, "because I didn't want to worry you, Isabel."

"What are you talking about?" Isabel asked.

"Mike's okay," Piper said.

The news was coming at Isabel in terrifying fragments. She groped for a question.

"Does Michael have to go to the hospital?"

"No, no," Piper said. "He'll be out of the dressing-room in a while. Why don't you wait for him in the lounge?"

Isabel obeyed. She waited through the rest of the third period and past the end of the game until Piper appeared at the door of the lounge.

"What's happening?" Isabel asked. "Does Michael need X-rays?"

"I'll see him in the morning," Piper said. "For now, just take him home, tuck him into bed, and give him a shot of Courvoisier."

Isabel stood outside the team dressing-room with Patty Dunn's wife, Marie. Inside, Mike tried to shower, but the splashes of water felt like pellets of pain to his body. He put his clothes on in the dressing-room which had now been emptied of everyone except himself and Dunn. Dunn asked Mike to come out for a drink, the two men and their wives. Funny, Mike thought, Patty's never gone drinking with me. Nice of him to ask, but strange. Robitaille agreed to the drink.

As Mike and Dunn emerged from the dressing-room, the lights were dimming in the arena. Only Isabel and Marie Dunn waited in the darkened corridor, and Isabel, seeing her husband for the first time since early in the game, his shoulders now hunched over and his right leg dragging, couldn't control a burst of panic.

"Oh, Michael, what's *wrong*?"

"Wait for now," Robitaille said, flashing annoyance. "We'll talk later."

The invitation to drinks surprised Isabel as much as it had Michael. The Dunns and the Robitailles never socialized together, and the party at the bar in West Vancouver turned out to be brief and grim. Mike couldn't grip his glass. He experimented with a couple of makeshift techniques and settled on clutching the glass between both wrists and lifting it to his lips. He made a mild joke about his problem. Only Dunn laughed.

"Listen, Mike," Dunn said as the unhappy group was leaving the bar, "I'll pick you up first thing in the morning and drive you for X-rays."

At home, Robitaille fretted over Dunn's offer.

"He never does that kind of job," he said to Isabel. "What's he being so attentive for, the drinks and everything? Something must be really wrong with me."

Isabel undressed her husband and brought him a bowl of soup in the bedroom. She left when he tried to eat it, too embarrassed to watch. Mike couldn't hold the soup spoon.

"Dr. Piper said something about a shot of Courvoisier," she said to Mike later.

"Yeah," Mike said. "I heard that line, too."

Robitaille was awake most of the night, shuffling back and forth to the bathroom. He vomited. He had diarrhea. And when he lay on the bed, he couldn't bear the pressure of a sheet on top of him. Its touch sent tingles of pain through his body. He rolled and sweated away the hours, and he would always remember this as the most wretched of all his terrible nights.

The next morning, January 20, Dunn picked Robitaille up at eight o'clock in the Canucks team truck and drove him to the Royal Columbia Hospital in New Westminster. Mike stayed there for nine days. It was a time of loneliness and secrecy and confusion. The loneliness grew out of Robitaille's realization that the rest of the Canucks, his teammates, had come to look on him as someone whose company was dangerous. Whatever management figured Mike had, the players reasoned, it might be catching. Just a single one of Robitaille's fellow Canucks, Dennis Kearns, dared to visit him at the Royal Columbia.

The secrecy came from the doctors. And they were responsible, too, for the confusion. Dr. Piper set the tone for Mike's treatment at the hospital when he phoned Dr. Termansen on that first day, January 20.

"What I think Mike has," Piper said to Termansen, "is conversion hysteria."

Termansen paused in disbelief. "Conversion hysteria" is medical jargon to describe a physical paralysis that originates in emotional troubles.

"Mike's beyond that," Termansen said. "I've been seeing him for months and he's responded positively to our sessions. Whatever he's complaining of is in his body. It's physical."

"Emotional," Piper said before he hung up.

Piper phoned Isabel.

"Mike's going to be under observation for a few days," he told her. "I don't know what's wrong, but we can't overrule the fact it may be psychosomatic."

Piper sent Robitaille to the X-ray room and asked Dr. Richard Grosch, a neurologist, to examine Mike and his X-rays.

"Well, the neurological signs are confusing," Grosch said. "But the problem could be essentially psychosomatic."

Next day, January 21, Piper dispatched another specialist, a neurosurgeon named John Porayko, to look at Mike. Porayko's diagnosis was different from Grosch's and Piper's. It was a diagnosis that was later to be confirmed by other specialists, a diagnosis that would haunt the debate over Robitaille's condition. But it was also a diagnosis that was almost immediately lost in the shuffle by everyone associated with the Canucks. It looks, Porayko said, as if this hockey player has a problem with his cervical cord. A contusion maybe, a severe bruising of the cord up near the C-5 or C-6 level, about mid-neck. Grosch considered what Porayko had to say and took another look at Robitaille's X-rays. He withdrew his view that Mike's injury was psychosomatic.

No one mentioned Porayko's diagnosis to Robitaille. No one reviewed his condition with him. No one offered satisfactory instructions or information or encouragement. Mike was left in the dark until the evening of his ninth day at the Royal Columbia when a nurse arrived at his door with instructions for him to move out within the hour. The hospital was short of beds. Mike went home, and all he had to show Isabel was a case of the blues and an appointment at Piper's office on February 3.

The day before the appointment, Piper made another of his phone calls to Dr. Termansen. Piper moved swiftly to the point.

"Robitaille," he told Termansen, "better get it together or he's going to find himself traded away from the Canucks."

Mike kept the February 3 appointment. Piper didn't. His associate, Dr. Richard Loomer, saw Robitaille. Loomer was, like Piper, an orthopedic surgeon. He was also, like Piper, a club doctor for the Canucks.

"These doctors," Mike said to Loomer, "they're not paying attention to what's wrong with me. They gotta quit thinking of me as some kind of head case. I'm a *patient*."

"You can't blame people for feeling the way they do when you consider all the circumstances," Loomer said.

"Huh?" Robitaille said.

Loomer tried to take a clear-eyed look at Robitaille's problems. He prescribed a program of physiotherapy. He told Mike to stay away from hockey. And he wrote on Mike's file that he should be "closely followed."

The words — "closely followed" — would strike Robitaille as ironic and cruel when they were repeated to him many months later.

One afternoon, during the time when Robitaille was in the Royal Columbia, Bill Good dropped into Greg Douglas's office at the

Coliseum. Good was a veteran sportscaster around town, the anchorman for the CBC's telecasts of Canucks games, and he made it a habit to touch base regularly with Douglas, a former reporter who now worked as Phil Maloney's assistant in charge of publicity and media relations. Douglas kept Good up to date on events around the team, feeding him material that sounded newsy on television. But this January afternoon, Douglas offered a tidbit that he asked Good to keep under his hat.

"The reason Mike Robitaille's not playing is kind of confidential, Bill," Douglas said. "He's undergoing psychiatric treatment. He's got emotional difficulties, and I'd really appreciate it if you held this in confidence. Don't broadcast it, Bill. It might hurt his family."

Good wasn't surprised. He'd been hearing the same whispers about Robitaille in the Canucks front office for a few weeks. Robitaille had mental problems. It seemed to be what Maloney and Hughes and Douglas and everybody were saying. But to play it safe, Good checked with a couple of other sports reporters. Oh yeah, Denny Boyd from radio station CJOR said, Robitaille's supposed to be in bad emotional shape, or anyway that's what they're giving out at the Coliseum. Okay, Good thought, I'll accept it. And I'll keep mum.

Robitaille stuck to the physiotherapy program that Dr. Loomer had prescribed. It helped. The pain remained in his back and shoulder, and the leg still lacked strength and co-ordination, but at least the exercises gave him a soothing sense of progress. He needed small encouragements. At home, he spent much of his time in front of the television set. His right hand kept clutching up. It was difficult to lift a glass or the car keys or the TV guide. Despair threatened him. He was cut off. No communication from the club. Nothing from Piper or Loomer. Porayko's diagnosis of a cervical cord contusion remained a secret to Robitaille. No one acted on it. No doctor checked his progress. Mike was on his own.

One day he laced up his skates at the Coliseum. He moved gingerly to the ice. This, he told himself, was an experiment. He began to push off in his familiar skating motion. Nothing happened. He couldn't stride on his skates. It was the right leg. The only way he could make it function was to throw it ahead of the left. Almost grab it with his hands and force it to move in the way it had done automatically for twenty years of hockey. Mike fell down. He got up. And fell down again. He looked like a clown on the ice. But Mike wasn't laughing. Nor was the man who was watching the performance from the stands. Phil Maloney.

In mid-February, Mike's pay cheque was a few days late. He phoned the Canucks office and reached Larry Popein, an assistant to Maloney. Popein had been Robitaille's first coach in pro hockey, back at Omaha in the late 1960s, and Mike regarded him with respect and affection.

"I'm looking for my cheque, Larry," Mike said into the phone. "Hasn't come yet."

Popein measured his answer in one sentence that devastated Robitaille. "We got cheques around here," Popein said, "only for guys who want to play hockey."

"Larry, you mean you feel just the same as the rest of them? *You*, Larry?"

"I guess I do," Popein said and hung up.

Robitaille drove to the Canucks offices in search of his cheque. He spoke to Dunn, who referred him to Orland Kurtenbach, who told him to see Maloney. Mike was in for his second lecture of the day from the Canucks management on the ethics of effort in hockey.

"I've been watching you skate," Maloney said to Robitaille when the two men were seated in Maloney's office. "What are you trying to prove? How come you're not trying? Who do you think you're kidding?"

"I can't help it," Mike said. "I'm trying to get back in shape. Maybe I can help the club later in the season."

"You're a con artist," Maloney said. Robitaille couldn't tell whether Maloney's anger was real or whether it was faked for Mike's benefit. Feigned anger was a favourite motivating tool among hockey coaches and managers.

"You're cheating your family," Maloney went on, rolling on the heat of his performance. "You're cheating your wife and the fans and your teammates. Jesus, the stuff you're pulling."

Maloney reached into a drawer of his desk and waved a familiar piece of stationery at Robitaille.

"Recognize this?" Maloney asked. It was the letter that Mike had written to Maloney before training camp several months earlier. "You promised me in this letter you were gonna give one hundred per cent. You said you wouldn't let me down. You know what you are? You're nothing but a con artist."

"Don't say those things," Robitaille said, furious. "Don't call me a liar."

Mike couldn't bear any more of Maloney's wrath. As he left the Canucks office, someone handed him the pay cheque. Mike hardly noticed.

Two days later he called on Kurtenbach at the Coliseum. Maybe, Mike thought, he'd understand.

"Well, y'know," Kurtenbach said, "sometimes you gotta learn to play with pain."

Not him too.

"Believe me, Kurt," Mike said as patiently as he could manage, "I want to play for you. I think the world of you. It's just that I can't work my right leg."

"Okay," Kurtenbach said, "here's what I want. I want you to come out with the guys tomorrow and practise with us."

Next day, Robitaille put on his skates in the Canucks dressing-room and took his place on the ice for the practice session. Kurtenbach called the first drill, a series of skate sprints. The team divided into two groups, half behind one goal, half behind the opposite goal, and when Kurtenbach blew his whistle, one player from each end would skate for the opposite end, pumping at maximum speed. Robitaille's turn came. He pushed off and floundered almost instantly. His right leg held like an anchor, and he'd reached only as far as the blueline in his own end when the player from the opposite end flew past him.

"Never mind, Mike," Kurtenbach called from across the ice. "Pack it in."

Kurtenbach's expression showed no anger. It was disgust that was written across his face. Anguish showed on Robitaille's.

Isabel let a few days go by, days of watching her husband in isolation and torment. Enough, she decided. If the club doctors weren't helping, she'd find someone who would. Mike was reluctant to turn to an outsider. There were channels to these things in hockey; a player gets hurt and he speaks to the trainer and the trainer calls in the team doctor. That's the traditional route, an order of priorities that a player learns from his first years in the game. But Isabel prevailed, and on February 21 she phoned Dr. Rod McGillivray. He was a general practitioner and had seen

Mike for checkups and other minor medical matters over the previous year. Isabel arranged an appointment, and when Dr. McGillivray had examined Mike and listened to his description of the pains on his right side, he decided that a specialist's attention was called for. He referred Mike to Dr. Brian Hunt, a neuro-surgeon.

Early in the last week of February, Mike took a phone call from Calgary. It was Joe Crozier on the line, Mike's old coach at Buffalo and now the general manager of the Calgary Cowboys in the World Hockey Association. Crozier said he'd heard from the Canucks. They were interested in working out a deal to send Mike to the Cowboys.

"Joe, I'd be honoured to play for you," Mike said. He couldn't make up his mind whether to laugh or to cry. He opted for the laugh. "If you got a need for paraplegics on Calgary, I'm your guy."

"What?" Crozier said. "You kidding me or what?"

"Joe, I can't even *move* my right leg."

"What?"

"I can't skate."

"What's Vancouver trying to pull on me?"

"I tried, Joe, and I can't skate."

"Well, *shit*."

On February 25, Greg Douglas, the Canucks assistant general manager, phoned the Robitaille house. Mike was out and Isabel answered. *Douglas?* He was like the rest of the Canucks people, insensitive to Michael, and Isabel went cold when she heard his voice. But his message to her didn't come from the front office. It came from Douglas's conscience.

"I just want to warn you that you ought to consider getting a lawyer for Mike," he said. "There's a lot of shit flying around down here, and I think Mike's gonna get hurt."

"Aren't you going out on a limb or something?" Isabel said. "I mean, should you be telling me this?"

"At this point, I don't care," Douglas said. "Mike's gonna be made the scapegoat. That's all I'm saying. The rest is up to you and Mike."

Bruce McColl, in his mid-thirties, was a lawyer in a Vancouver firm, Macaulay, McColl & MacKenzie, where the others were like him, young and bright and gung-ho. He acted for a number of Vancouver players in negotiating contracts with the Canucks management. He'd handled a few matters for Robitaille and would be working out the new deal for Mike as soon as his original three-year contract expired over the next few months. McColl liked Robitaille, and when Mike phoned him with his troubles on February 26, his mind latched immediately on to legal tactics.

"More medical information," he said. "Mike, the only way we can deal with the Canucks people is if we have solid medical information."

"Something bad's going on," Robitaille said. "I heard from Joe Crozier. Maybe they're trying to trade me. But more likely they're gonna suspend me. That must be what Greg Douglas is talking about."

"All right, Mike, okay," McColl said. "Think about the medical stuff. You got to see an orthopedic specialist or a neurologist, somebody like that. Brian Hunt? Is that the specialist Dr. McGillivray wants you to go to? He's good. Get a report on your real condition, and I'll take care of business with the Canucks."

At last, Mike thought, *somebody*'s listening to me.

On February 28 Dr. Hunt examined Robitaille. His diagnosis was a rerun of Dr. Porayko's. Mike had sustained a severe injury to his spinal cord and was suffering from a physical disability that ranked in the critical category. Hunt couldn't be immediately certain of the disability's nature or origin, but he could draw a couple of obvious conclusions. One was that Mike needed long-term treatment. And the other was that he shouldn't put his body under the strain of physical activity. No hockey. No skating.

On Friday, March 4, Bruce McColl got on the phone. He talked to Dr. Hunt, who ran through his diagnosis and offered the opinion that Robitaille shouldn't have played in the game of January 19. His troubles in the spine probably predated the January 19 check from Dennis Owchar. "God knows," Hunt said to McColl, "what would happen if Robitaille fell on the ice again." McColl phoned Dr. Termansen. Of course, Termansen said, growing exasperated over his constant repetition of the obvious, Mike has no more emotional problems. It's his *body*. McColl phoned Phil Maloney at the Canucks offices. Maloney was on the road with the team. McColl left a message. Greg Douglas spotted it and returned McColl's call. He knew that if Bruce McColl had phoned, something heavy was in the air.

"I've been doing a lot of work with the doctors," McColl told Douglas, "and I think we're into matters that are very serious for Mike and for you people."

Douglas reached Maloney in Toronto, and later that day, four o'clock Vancouver time, Maloney phoned McColl.

"What's Robitaille's doctor say?" Maloney asked.

McColl sketched Dr. Hunt's preliminary diagnosis.

"Look, Mike Robitaille's a con artist," Maloney said. "Nothing but a crybaby."

"What concerns me in this business, Phil," McColl persisted, "is that Mike was made to play a game when he was already suffering from some injury. I'm talking about the January 19 game. That really concerns me."

Maloney began to retreat. "It wasn't me. The pressure comes from the top. Bill Hughes wants his players on the ice. I won't put any more heat on Mike if he's really hurt bad."

"I'm gonna get Dr. Hunt's written report," McColl said. "When it's ready, I'll get back to you people, and we'll go at the whole thing again."

McColl had pushed the Robitaille situation one long step closer to confrontation.

Al Davidson represents the Howard Cosell tradition of sports broadcasting in the Vancouver area. He insists on calling them the way they are, and on his sportscast over radio station CKNW on March 4, he spoke out fearlessly on the Mike Robitaille case. "Some hockey players like the great Frank Mahovlich and Mike Walton had the same thing happen to them, nervous breakdowns," Davidson told his listeners. "I have known Mike Robitaille for a couple of years now and he's a fine boy. Let's get everybody behind him and hope some day he'll be normal."

Robitaille didn't hear the broadcast, but a friend paraphrased it for him. Mike phoned Bruce McColl, and next day the two went to CKNW and listened to a tape of Davidson's words. McColl arranged a meeting with Davidson and asked for a retraction. On his next broadcast, Davidson took it all back. Robitaille wasn't like the great Frank Mahovlich or Mike Walton. He'd not had a nervous breakdown. His trouble was physical. Mike listened to the retraction and felt weary. He appreciated Davidson's apology, but he knew the word was out that hockey people thought of Mike Robitaille as a head case.

The Canucks were playing a home game on March 9, a Wednesday, and an hour before the start of the first period, Bruce McColl arrived at the Coliseum. He was carrying Dr. Hunt's written report on Robitaille's condition, and he took it to a meeting in Maloney's office. Maloney, it was immediately clear to McColl, had returned to his familiar stand on the whole bothersome Robitaille mess. There was no more mention of "pressure from the top" and of "not putting heat on Mike."

"I don't know this guy Hunt," Maloney said to McColl, "but I know Mike Robitaille. I've been in his house. He's got all these medical journals that he reads, and if you ask me, he simulates the injuries you're talking about. I wouldn't be surprised if he conned your Dr. Hunt."

"Phil, the main reason I'm here discussing this with you is to avoid a lawsuit," McColl said. "Unless somebody pays attention to Mike, we're going to end up in court. I'm telling you, there could be a basic problem of negligence here. Negligence by the Canucks."

It was the first time a legal term — "negligence" — had been used in connection with Mike Robitaille's problems.

Maloney lost his cool. "I'm used to your types," he told McColl. "You're not interested in Mike Robitaille. You're not interested in the Canucks. You're not interested in anything except yourself. You want to make a big public deal of this thing. You want to flog it out there."

Maloney left to watch the hockey game, and between the second and third periods McColl returned to Maloney's office for a second meeting. Dr. Piper was in the room. So were Greg Douglas, Maloney, and the third team doctor, a general practitioner named Lough. Piper took the spokesman's role.

"I hear you're making allegations of negligence," he said to McColl. "Maybe you should just wait a minute and hear our side of the story."

"Well, first," McColl said, "I might suggest that you should speak to the Canucks lawyers before you go any further."

"Never mind the lawyers," Piper said. "The point is that Mike Robitaille has deep psychological problems and he's under treatment right this minute."

"Wait, wait," McColl said. "I spoke to Mike's psychiatrist. I spoke to Dr. Termansen and he says there's no psychological problems at all."

Piper had a curious answer. "Eric Termansen tends to get carried away with himself."

"But what about the lack of treatment that Mike got?" McColl said. "I understand you saw him on different occasions, Dr. Piper, and you heard him making complaints. I'm talking about January 12 and later on. What about the lack of treatment?"

"On that point," Piper said, "we go back to the question I raised in the first place. As far as I'm concerned, Michael's problems are all in his head."

"Dr. Hunt told me that Mike might never play hockey again."

"Well," Piper said, giving a reprise to a favourite line. "Brian tends to get carried away with himself."

McColl shifted his approach. "Okay," he said, "why don't we get another opinion besides Dr. Hunt's? How about that? I know Barbara Allan. She's a neurologist, and she's on a top team at the Vancouver General. We get her and then we see what Mike needs, an operation or what."

"We'll go along with that," Piper said.

The buzzer had already sounded to signal the beginning of the third period, and the meeting in Maloney's office broke up.

On April 4, Isabel gave birth to a baby, a second daughter for the Robitailles. They named the little girl Sarah.

On April 17, Dr. Barbara Allan, a practitioner in clinical neurology, submitted Robitaille to the most thorough examination that he had so far received. She recognized symptoms of trouble, enough to offer a diagnosis that she would stand by. From that moment of decision, Dr. Allan became a major protagonist in the debate over Robitaille's condition. She emerged as Mike's medical voice in the struggle with the Canucks that was to stretch over another four years. The hockey team later came forward with other medical voices that sought to put the lie to Dr. Allan's diagnosis of April 17. But she held firm, and it was her word that formed the small, hard core at the centre of Mike Robitaille's cause.

"This man," Dr. Allan wrote in her report, which was dated April 27, "has symptoms of cervical spinal-cord abnormality, the first symptoms of this that one can be definite about occurring during the game of 12 January 1977, but prior to this time from January 1 on, he had symptoms of neck pain with cervical root irritation judging by the radiation of pain to the right arm."

What Mike must have suffered in the January 12 game, she concluded, was a hemorrhaging or severe bruising of the spinal cord. The electrical-shock sensation that Mike had felt earlier in the season, the pain in the elbow and shoulder, the shooting spasms down his arm and leg — all of these indicated that he was already suffering some sort of protrusion in a cervical disc. But the bang he took in the January 12 game was the clincher. If she had seen Mike's condition after that game, Dr. Allan would have immediately admitted him to hospital. She would have ordered a myelogram, a painful process in which dye is injected inside the spinal canal and the canal photographed. She would have kept him away from hockey, and certainly she would have forbidden him from playing in the game of January 19 when Mike was patently at risk.

Her April 26 report drew a line under the dangers Robitaille faced in the later game:

"How did the injury on January 19, 1977, relate to the injury on January 12, 1977?

"Answer: It made it considerably worse according to his history; on January 12, 1977, he had relatively transient and less severe symptoms of cervical cord abnormality while on January 19, the symptoms suggested more extensive cervical involvement and the symptoms failed to clear."

The body check Mike took from Dennis Owchar on January 19 aggravated the injury of January 12. The blow was to the very same area of the spinal cord, at the C-5 and C-6 level in mid-neck, that was giving Mike such excruciating pain, and what happened was the precise injury that Dr. Allan, if she'd seen Mike on the twelfth, would have set out to avoid by keeping Robitaille away from hockey. Now Mike was paying a penalty in pain and suffering. It would take extensive rest and treatment to relieve his agony, and he would never be free of some disability for the rest of his life. Would he play hockey again? Not a chance.

The 1976-77 NHL season ended in late April. The Canucks had sixty-three points, a total that tied the team with the Chicago Black Hawks for third place in its division. But Chicago had managed to show one more game in the win column than Vancouver and took the last spot in the Stanley Cup playoffs. A few weeks later, the Canucks fired Phil Maloney as general manager. He found a job in Vancouver as a car salesman.

In the summer of 1977, Mike and Isabel and the two little girls moved from Vancouver to Buffalo. It was good to get away from a city where people thought of Mike as some kind of nut. The Al Davidson broadcast had hurt his reputation. The Canucks players were avoiding him. And he felt isolated in Vancouver. Buffalo, on the other hand, was a city where Mike had played good hockey, a community where, as he said, "I feel socially comfortable." Physically, Mike was in agony. His right hand would fold involuntarily into a painful claw. His right leg turned inward and developed a tremor. Simple activities — a short walk, an hour of driving around the city — left him exhausted. He kept up sessions of physiotherapy that brought some relief. But the strength he took such pride in during his career in hockey had fled from his body.

The Canucks sent Mike a letter in early August. The team was releasing him because, as Robitaille's own doctors advised, he was incapable of playing hockey. The release took Mike off team medical coverage, and when his hospital bills came back unpaid, he turned to his savings.

"I had to use money from the bank account," he said. "I mean, a job? I couldn't even dial the phone to ask anybody for a job."

Robitaille was bitter.

"You're an NHL hockey player and people you meet promise the sun and the stars," he said. " 'Sure, Mike,' they'd tell me, 'when you quit hockey, I'd like you to work for me at my restaurant, in my business, public relations stuff.' Those people, what I thought of as friends, they've vanished out of my life."

Meanwhile, Bruce McColl chased after legal remedies for Robitaille. He flew to Toronto for discussions with Alan Eagleson, the lawyer who runs the NHL Players' Association. The situation was dicey, Eagleson said, and a court case, if that's what it came to, wasn't the association's proper role. McColl negotiated with the Canucks. The talks yielded nothing, no offer of settlement, no admission of an obligation to Robitaille. It was becoming clearer to McColl with each frustration that action in the courts was reaching the stage of inevitability. He organized his weapons. He instructed Mike to submit himself to one more examination, and in November at a Buffalo hospital a neuroradiologist named Kenneth

Kaan and a neurosurgeon named Lawrence Jacobs X-rayed Mike's spinal canal and put him through the ordeal of another myelogram. The Kaan-Jacobs report confirmed in every major respect Dr. Barbara Allan's earlier analysis of Mike's condition. With that news, McColl decided it was time to take the Canucks to court, and as counsel for Robitaille he briefed a Vancouver barrister. His name was John Laxton.

When John Laxton talks, he runs his right hand through his hair in a gesture that's decidedly sensuous. The hair is thick, black turning grey, and would inevitably be described in a man more pretentious than Laxton as leonine. He's in his late forties, medium height, wears smart moustaches, and has the sturdy good looks of the hero of a Thomas Hardy novel. His style, at work or play, is casual. The receptionist in his firm, Laxton, Pidgeon, calls him by his first name. So does everybody who has known him for at least five minutes.

Laxton's office is in a ten-storey building in downtown Vancouver that opened in 1980 and cost ten million dollars to put up. Laxton raised the money, and the building reflects his tastes and inclinations. Designed by the celebrated Vancouver architect Arthur Erickson, it slopes away on three sides in a series of pyramid-like levels. Plants tumble from the tiered balconies and look lush against the building's concrete and glass. A YWCA branch, sleek and fully equipped, takes up most of the third floor. Its presence was arranged by Laxton, who is a fitness freak and marathon runner. His devotion to a sound body does not stop him, however, from pointing out in an aside that's both proud and puckish that his Y is the only branch in the world boasting a beer and wine bar.

Laxton, Pidgeon occupies the building's top floor, and the view from Laxton's office through the window that fills the entire north wall looks across Coal Harbour and its traffic in freighters and seaplanes to the mountains, Grouse and Seymour, that define the boundary between Vancouver and the wilderness. Inside, the office runs to maroon walls, black furnishings, and light-grey carpeting. A wood fire burns in the grate, and invisible behind the panel to the right of the fireplace there's a bar that is stocked to meet everybody's drinking preference. Laxton's is Scotch, and each Friday, come five o'clock, he breaks out the drinks and the conversation.

"Maybe the muff-diver case was the craziest I ever took," he might say with very little prompting. "Back around 1970, Vancouver was death on hippies, really hated them, and I acted for the *Georgia Strait*, which was the hippie newspaper of the day. One of the guys in the crown attorney's office used to lay charges against the *Strait*, out of some sort of wild moral fervour, at the rate of about one a week, and I'd parade back and forth to court trying to fight off the attacks.

"Things got utterly ridiculous when this crown slapped the paper with an obscenity charge on the basis of an ad that ran in the *Strait*'s personals section. The ad read something like 'Young man wants to meet young woman for muff diving, etc.' So we went to court, and the crown and the police pretended to be scandalized by the printing of the phrase 'muff diving,' which everybody knows, but nobody was coming out and saying, is a colloquialism for cunnilingus. All right, what was I supposed to do for a defence? By great good fortune, about the time of the trial I happened to run into an old friend from back in my Lancashire days, Fred Bowers, who was teaching English at UBC. He told me his specialty was the structure of the English language. Marvelous, I said, you're my expert witness in the muff-diving case.

"Fred was fantastic. He got on the stand and he talked for two hours. He told the court he'd researched the word in question, 'muff diving,' through every source available to him. He reviewed ancient slang and the modern vernacular, obscure sources and serious literature. It was a virtuoso performance. He gave a bloody lecture in this thick Lancashire accent that he's never lost, and the judge, my god, he was absolutely enthralled. He hung on every word that Fred uttered. Fred said the faintest trace he could find of the word was from an eighteenth-century source that described 'muff' as a term for female private parts. But that in his considered opinion 'muff diving' had no identifiable and established meaning in the English language.

"The judge loved it. He said in his judgment he adopted the views of the expert witness in whole. He found that 'muff diving' was without meaning and that therefore the *Georgia Strait* had committed no crime in publishing the said non-word.

"Case bloody dismissed."

John Laxton's first job in Canada was as a Montreal vacuum-cleaner salesman. He and his wife Valerie had paused on a bumming-around trip to the South Pacific. They'd come from

England, where Laxton grew up in Lancashire, the son of a coal miner who read Karl Marx. When Laxton headed out from his home country, he took along his father's affection for socialism. He also packed a degree in law from King's College of Durham University. He and his wife drifted west from Montreal and the vaccuum-cleaner business, and as soon as their eyes fell on Vancouver, they decided that the South Pacific could wait.

"Vancouver looked like paradise," Laxton says in a voice that has shed most of the Lancashire accent. "What I remembered about home was the chimneys. Everywhere you looked in Lancashire, you saw those goddamned dirty, smoking chimneys. But in Vancouver it was open and clean and free and beautiful."

Valerie Laxton took a job — $200 a month — and the couple rented a humble apartment — $70 a month — while Laxton went through the tedious one-year routine of meeting the educational requirements for the British Columbia bar. He got his call in 1960 and went to work with a Vancouver firm, Shulman & Company, that had a lock on labour cases up and down the coast. In the atmosphere of the Shulman firm, knocking over the establishment on behalf of the workers, Laxton blossomed.

"There was a grand Irishman in the firm, Tom Hurley, who taught me one of the great secrets of arguing in court," Laxton says. "We used to have these Saturday-morning sessions in the office. One of the lawyers would have to be on deck the following Monday for a case in the Supreme Court, and we'd sit down and try to cover all the legal points to help the guy get a handle on his case. Talk'd fly around the table, stuff about precedents and theories and cases on point. Hurley used to sit in his chair, very quiet at first, absorbing all the babble, and then he'd go to work. His method was to distil an argument by putting it forward as if, right there in the office on Saturday morning, he was actually talking to a judge. He'd get past the academic junk and set the scene in the courtroom. It was amazing how that technique focussed the mind. Tom had the facility for conceiving wonderful phrases that would sum up an hour's argument and put the shaft to the other side. It'd be all wrapped up in a single sentence, and the lawyer who was due in court on Monday would write it down and construct his whole argument around the one sentence. Ever since those days, in my own office, I've followed Hurley's approach. I imagine I'm addressing the judge, and I don't waste words or build silly ideas. And I usually win the case."

Whatever his technique, Laxton developed into a persuasive counsel. He was made a partner in the Shulman firm in 1963, stayed another eleven years, then left to found his own firm in 1974. Labour law still keeps most of Laxton, Pidgeon's partners and associates busy, but Laxton has branched out to take on criminal charges, compensation work, and negligence cases. Away from the office, he has worked for the NDP and served as the party's B.C. president through the late 1960s. At the same time, socialism hasn't prevented him from turning a big dollar. Laxton exudes style and the golden touch. In the mid-1960s, he and Valerie spotted a piece of lovely seaside land on a sloping lot on Marine Drive in West Vancouver. Laxton picked it up for $10,000, persuaded Arthur Erickson to design a house that would blend into the setting, and hired a friendly contractor to take on the building job at a bargain price. The home, graceful in the laid-back west coast manner, cost less than $50,000, and today, when Marine Drive is a showcase for some of the most spectacular domestic architecture in Canada, it would go cheap at a million and a quarter. And Laxton has been just as astute in his ventures into commercial-land investment. In all things, he's a dealer with good instincts, disciplined follow-through, and an eye for the main chance.

Case number C782249 in the Vancouver Registry of the Supreme Court of British Columbia: Michael Robitaille and Michael Robitaille Investments Ltd., plaintiffs, and Vancouver Hockey Club Limited, defendant.

Laxton issued the writ in August 1978, and legal language took over from sports jargon. The plaintiff claimed damages in loss of income and in pain and suffering from the defendant for an injury that ended the plaintiff's hockey career and left him permanently disabled to a serious degree. The injury resulted from the defendant's negligence, which took a variety of forms: failure to respond to the plaintiff's complaints and to his clear symptoms of injury, failure to keep the plaintiff out of hockey games, and the ultimate failure to provide the plaintiff with proper medical care.

Laxton brushed up on his negligence law. In order to prove his claim that the Canucks were responsible for Robitaille's injuries through their negligence, he would first have to satisfy the court that the Canucks owed Mike a "duty of care." That concept

— duty of care — is fundamental to a plaintiff's claim in the law of torts, running through Canadian cases on negligence and further back to the leading cases in British courts which established the first principles in tort law. "First," Lord Wilberforce, a law lord, wrote in *Anns* v. *London Borough of Morton*, a leading English appeal case on duty of care, "one has to ask whether, as between the alleged wrong-doer and the person who suffered damage, there is sufficient relationship of proximity or neighbourhood such that, in the reasonable contemplation of the former, carelessness on his part may be likely to cause damage to the latter, in which case a prima facie case of duty of care arises."

It made perfect sense to Laxton that the Canucks knew their failure to provide proper protection and medical attention for Robitaille would inevitably expose him, an employee who was in a position of relying on their protection, to the reasonable possibility of injury. It made sense, but, alas, there were no earlier cases that offered a comforting precedent in Robitaille's special set of circumstances. No factual situation in any reported case, Canadian or English, approached the facts in the Robitaille case. It was unique. On just a single previous occasion had a professional athlete sued his team alleging that its negligence left him vulnerable to physical harm. The case was American, a football player named Dick Butkus versus the Chicago Bears of the National Football League, but it had been settled out of court with a payment of $50,000 to Butkus and therefore gave Laxton no assistance in judge-made case law. He was on his own, blazing legal trails, up against the establishment of professional hockey. For Laxton, it was hardly a new role.

He researched the law, interviewed witnesses, and began to build a case that would, in fact and in law, establish the Canucks' negligence. He leaned on Robitaille in a series of interviews, ransacking Mike's memories for every detail of his long ordeal. In the course of two years, Robitaille made nine plane trips to Vancouver for sessions with Laxton. The journeys were arduous, but they gave Mike a sense of ongoing accomplishment, something that was missing from his life in Buffalo. He had tried a couple of jobs that cost him in finances and pride. He lost money in a wine-and-cheese importing operation, and he abandoned a plant and tree business when he couldn't handle its modest physical demands. He found a job as a salesman with a machinery firm, earning $12,000 a year plus commissions, but it tired him, the car-driving and the socializing, and he would knock off work each day, exhausted, by two in the afternoon. His body was a burden to him — the lack of co-ordination, the tightness and pounding in his right arm and leg, the extreme sensitivity in parts of his body that often made sex with Isabel a painful impossibility. Life came hard for Mike, and while helping Laxton build his case, he opened himself to one more blow.

Laxton asked Robitaille to contact a group of players from his NHL years and persuade them to testify on his behalf at the trial. Laxton needed evidence that Mike wasn't a malingerer who was likely to fake injuries and that, except for the career-ending injury, he had the skills to play in the NHL for several more money-making years. Robitaille wrote letters to thirty of his former teammates and waited for the answers to roll in. But of the thirty, only two players volunteered to testify, Syl Apps, Jr., and Ab DeMarco. Two more, Jim Schoenfeld and Jerry Korab, came forward on their own, volunteering support in court. The rest shied away from Robitaille, and one player let him know that, if he were subpoenaed to testify, he would give evidence in a way to deliberately hurt Mike's case. Robitaille's morale was shattered.

"These were guys that Isabel and I spent Christmases with," he said, uncomprehending. "I thought of them as my special friends. But they were scared of what the hockey owners would do to them. The guy who said he'd testify to hurt me, he was trying to get a job as an NHL scout. He'd never get it if the owners thought he was on my side. The guys figured my friendship wasn't worth bucking the big shots."

Robitaille soldiered on.

So did Laxton, and as he moved further into his research and deeper into his construction of the case, he grew confident that he would lick the Canucks in court. A breakthrough came with his examination for discovery of Phil Maloney. Discovery is a pre-trial process in a civil action that permits lawyers for plaintiff and defendant to question the other side's witnesses under oath before a court reporter. Though Maloney was a potential witness for the Canucks, he had no axe to grind for the team that had fired him, and he willingly yielded pages of valuable material under Laxton's examination. He admitted that he considered Mike's problems more mental than physical and for that reason had ignored Robitaille's cries for help. This view, Maloney testified, wasn't exclusive to him. It was shared by others around the Canucks office, by people like Michael Piper. Maloney's testimony amounted to an admission of negligence, and, buoyed by the revelations, Laxton approached the Canucks lawyer and offered to settle the case before it went to trial.

"We'll take $350,000," Laxton said.

Barry Kirkham was acting for the Canucks. He's a short, slim, good-looking man in his late thirties. He has a high-pitched voice and his manner speaks of an establishment background. He practises with Owen, Bird in Vancouver, a firm that Laxton had plenty of reason to remember. The very day after he was called to the B.C. bar in 1960, Shulman & Company dispatched him to his first court appearance. He was to argue the appellant's case in the Court of Appeal, and on the other side, for the respondent, was a senior Vancouver counsel, Walter Owen, who had two juniors in tow. "The case," Laxton says, "represented twenty-four hours' experience at the bar against sixty-seven years'." Laxton had one strong point that he put to the three appeal-court justices in his argument, but when Owen's turn came to speak, he refused to address himself to the point, even under the prodding of the three judges. "He was courtly and wise and very evasive," Laxton remembers. "He talked for a day and a half, and eventually the court gave up trying to bring him around to my one point." The judges in effect said to hell with Laxton's point and found in favour of Owen's client. Owen bestowed a patrician smile on Laxton, and a few years later he retired from practice to be named British Columbia's lieutenant-governor.

"Three hundred and fifty thousand," Laxton said.

"Out of the question," Kirkham told him. "I've already assured my people we're going to win."

As events later unfolded, $350,000 may not have been an offer that deserved to be refused.

On April 10, 1979, Dr. Gordon Thompson re-entered the Robitaille case and came close to destroying it for Laxton. It was Dr. Thompson who had sat beside Michael Piper at the Coliseum on the night of January 19 when Robitaille took the infamous check from Dennis Owchar. Now the Canucks were calling on him to examine Robitaille on their behalf. They had the right to satisfy themselves as to Robitaille's condition, and on Piper's recommendation they chose Dr. Thompson for the job. He possessed the qualifications. A man close to sixty, grey-haired and ruddy, distinguished and imperious, he ranked as the leading neuro-surgeon in Vancouver. He was neurosurgeon-in-chief at the Vancouver General Hospital, taught the subject at UBC and served as chief examiner in his speciality for the Royal College of Physicians and Surgeons. He also enjoyed close connections with the Canucks. He'd been a season ticket holder since the team entered the NHL in 1970, and after he performed a successful operation on Coley Hall, a former Canucks owner, he was rewarded by having his season tickets moved into more exclusive territory in a row just above ice level next to seats that came to be occupied by Michael Piper.

Thompson's examination of Robitaille on April 10 didn't err, as such medical matters go, on the side of length. "We got talking about hockey," Mike remembers, "and the actual check-up and everything else lasted about an hour." That was time enough for Dr. Thompson to arrive at some opinions that brought him into a head-on difference of diagnosis with Dr. Barbara Allan.

"I do not think there is any question in my mind," he wrote in his report to Kirkham, "that this man sustained his injury to the cervical cord on January 19, 1977, when he was heavily checked. He sustained a hyper-extensive injury to the cervical spine at the time with attendant contusion of the underlying cervical cord, the residual of which is present today. I am of the opinion that his complaints prior to January 19, 1977, in the region of the neck and shoulder are unrelated as a pre-existing condition to the incomplete spinal cord injury sustained on that date."

So, Dr. Thompson was saying, the January 19 injury was independent of earlier injuries. It had no connection with the bang that Mike took to his back on January 12. There was no causal link between the two. It was, Thompson insisted, "most unusual" for one cervical-cord injury to be aggravated by another. That view contradicted Dr. Allan, who concluded that the blow of January 19 had been to the same area of the spinal cord as the blow of January 12, with the obvious disastrous consequences. No, no, Thompson said, staking out his territory, the Dennis Owchar body check of January 19 was isolated as the sole and only cause of Robitaille's troubles.

From the Thompson version, one major consequence flowed that spelled death to Laxton's case. If the January 19 incident stood alone, then Robitaille was in no jeopardy when he went into the game. He was free of serious symptoms that doctors or trainers should have been treating. No red flags had gone up, putting Dr. Piper on alert. Hence, there was no negligence on his part in allowing Mike to play, none on Patty Dunn's part or Phil Maloney's or any other Canucks agent. No negligence. And no case against the Canucks.

Dr. Thompson's opinion formed the basis of the argument that Barry Kirkham considered with good reason to be his most convincing. Still, he prepared other, necessarily lesser points in his client's favour. He would argue that Robitaille, in his own relentless play, was sadly the author of his own misfortune. He'd contend that the Canucks provided Mike with the services of team doctors and if they failed to treat him properly, then the club was not at fault. It had carried out any duty of care it owed Robitaille, and whatever action he had at law lay against the doctors, not the Canucks. Kirkham would argue, touching all the alternatives available to him, that Maloney alone should shoulder the blame, that other Canucks officials and employees acted honourably toward Mike, all but Maloney, and that Robitaille must seek his relief against him. Kirkham would raise all of these arguments in his defence of the Canucks, but ultimately it would be Dr. Thompson's diagnosis that he depended on as the most persuasive of his submissions. Dr. Thompson would shoot Laxton out of the water.

On the evening of the day after he examined Robitaille, Dr. Thompson went to dinner with his brother-in-law and the two men's wives at the Arbutus Club, a members-only club for sports and dining that caters to Vancouver's upper crust. The couples settled first in the lounge, sitting over drinks at a large L-shaped sofa. Thompson dominated the early conversation, and it was Mike Robitaille who was on his mind.

"This chap Robitaille is seriously hurt, you know," Thompson said. "I've examined him and he isn't good for anything. I doubt if he could drive a garbage truck."

Directly opposite Thompson, about twenty feet away at a matching L-shaped sofa, another man, much younger, sat with his wife. The young man came alert when he heard Robitaille's name dropped into the neighbouring conversation.

"Bruce McColl's dumped Robitaille as a client," Thompson went on. "He went somewhere else, and now he's in the hands of this Laxton. You know him, the socialist lawyer who drives the big car?"

By an astounding coincidence that Dr. Thompson would come

to regret, the young man opposite him, in easy earshot, in the wind of Thompson's pronouncements, was a lawyer named Robert MacKenzie. His firm was Macaulay, McColl & MacKenzie. He was Bruce McColl's partner.

"I was at that game with Piper," Thompson continued. "I saw the hit and I heard the crack as he went down. I said, 'That man has been seriously hurt. Somebody should go down right away.' I said this to Piper. I was sitting at the game talking to him and I nudged him. Piper had just lit a cigarette."

Robert MacKenzie felt gauche. What did social protocol demand in the situation? He was sitting in the Arbutus Club twenty feet from a man who was skirting close to insults directed at one of his law partners and the partner's client. The man was talking about fairly confidential matters that touched on a trial scheduled to start in a couple of months. MacKenzie decided to assert himself. He stood up and walked across to the Thompson group.

"I don't mean to be rude," he said, addressing Thompson, "but I'm Bruce McColl's partner."

He got no further. Thompson gave MacKenzie what he later described as "the coldest stare I ever received."

"We're not talking about that," Thompson said.

The freezing look, the clipped tone, Thompson's forbidding manner, and the intimidating atmosphere of the setting — nobody raises a voice in the Arbutus Club — combined to discourage MacKenzie. He felt his face go pale, and he turned away without speaking again.

"Who is that man?" he heard Thompson ask his brother-in-law.

"He's Rob MacKenzie," the answer came.

Thompson shifted the topic of conversation, and while they finished their drinks, the four people talked of tax matters.

The day after the encounter, MacKenzie repeated the details of his bizzare evening at the Arbutus Club to Bruce McColl. *Fantastic*, McColl said, and phoned Laxton.

"What's he mean 'socialist lawyer with the big car'?" Laxton said. "It's a 1972 Jaguar that I got for a thousand dollars, and it spends most of its time going from garage to garage for repairs."

After Laxton had given his indignation a mild and comic workout, he told McColl that he could envision a situation down the line in the trial where he could use MacKenzie as a witness.

Yes, he said, it wouldn't surprise him at all if Rob contributed valuable testimony. It was looking like a rough case up ahead.

Mr. Justice William Esson drew the assignment at the spring non-jury assizes for *Robitaille* v. *Vancouver Hockey Club Ltd.*, a choice that came as a mild surprise. Esson had been appointed to the B.C. Supreme Court only within the previous year, and the case, which would clearly take the court into uncharted legal regions, was made to order for a veteran member of the bench. Esson was in his mid-forties, strait-laced, diligent, and plucked for the court from a large downtown Vancouver firm. He blocked out the month of June 1979 to hear the Robitaille case, and when his clerk called the court to order on opening day, Monday, June 4, 1979, he was feeling a few butterflies of nervousness. Nobody in the courtroom on that day was entirely calm.

Laxton called his first witness, Dr. Barbara Allan. She told the story that Laxton knew by heart. How, as her examination of Mike two years earlier had revealed, he showed symptoms of nerve-root irritation at different levels of his spine at least as early as January 1, 1977. And how hemorrhage or severe bruising of the spinal cord occurred initially during the game of January 12 and to a more marked extent in the January 19 game. Under Laxton's careful questioning, Dr. Allan spelled out her analysis of Mike's condition and its causes for Mr. Justice Esson. She repeated her declaration that if she'd seen Mike's symptoms on January 12, she would have hustled him to hospital care. He was, she said, clearly in trouble by that date. Laxton was satisfied that Dr. Allan's voice gave off the ring of conviction. She appeared confident but not pushy or overbearing. She seemed believable, Laxton thought, and surely the frightening opinion with which she ended her examination-in-chief must have moved Esson to sympathy for Robitaille's plight. It was unlikely, Dr. Allan testified in her level-headed way, that Mike's present disabilities would ever grow less painful and inhibiting, not in all the years that were left to him.

On cross-examination, Barry Kirkham couldn't budge Dr. Allan from her views. He presented her with the defence's thesis, the notion that Dr. Thompson would introduce later in the trial. "I suggest to you," Kirkham said, "that the mechanism that caused this man's spinal-cord injury was what happened on January 19 and only what happened on January 19." Dr. Allan countered with *her* thesis, that the January 19 body check aggravated the existing injury from the January 12 game. Dr. Allan held firm, and Laxton had successfully planted with the court the seed of his case.

In the next few days, Laxton summoned thirteen more witnesses. First came three hockey players, Jim Schoenfeld, Syl Apps, Jr., and Ab DeMarco. "One of the best hip checks in the league," Schoenfeld said of Robitaille. He ought to have lasted with an NHL club till he was thirty-four or thirty-five, and his next contract should have given him, minimum, a half-million dollars over five years. Apps and DeMarco spoke of other financial possibilities for Robitaille, playing in the European leagues, coaching in minor hockey, perhaps working a job behind an NHL bench. Mike had the right temperament to handle other guys.

Alan Eagleson, the head of the NHL Players' Association, flew from Toronto to speak for Robitaille. He testified two days after the June 11 issue of *Sports Illustrated* hit newsstands with a feature article entitled "Playing Hurt — The Doctors' Dilemma." The piece dealt at length with the role of the team physician: "Is his paramount concern the health of the athlete or is it the welfare of the club?" And Laxton used it as a jumping-off point in his examination of Eagleson. Athletes feel pressure to play when they're hurt, Eagleson said, pressure from management and sometimes from physicians. But there's a distinction to be made. On a hockey-team roster of twenty players, the top five don't take the heat. "If Darryl Sittler says he doesn't feel like playing tonight," Eagleson said, "there's no question from management." But, he went on, "if the others from five to twenty say the same thing, then the question from management is, why? Those players feel if they don't do what management says, they won't be around long."

And where did Mike Robitaille fit in the range of players? Top five? Or five to twenty?

"Five to twenty."

Next came the doctors. Rod McGillivray, Mike's general practitioner, told of Robitaille's medical background and of his examination of Mike in early February of 1977. Eric Termansen ran through Mike's psychiatric history and the positive ways in which he took to Termansen's treatment. And Brian Hunt testified to his diagnosis of Mike's cervical injury, his examination of February 28, 1977, supporting Dr. Allan's later diagnosis.

Two sportscasters, Bill Good, Jr., and Denny Boyd, told the court of the word that Canucks management had been spreading through late 1976 and early '77, that Robitaille was in deep emotional trouble, a head case. Bruce McColl, the lawyer, relived his encounters with the Canucks officials, with Phil Maloney and Michael Piper, and testified to their intransigent attitudes towards Mike. Isabel took the stand and traced the events of early 1977, focussing on the horrors that her husband endured when he returned home, hurt and baffled, after the January 12 and January 19 games.

Mike Robitaille limped across the courtroom to testify on his own behalf. He made a compelling witness, speaking in great swelling rushes of sentences, the words tumbling over one another. Mike was eager after years of frustration to get out his version of all that had happened to him. He began with his earliest ambitions: "I knew I had to do well because I saw my dad and I didn't want to have the life he led. I was going to be a special player because that was my only way out." And he didn't finish, after almost three days of testimony, until he'd reached the circumstances of the end of his life in the NHL: "Nobody, not management, wants to listen to stuff about injuries. Just win the hockey games and tell me your excuses afterwards. You're getting paid a lot of money. You should be able to perform like the Almighty out there."

As Robitaille spoke, and Isabel and the doctors and players and sportscasters, a piece of magic unfolded in Mr. Justice Esson's courtroom, no less dazzling because of its familiarity. It happens in all courtrooms in all trials when gifted counsel are at work, the magical transformation of cold facts into a tale as gripping as a piece of fiction. Characters emerge, heroes and villains and innocent bystanders, and the elements of story-telling fall into place, cohesion and plot development, a climax that's logical and human. The story comes in many voices and falls from a variety of points of view, and yet one man, the counsel, arranges the sequence of paragraphs and chapters. He asks the questions that evoke the answering lines, but in the end, the questions are rubbed out, and all that remains is the flow of the narrative, the story in its simplicity and drama.

So John Laxton acted as amanuensis in the recounting of the Mike Robitaille story. Disparate events from years earlier were woven into a piece of wonderful consistency. It started at young

Mike's torturous boyhood and skipped forward, touching on the essences of his hockey career to the point when, in the autumn of 1976, life and career began to come unravelled.

Encounters and conversations clicked into the story. Bill Good's conversation with Greg Douglas, Michael Piper's conversations with Eric Termansen, Phil Maloney's with Robitaille, Larry Popein's one-sentence talk with Robitaille ("We got cheques around here only for guys who want to play hockey"). Perhaps one party to the conversations may have lost them in the swirls of memory, but the words survived and were brought back to life in the courtroom. And they made, as Laxton intended them to, an insistent point: that the Canucks management had adopted throughout a view of Robitaille that he was a faker, a man whose emotions were in disarray, sicker in mind than in body, a player unique for being, in Maloney's indelicate phrase, "a con artist."

Nothing from the past escaped the story that Laxton coaxed from his witnesses. Al Davidson's radio broadcast. Dr. Piper's stroll past the aching Robitaille in the Coliseum dressing-room after the January 12 game. His advice following the January 19 game, given once and repeated a second time, to take a shot of Courvoisier. Maloney's disparagement of Bruce McColl at the Coliseum on March 9, 1977 ("I'm used to your types"), and Piper's challenge to McColl on the same night. Incident piled on incident. The Canucks' efforts to trade Robitaille to Calgary when they were aware he couldn't skate. The doctors' neglect to follow up on Dr. Porayko's January 21 diagnosis, correct as it turned out, of Mike's cervical problems. Did Laxton leave out any stray fact? Mr. Justice Esson could hardly have imagined so. Piper's January 20 phone call to Isabel ("We can't overrule the fact it may be psychosomatic"), and the team's failure the night before to carry Mike from the ice on a stretcher rather than on the shoulders of a trainer and a player. It was all in place, every last word of the story.

"When I finished," Laxton said later of his presentation of the plaintiff's case, "I was at least sixty per cent certain we'd win everything we asked for. Probably seventy per cent."

The story had been long and complex and colourful in the recounting, but Laxton's request of Mr. Justice Esson was simple: he must hold that the Canucks, in ignoring Robitaille's real symptoms because of their dismissal of him as a sort of charlatan, had caused Mike's crippling and permanent injuries, for which they must recompense him in a sum covering his suffering and his loss of past and future income.

When Barry Kirkham opened for the defence, he called Michael Piper as his first witness. Piper promptly lobbed a bombshell into Laxton's case.

KIRKHAM: "What do you know about the evening of January 12, 1977?"

PIPER: "I know I wasn't at the hockey game on that night."

KIRKHAM: "How do you know that?"

PIPER: "Because I was at a meeting of the board of directors of the Westminster Medical Building of which I was member of the board at the time and that meeting was held at the office of Touche, Ross, and the meeting began at eight o'clock and adjourned at 11:30, and I was in attendance at it."

KIRKHAM: "All right, were minutes kept at the meeting?"

PIPER: "Yes."

KIRKHAM: "When did you obtain such minutes?"

PIPER: "The minutes would have been mailed out, you know, a week or two after and filed."

KIRKHAM: "You produced them to me last week?"

PIPER: "That's correct."

KIRKHAM (showing Piper some sheets of paper): "Are these the minutes in question?"

PIPER: "Yes."

KIRKHAM (turning to Mr. Justice Esson): "May the minutes be the next exhibit?"

ESSON: "Any objection, Mr. Laxton?"

The minutes came as a shock to Laxton. They represented a piece of eleventh-hour evidence that placed Piper miles away from the Coliseum on the night when Robitaille had suffered the first of his two crucial injuries. It was of course Piper who, according to Laxton's case, had walked through the Canucks dressing-room after the game and ignored Robitaille's obvious distress. This was one of the principal instances of the Canucks' negligence. But if Piper wasn't in the dressing-room, or even in the building, then a substantial section of the plaintiff's case lost its persuasive power. So much for Piper's negligent behaviour on January 12.

Laxton objected that Kirkham was introducing the minutes at an improper time. They should have been produced to the plaintiff months earlier when the rest of the defendant's documents had been handed over. "It makes it a bit late in the day," Laxton told Esson, "for us to check on whether Dr. Piper did attend the meeting." Kirkham countered with the point that Piper had revealed the existence of the minutes only a week before. "Dr. Piper," he said, "obviously forgot about them, and they came up when I was trying to pin him down whether there was any way he could say he was at the game of January 12 or not." Mr. Justice Esson considered the lawyers' points and ruled that he'd order the minutes marked for identification by the court clerk and would then hold them, not yet admitted as an exhibit, until both lawyers could prepare more argument on the admissibility question. Laxton was given breathing-space.

But, he fretted, what good would it do him even if he kept the minutes out of the trial? As Kirkham himself had indicated, he had at least one other way of establishing Piper's absence from the Coliseum on January 12. He could call to the witness-box the other directors of the Westminster Medical Building, a bunch of doctors presumably, and they'd testify that Piper had attended the meeting until 11:30, long after the end of the hockey game. Laxton was already beginning to write off the evidence of Piper's negligence on January 12.

The day's testimony ended, and Laxton, his optimism dampened, sat at the plaintiff's table gathering his papers. The courtroom had emptied of everyone except Laxton, his junior, and the court clerk.

"Let me show you something you'll be interested in, Mr. Laxton." It was the court clerk.

"I used to be a policeman," he went on, "a detective, and I'm kind of fascinated by this case of yours."

"Yes," Laxton said. "So?"

"So I was looking pretty close at the minutes, the ones you were arguing about today. Show you what I mean."

The clerk put the minutes on a light-box that had been set up in the courtroom to illuminate X-rays of Robitaille's spinal cord. The box blew the typing on the minutes into large, transparent letters and figures. Laxton studied them.

"Get my point?" the clerk asked.

Laxton got it. The numerals "11:30 p.m.," indicating the time when the meeting was supposed to have ended, had been rubbed out and typed over, and the original time, under the "11:30 p.m.," shone through as "7:30 p.m." The earlier hour gave Piper plenty of time to drive to the Coliseum for the hockey game.

Laxton considered the series of possibilities. Someone had tampered with the minutes. Someone had pulled a small forgery job. Someone was lying. Someone was trying to run a bluff past the court. Or it could have been something as innocent as a typist's error.

"What is this?" Laxton said. "A trial or a Sherlock Holmes mystery?"

He thanked the clerk and tucked away the revelations of the light-box for future reference.

As Barry Kirkham continued to present his defence over the next few days, the court's attention swung to two dominant issues. One had to do with medical matters and the other with credibility. The defence's doctors, Michael Piper and Gordon Thompson, figured in both.

Almost unwittingly, Laxton set a challenge for Piper and the believability of his version of events when he cross-examined him on his actions on the night of January 19. Laxton was dealing with an ace up his sleeve. He already knew what Piper had said and done on the nineteenth. He had Thompson's word for Piper's actions, Thompson who had spilled the story of the nineteenth at the Arbutus Club on an evening when Rob MacKenzie was unexpectedly privy to Thompson's conversation. Laxton had no notion of putting Piper's credibility to the test when he began his cross-examination. His intention was in a sense more innocent — to establish that Piper had been slow to react to Robitaille's injury on the ice, that he lingered over his cigarette before going to Mike's aid, that he had therefore been negligent. Laxton began cross-examination on the point by asking a simple question — who was Piper sitting beside at the January 19 game? — and he got an answer he didn't expect, an answer that would later get Piper in deep waters.

LAXTON: "Were you sitting beside Dr. Thompson at the game of January 19?"

PIPER: "No, I was not."

LAXTON: "Who were you sitting with?"

PIPER: "I imagine probably my wife. I know it was not Dr. Thompson because his seats were about six rows behind ours at that stage. I imagine Dr. Thompson was probably sitting about six rows behind us and ten or twelve seats over. I wasn't aware of him at the game."

LAXTON: "Well, I suggest you were sitting next to Dr. Thompson or very close to him when this accident happened on the nineteenth of January."

PIPER: "Well, I assure you I was not sitting next to him because the seats I was sitting in at that time were row three and Dr. Thompson's, I think, are in row nine."

Slightly baffled, Laxton let the point pass, but he returned to it a few days later when his turn came to cross-examine Dr. Thompson. He zeroed in on Thompson's whereabouts on the nineteenth.

LAXTON: "You were sitting next to Dr. Piper on January 19 when this incident happened, weren't you?"

THOMPSON: "Yes."

Once having made the admission, however, and put the lie to Piper's earlier testimony, Thompson lit out for the hills in the questions that followed. He wouldn't deny that Piper was next to him, but he would fudge on Piper's behaviour in the minutes immediately after Robitaille was crushed to the ice by Dennis Owchar's check.

LAXTON: "You remember seeing the accident, don't you?"

THOMPSON: "I really don't know that I did."

LAXTON: "Well, I suggest to you that you noticed how serious the accident was and you said to Dr. Piper, 'Mike, that man has been hurt. You better get down there.'"

THOMPSON: "Well, if I did, I don't recall."

LAXTON: "Why not?"

THOMPSON: "I don't know. I suppose there are many aspects to watching a hockey game."

LAXTON: "Didn't you nudge Dr. Piper and say, 'Mike, you better get down there. He's really hurt.'"

THOMPSON: "I don't recall."

LAXTON: "And didn't Dr. Piper continue to sit there?"

THOMPSON: "I really don't know."

LAXTON: "That's possible, though, isn't it?"

THOMPSON: "I don't know. That's two years ago and I don't know."

LAXTON: "Mike Piper didn't go down to the ice immediately, did he?"

THOMPSON: "I don't know that."

LAXTON: "You mean you can't remember?"

THOMPSON: "I really don't know. I can't remember. That really wasn't of any concern to me."

Laxton decided it was time to slip the ace from his sleeve. He hadn't yet introduced Rob MacKenzie's name to the court. Now he'd spring him on Thompson.

LAXTON: "Doctor, did you attend the Arbutus Club on April 11, 1979?"

THOMPSON: "I really don't know. I could have been."

LAXTON: "Do you remember that someone came over to your table when you were sitting there on April 11, 1979, and introduced himself as Mr. Rob MacKenzie?"

THOMPSON: "No, no one introduced himself as Rob MacKenzie."

Laxton persisted, and Thompson eventually allowed that *someone* had approached his party at the club.

THOMPSON: "I remember someone coming up and asked if we were doctors, and I said, it just happens the person here happens to be a lawyer, and that was the end of the conversation. He didn't introduce himself. He didn't say anything else."

The chase was on, Laxton hounding Thompson with questions about his words and actions at the Arbutus Club and Thompson stepping a stride or two ahead with his denials. Then Thompson slipped.

LAXTON: "Did you say anything to [MacKenzie] in respect of we were not talking about Robitaille's case?"

THOMPSON: "I didn't say anything about that. He came and introduced . . ." Thompson caught himself in mid-stumble. "At least he didn't introduce himself. He just spoke to me and wanted to know if we were two doctors."

Thompson was off again, just out of reach of the pursuing questions. The purpose behind Laxton's line of interrogations was plain — to show that Thompson had talked in MacKenzie's hearing at the Arbutus Club and had described Piper's behaviour on the nineteenth in terms that brought Piper close to negligence. Piper was the ultimate target, but Thompson, denying memory of any such conversation, acted as his shield. Thompson remained unyielding, and Laxton at last gave up the pursuit. He abandoned his questions about the great Arbutus Club run-in. He shoved the ace into his deck of cards and held it there for a few days until Barry Kirkham told the court that he had concluded the defence's case. Laxton rose and asked Mr. Justice Esson's permission to call one more witness for the plaintiff, a witness whose evidence would go to the delay of Dr. Piper to attend to Robitaille on the ice on the nineteenth and would also bear on the credibility of Dr. Thompson in parts of his testimony. Kirkham objected that Laxton had closed for the plaintiff and wasn't entitled to reopen his case. The judge listened to the arguments and came down on Laxton's side. The new evidence was admissible, he ruled, because it would apparently deal with a prior inconsistent statement by an earlier witness, Thompson. Laxton's ace was out of the deck. He called Rob MacKenzie to the witness-box.

"We were sitting in what might be described as the lounge area in the Arbutus Club," MacKenzie began, "which is like a livingroom with chesterfields in an L-shape. Every twenty feet away there is another chesterfield in an L-shape. The end result is I am facing Dr. Gordon Thompson. . . . I didn't pay any attention to anything except all of a sudden I hear the name Robitaille. . . ."

Mackenzie told his story, the tale of the astounding coincidence, a version of events that differed dramatically from Dr. Thompson's memory of them, a stunning piece of contradiction. Laxton was content that MacKenzie came across as a formidable witness, unfaltering and detailed in his recollections of an encounter that had, after all, taken place a mere ten weeks earlier. Mr. Justice Esson listened in silence to the testimony. Neither Laxton nor Kirkham would know what Esson made of it until many months later when he analysed it in his written judgment. Kirkham wouldn't care for the analysis. Neither would Dr. Thompson.

Dr. Thompson found himself at the storm centre of another controversy that took over the trial for several more tense and critical hours. The issue this time was medical, though it ultimately turned on a point of credibility, and it surfaced during the course of the proceedings, not as something that Laxton could anticipate and prepare for. The issue grew out of the examination at the trial of two sets of X-rays that had been taken of Robitaille's spinal canal, the first at the Royal Columbia Hospital in New Westminster in the days after Mike's last game on January 19, 1977, and the second at a hospital in Buffalo in November 1977. During Dr. Barbara Allan's testimony, she looked at the X-rays and gave it as her view that Robitaille's spinal canal was abnormally small. In a written report that was prepared at Laxton's request as the trial was proceeding, Dr. Kenneth Kaan, the Buffalo neuroradiologist, agreed with Dr. Allan's assessment. The spinal canal is the channel that encloses and protects the spinal cord, and its normal width is about eleven millimetres. Robitaille's was narrower, critically narrower at approximately 8.5 millimetres. The reason for the narrowness couldn't be determined — a congenital condition perhaps or the result of degenerative change — but its significance was apparent and crucial. When the canal is narrow, the cord is crowded for space, and if the canal takes a blow from the outside, then the chances are greater for the cord to come into such jarring contact with the hard surface of the canal that it will suffer serious damage. Thus, the narrowness of Robitaille's spinal canal increased the odds on injury to his spinal cord. More than that, given Dr. Allan's contention about the connection between Robitaille's injuries of January 12 and those of January 19, it stepped up the odds on two *related* injuries to his cord.

For the defence, Dr. Thompson studied the X-rays and pronounced himself satisfied that there was nothing dangerously narrow about Robitaille's spinal canal as revealed in the January 1977 X-rays. If there were signs of narrowing in the later X-rays from Buffalo, then the degenerative changes had taken place in the ten months from January to November 1977. Thompson was firm, defiant even, in his interpretation of the X-rays, and Laxton swooped in to cross-examine him on the point. He had no difficulty in getting Thompson to agree that eleven millimetres was a normal width for the spinal canal and that anything under nine millimetres was "in the critical area." Then Laxton had the January X-rays placed on the light-box. They showed Robitaille's spinal canal in a blow-up that had been examined by Dr. Kaan in Buffalo in preparing his report for the court. Dr. Kaan had written a measurement of the canal on the X-ray: eleven millimetres. Laxton asked Thompson to confirm the measurement. Thompson stepped up to the light-box, worked his measuring instrument, and announced that he agreed with the figure Kaan had written in: eleven millimetres.

LAXTON: "Do you see narrowing of the diameter of the spinal canal?"

THOMPSON: "No, I don't see any narrowing. I see a measurement that he's got there of about eleven millimetres. But I think that's within acceptable limits. I don't call that narrowing."

LAXTON: "Now you say there is a measurement there that shows eleven millimetres but that is not evidence of a narrow canal?"

THOMPSON: "I would accept that within my range of normal."

Laxton was proceeding at a slower rate than the one at which he usually conducted his cross-examinations. He was repeating himself, going over the same territory one or two times more than he needed to. The repetition and the leisurely pace weren't the product of any confusion on Laxton's part. They sprang from excitement. Thompson, Laxton recognized, had dug himself into a hole. Laxton knew that the eleven millimetres shown on the X-ray in Kaan's handwriting, the eleven millimetres confirmed by Thompson's own calculation, wasn't an absolute measurement. It was a preliminary figure. It didn't take into account something essential called the magnification factor. Before the real width of Robitaille's spinal canal could be computed, a figure had to be worked into the equation that allowed for the amount by which the width had been magnified by the process of X-raying. When that factor was thrown into the mathematics, the final, authentic, physical width of Mike Robitaille's spinal canal came to a measurement close to 8.5 millimetres. Dr. Thompson had not mentioned the magnification factor to the court.

"When I realized what Thompson was doing," Laxton recalled long after the trial, "I got so excited I almost blew it. These Perry Mason things aren't supposed to happen in real trials. Here I had this witness clearly trapped in a contradiction and I couldn't believe it was happening."

Laxton pulled his excitement under control and put the direct question to Thompson.

"How," he asked, "could you work out the true or absolute measurement without knowing the magnification factor?"

"Well, this is what I said about the Buffalo film," Thompson began, looking for solid ground and not finding it, "and I don't know about the ratio, the multiplying." He stopped and started again. "I don't know what the ratio is, the multiplying factor is."

LAXTON: "You would have to go to an expert like Dr. Kaan, wouldn't you, to know the fixed rate of magnification?"

THOMPSON: "Well, I would expect I would have to go to the area or the place where the radiograph was done, that's correct."

LAXTON: "What you're telling me, doctor, is that you can't look at that film and work out the true spinal cord measurement because you don't know the ratio of magnification."

THOMPSON: "You can't work out the true diameter of the spinal cord."

LAXTON: "You can't do that?"

THOMPSON: "No, there is a multiplying factor on all magnification."

LAXTON: "You say you looked at that and it showed eleven millimetres and that's normal."

THOMPSON: "No, I didn't say that. I said there's a number written on there, eleven millimetres."

LAXTON: "And that's within normal? You're satisfied with that?"

THOMPSON: "I accept a measurement of that."

Laxton was still struggling to control his excited delight and to nail Thompson once and for all. The focus of his questions wavered. Then, finally, again: "Do you know that you had to take into account the magnification factor?"

THOMPSON: "Always, that's correct."

LAXTON: "Now, when you take into account the magnification factor, that eleven millimetres comes down to 8.46 millimetres. Does that sound reasonable?"

THOMPSON: "Yes, that sounds reasonable."

LAXTON: "Because the magnification factor is 1.3 times actual size?"

THOMPSON: "That sounds quite reasonable."

Laxton worked over the same ground with two or three additional questions, and then pounced on what he considered the gap in Thompson's earlier testimony.

"You see, the impression you gave me," he said to Thompson, "was that you looked over the X-ray, you made a measurement, you assumed eleven millimetres was right, and that was the width of the spinal canal."

"I said," Thompson told Laxton, "that was the number written on the film."

LAXTON: "Yes, and you assumed that was within normal limits?"

THOMPSON: "No, I didn't assume that. I said that was the number written on there and I measured it, and it was eleven millimetres, and I know there is a magnification factor."

Mr. Justice Esson seemed satisfied that the fly had been pinned. He interrupted Laxton's questions with one of his own.

"Well," he said to Thompson, "was there any meaning to your saying it was within normal limits if you didn't know the magnification factor?"

THOMPSON: "No. All I mean, it would be less than the eleven millimetres that was on there but, and I made this point about the

Buffalo films because they are not comparable films to the Royal Columbia's."

Thompson's testimony on the point fizzled to an end.

Barry Kirkham's case was developing pock-marks. Piper and Thompson were caught in contradictory testimony. When Kirkham summoned another witness, John Chessman, the Canucks comptroller, he gave the plaintiff more ammunition by conceding under cross-examination that, sure, it was common practice to attempt to peddle an injured player, Robitaille for example, to another team, the Calgary Cowboys, without mentioning the injury. With Chessman as his vehicle, Kirkham's own witness, Laxton scored an easy point: the Canucks were callous. Kirkham was treading water, in danger of going under. He called fewer witnesses than he had indicated to the court at the outset of the trial that he would call. And he failed to return to Dr. Piper's alibi for January 12. He didn't offer witnesses to vouch that Piper was at a meeting in New Westminster rather than at the hockey game, and it never became necessary for Laxton to trot out the revelations of the light-box. Had Kirkham cottoned on to a possible forgery? Laxton couldn't be certain. All he knew was that his fears for the twelfth had fled. And his confidence about the outcome of the trial took a quantum leap.

"If I felt seventy per cent positive I'd win after my own case went in," he said later, "I felt one hundred per cent sure after the defence's case was finished."

The last three days of the trial were devoted to counsel's argument, and Laxton took most of the hours in those days, Kirkham preferring to present the bulk of his argument in written form. Laxton was assured as he waded through his presentation, and if he'd been more alert during a curious and possibly telling exchange with Mr. Justice Esson at the beginning of his third day of addressing the court, he might have been fairly bursting with certainty.

"I'm making a supreme sacrifice," he said to Esson in an offhand remark as he organized the documents in front of him for the day's session. "The principal where my twelve-year-old daughter goes to school asked me to come to the prize-giving today. She's going to receive the top prize for academics, sports, and citizenship."

ESSON: "Please convey my regrets and congratulations."

LAXTON: "Thank you, my lord."

ESSON: "Hopefully I can do more for you than that."

Had Esson signalled his verdict? Was he saying his decision would bring a few smiles and a few bucks for Laxton and Robitaille? Laxton had no idea. He wasn't listening.

"I was so busy getting my papers in order," he said later, "that I didn't pay attention to what Esson was saying. It wasn't until months later, a year and a half later, when I read over the transcript that I realized what he'd told me. Even then, I wasn't really sure that he was sending me a particular message."

Laxton was his thorough self in serving up the case for the plaintiff, ticking off the strengths in his own argument and the weaknesses in Kirkham's. He covered all witnesses, all events, but it was in his third day of presentation, near the end of the time on his feet, that he grew most passionate. He put a unique request to Esson. He asked that exemplary damages be awarded to Robitaille. Exemplary damages go beyond simple damages for pain and suffering and loss of income. They're special and rare punitive damages that are given only when the court decides to censure a defendant for its outrageous conduct or for the cruel way in which it has harmed the plaintiff. Laxton argued that the Canucks had behaved so abominably in their treatment of Robitaille that this, of all cases, was an appropriate occasion to invoke exemplary damages. He listed the outrages: the careless handling of Robitaille on the night of January 19; advising the press on the sly that Mike's problems were caused by a faulty psyche; branding him a "con artist" and subjecting him to a variety of indignities. Even in the conduct of the case itself, Laxton argued, the defendant was shown to be uncooperative and contemptuous. He cited the abortive try at developing an alibi for Dr. Piper on January 12. "I was astonished," Laxton said, taking a poke at Barry Kirkham, "that when my friend closed his case, he didn't call the people at the January 12 meeting." Laxton hardly missed a bet. How much should Esson award in exemplary damages? Laxton cited the highest amount that had so far been given under that head in a British Columbia court, $30,000, against the International Association of Bridge Structural & Ornamental Ironworkers Union for their high-handed conduct in dismantling a challenging union, the Canadian Ironworkers Union No. 1. Laxton knew the case intimately. He had acted for the plaintiff, the Canadian Ironworkers, and he'd secured the exemplary damages. He asked Esson to give at least as much to Robitaille.

Once done with the special plea, Laxton wound up his argument in *Robitaille* v. *Vancouver Hockey Club Ltd.* with a small flourish. "The case itself," he said, "is a classic one." Why, he went on, "it could maybe form the basis of a great Canadian novel."

Mr. Justice Esson, as his law clerk for 1978 remembered, "sweated blood over the writing of the Robitaille decision." He kept at it, evenings and weekends, through much of the six months after the end of the trial. He wrote and rewrote. In one draft, he came down hard on the defence's medical witnesses. Then he reconsidered and softened the passages that dealt with the doctors. The decision was ready by December, but even then, Esson was revising the judgment, a fat 143-page document, up to the last possible moment. Finally, he released it to the waiting plaintiff, defendant, and public. The date was December 18, 1978, and Mr. Justice Esson's hard-wrought words arrived at last as a glorious triumph for Mike Robitaille — and for John Laxton.

Legal judgments are rarely works of literature. They're pragmatic documents, delivered in prose that's usually plodding, sometimes fussy, and always painstaking. Esson's judgment was no exception. Its major virtue was its clarity. The wording may not have been elegant, but the meaning was forever plain, and the judgment represented a remarkable display of cool control. Occasionally Esson's natural indignation popped through the flow of legalese, through the laborious construction of sentences and paragraphs. But for the most part he kept a proper rein on his emotions and concentrated on conveying fact and interpretation — *his* interpretation — in language that no one, plaintiff or defendant or appeal court, could misread.

By necessity, Esson made the issue of credibility one pivot of his decision. Who was he going to believe? Robitaille and his fellow witnesses for the plaintiff? Or the representatives and agents of the Canucks? Which set of doctors would he accept? Dr. Barbara Allan and friends? Or Piper, Thompson, and company? Esson arrived almost effortlessly at his choice.

Of Robitaille he wrote: "He has not been shown to have been wrong to any significant extent in the course of the lengthy evidence in relation to any verifiable fact to which he testified, i.e. those facts which relate to events external to his feelings, sensations and injuries and which were capable of being checked."

The Canucks' witnesses, on the other hand, especially the doctors, offered evidence that Esson found less than acceptable, and he handed out rebukes that ranged from mild to stern.

On Dr. Piper's alibi for January 12: "At trial, an attempt was made to establish that Dr. Piper was elsewhere on the evening of January 12. That attempt did not succeed. After considering all the evidence on the point, I find that Robitaille was right in saying that it was Dr. Piper who walked through the dressing room."

On Piper's seat at the Coliseum on the night of January 19: "Dr. Piper denied in his evidence that he was sitting beside Dr. Thompson at the time of the injury to Robitaille. On that conflict, I prefer the evidence of Dr. Thompson who could have no reason to be wrong on that point."

On Dr. Thompson's testimony about the width of Robitaille's spinal canal: "He said that the measurement was eleven millimetres and 'within acceptable limits,' anything over ten millimetres being outside the range of critically narrow. That was a misleading answer because, as he must have known, the eleven millimetres figure involved a magnification factor and indicated an actual width of under nine millimetres. The matter of magnification had not been mentioned to that point in the trial. I concluded that this could not have been a matter of oversight or forgetfulness but was a matter of the witness taking a chance on not being caught out rather than admitting a fact unfavorable to his basic thesis."

On Thompson's conversation at the Arbutus Club on the night when Rob MacKenzie was sitting in earshot: "[Dr. Thompson denied] having made at a dinner party certain statements as to the conduct of Dr. Piper, who was sitting beside him as a spectator at the January 19 game when Robitaille was injured, and as to his opinion as to the seriousness of Robitaille's injury. The occasion was within a day or two after Dr. Thompson had examined Robitaille in preparation for giving evidence. He denied making those statements. I do not accept that denial in face of the evidence led for the plaintiff, which evidence I find was true as to what was said on that occasion."

Esson seemed downright shocked by Dr. Thompson's testimony on the Arbutus Club incident, and he used it as ground for throwing doubt on much of the rest of Thompson's evidence. "Had that false denial [of the Arbutus Club statements]," Esson wrote, "been motivated only by embarrassment at a social and professional faux pas, it might have little importance in relation to the question of the weight to be given to the witness's opinion in the field in which he is so highly qualified. But it goes beyond that. I find that he was motivated, at least in part, by his desire to protect the defendant, with the owners of which he had a friendly relationship, and by his desire to protect Dr. Piper, who incidentally was the person who arranged on behalf of the defendant for him to act. Whatever the reason, I find that he allowed himself to become a partisan on behalf of the defendant and allowed that attitude to affect his opinion evidence."

Thus, with Dr. Thompson's credibility as an objective witness shot to pieces, wherever his medical testimony differed from Dr. Barbara Allan's, Esson accepted the Allan version. Robitaille's January 19 injury *was* an aggravation of the injury that dated back to January 12 and probably earlier. The Canucks, through their doctors, general manager, and other agents and employees, had been negligent in their treatment of Robitaille, blaming his non-existent emotional troubles for his real physical ailments. The defendant, Esson held, owed the plaintiff a duty of care, and it had failed to carry out the duty. The defendant must pay damages to the plaintiff, and by page 119 of his judgment, Esson was ready to add up the bill.

Loss of opportunity to earn income as a major-league player after the 1976-77 season: $175,000.

Loss of opportunity to earn income for the rest of his life: $185,000.

Damages for pain and suffering and loss of enjoyment of life: $40,000.

Then Esson took up Laxton's request for exemplary damages. Yes, he wrote, he agreed with Laxton. Indeed, in the strongest language of his judgment, he may have exceeded Laxton in announcing his wrath at the Canucks' treatment of Robitaille. "The conduct of the defendant can fairly be described as high-handed, arrogant and as displaying a reckless disregard for the rights of the plaintiff. . . . In carrying through their chosen treatment [the management and medical team of the defendant] showed a callous disregard for his feelings and his well-being — they ignored the dictates of common decency as well as commonsense." After unloading his blast, Esson proceeded to award Robitaille the highest amount for exemplary damages in B.C. judicial history, topping the award in Laxtons old Ironworkers case by $5,000: $35,000.

Total damages for the plaintiff against the defendant: $435,000 plus costs.

Esson dangled the award in front of Robitaille. Then he snatched some of it back. Robitaille, he wrote, must bear partial blame for his own misfortune. Esson recognized that a professional hockey club puts such pressure on its players that they surrender much of the will to act on their own. Still, Esson ruled, Robitaille should have begun taking steps to protect his health and his interests in the week before January 19. In not doing so, not consulting a doctor on his own hook, he must be faulted. The passage in Esson's judgment dealing with Robitaille's lack of initiative was sketchy, a mere four pages out of 143, but Esson was satisfied that Mike had contributed his own negligence to the mess and horror he found himself engulfed in. Esson estimated the contributory negligence at twenty per cent and reduced the award by that amount, or $87,000.

Total damages: $348,000, plus Robitaille's court costs.

Every Christmas season, Laxton takes his wife and three daughters to Hawaii for a combined holiday and birthday celebration. Laxton's natal day is December 25, and all his Vancouver friends, the lawyers and politicians and old pals who make the islands the scene for their winter break, know that Christmas Day is open house at the Laxton retreat.

Christmas of 1978, shortly after the publication of the Robitaille judgment, was no exception to the family tradition, and all the Laxtons flew to Hawaii, where they sunned, swam, jogged, and partied. The head of the house, husband and father, was especially ready to unwind. It had been a long year in the courts, what with Robitaille and a couple of other demanding cases, but in a few days Laxton was feeling tanned and relaxed. He liked to take his ease on the balcony of the family's hotel suite, and one afternoon when he was surveying the horizon from his favourite perch, he spotted a familiar figure in the driveway below. It was none other than Mr. Justice William Esson of the B.C. Supreme Court. Laxton had the notion that Esson was deliberately hanging around, keen to run into Laxton but reluctant to approach him directly. Just about everybody from Vancouver knew where

Laxton stayed, and it would be no trouble for Esson, another vacationer from the mainland, to locate him. Laxton shouted down and invited Esson up to the balcony for a drink.

"Naturally we didn't talk about the case," Laxton remembers of the amiable hour or so he passed with Esson. "We couldn't because it was still open for appeal. But I think Bill felt the way I did, that it was nice just to sit and kind of bask in the memory of the trial. Both of us had performed pretty damn well through all those weeks in court. We took pleasure in that even though we didn't dare say anything much about the case. God knows I kept thinking that Bill Esson had done a hell of a fine job of running a trial and writing a judgment."

Barry Kirkham wasn't so sure of the quality of Esson's work, and he elected to take the Robitaille decision to the B.C. Court of Appeal. Laxton cranked up and went back to court, arguing with Kirkham before a three-man appeal court that was headed by Chief Justice Nathan Nemetz. The three listened patiently to the two counsel's arguments, pondered their points over several months, and on April 10, 1981, handed down a 42-page decision that offered bad news to the Canucks and a slight increase in damages to Robitaille. The appeal court agreed in every particular but one with Mr. Justice Esson's decision. They accepted his findings of negligence, his doubts of the defence doctors' credibility, his apportionment of damages. They adopted all his findings and rulings, all except his reasoning on exemplary damages. Yes, the appeal court said, the defendant's despicable actions entitled the plaintiff to exemplary damages. Of course. But Robitaille should get *more* under that head, *more* exemplary damages. The trial judge, according to the appeal court, erred when he applied Robitaille's contributory negligence, twenty per cent, to all damages. The twenty per cent shouldn't bear on exemplary damages. "There is no evidence," the court held, "that Robitaille's negligence contributed to the conduct of the Club which gives rise to the award under this head of damages." The Court of Appeal added $7,000 to Robitaille's bill, and the Canucks now owed him $355,000 and costs.

On May 14, 1981, the Canucks announced that they would not take the case on appeal to the Supreme Court of Canada. Almost three years after John Laxton had issued the writ, four and a half years after Mike Robitaille had felt the first pains shooting down his back and leg, *Robitaille* v. *Vancouver Hockey Club Ltd.* had dwindled to its conclusion.

Near the end of the first week in July 1981, Mike and Isabel flew from Buffalo to Vancouver. It was their first trip to the coast in years that wasn't burdened by a lawsuit and anguish. They planned to visit friends, the ones who'd survived from the Canucks days. They'd call on John Laxton. And they would pick up a cheque from the Supreme Court of British Columbia written on moneys that the Canucks had delivered into court in settlement of Mike's judgment against the club. Payment in full.

"The money came at the right time," Isabel said. "After all the years of suing people, we were running out of cash."

What the Robitailles weren't going short on, given the bleak times, was optimism. The world had begun to break Mike's way shortly after his trial. He took a public relations job with the Buffalo Stallions indoor soccer team that suited his gifts for talk and sports and enthusiasm. He found himself growing closer to his family and his church. "I understand people better now, my wife and kids and everybody, after what I went through," he said. "And I go to mass every day." His strength and stamina began to return. He couldn't play hockey, not with the right hand that clutched up when he was tired, not with the right leg that turned inward and developed a tremor. But he could coach hockey, and in the winter of 1979-80 he spent his nights and weekends with the Lockport Wolves, a junior team in a suburban Buffalo community. He coached, he managed, he led the cheers, and he blossomed into a personality around Lockport. Everybody knew Mike Robitaille. Everybody warmed to his open ways. When he ran the Wolves again the following season to the same reaction from everyone in town, a large group-insurance company in the area — "a good Christian business," as Isabel describes it, Isabel who sets the family's religious and psychological tone — took a calculated look at Mike's local popularity and made him an offer. They'd set him up in his very own insurance agency. He accepted, and in the late spring of '81, Mike Robitaille Insurance opened for business in downtown Lockport.

"Look at *that*!" Mike's older daughter, Anique, said when he drove her past the spanking new office. "Daddy's name's up in lights!"

Mike felt high in Vancouver, the lawsuit behind him and a fresh career ahead. And then the call came from Toronto. Geraldine Robitaille had died at St. Michael's Hospital on Wednesday, July 8. Mike's mother was dead, the woman who had, years earlier, been the victim of two nervous breakdowns, the woman who had brought disorder and tension into the childhood of her youngest. It was a difficult period for Mike. His lawsuit was finished and his mother was dead.

"It was okay," Isabel said later of the news from Toronto. "Mike was deeply saddened. Of course he was. But he'd made his peace with his mother. He understood that his anxieties as an adult had grown out of his experiences with her as a boy. He'd come to grips with all of that before she died."

As for John Laxton, the Robitailles didn't see much of him in Vancouver. He was busy. An NDP Member of Parliament named Ian Waddell was suing the Governor General and all the members of the federal cabinet. He contended that orders-in-council passed by the cabinet which made certain alterations in the construction of the Alaska Highway natural gas pipeline had usurped the role of Parliament. Waddell retained Laxton to take the matter to court. Laxton was back in his natural element.

VERDICT

HAVE I MADE IT CLEAR in the preceding chapters that the nine men and one woman I've written about are among my favourite people? I spent much time with those ten lawyers, more with some than with others. I trailed them into court, recorded their adventures, observed them in action and in their rare moments of ease. And I came away respecting their talents and appreciating their personalities. Courtroom lawyers, I recognized, are special and apart. Like my other favourite group of people, jazz musicians, they are obsessed and irrepressible. They too belong to a profession that puts a premium on a rare talent — improvisation. Judges and juries make immediate demands on counsel — "Give us a reason, right now, why we shouldn't punish your client" — and counsel must respond with their wits, building an answer to rescue the client, calculating and constructing and improvising. Courtroom lawyers operate on the edges. It's a tricky and daring life that they lead in their courts, and I, for one, admire the nerve and brains that they display in triumphing over it.

There are also, I realized in researching the book, more mundane virtues that good counsel require. Patience is one. The moments of high drama in any trial are separated by long stretches of routine and tedium. But counsel must stay alert to the nuances that show up in a witness's apparently boring recitation of evidence or in an opposing counsel's argument on an obscure point of law. Cases are often won on dull facts or subtle law, and the best counsel have a large gift for paying attention. It helps that courtrooms are, in effect, their offices and their clubrooms. Courts may seem august places to outsiders, too intimidating by far, and it's true that there are formalities to be observed, especially in deferring to the judges on their high benches. But for counsel, at home in their natural habitat, courtrooms turn into surprisingly casual theatres. Crucial matters of freedom and money and justice are to be decided, but lawyers, those remarkable performers, frequently invest trials and hearings with as many elements of comedy as of tragedy. The court is their stage, and they strut it well and confidently.

It occurred to me as I was watching them and listening to their performances that we Canadians have rarely celebrated our great counsel. We read books about Melvin Belli and Louis Nizer and Richard "Racehorse" Haynes, Americans all. We see F. Lee Bailey, another American, turn up on our television screens, and we sit through movies that hail the legend of Clarence Darrow, yet another American courtroom giant. But we've permitted few home-grown counsel to lodge themselves in our consciousness.

That's an omission in our social history that I hope this book has helped to correct. Our counsel are as crafty and colourful as their American counterparts, as gifted and spellbinding as the Darrows and Nizers of the U.S. Dave Humphrey, master with a quip and a jury, can shift gears with the expertise of a Belli. John Robinette has towered over the profession in all of North America. And the others in the book rank alongside the acclaimed Americans in persuasive skills — smooth Bert Oliver, relentless John Laxton, canny Joe Sedgwick.

Sedgwick died during the time I worked on his chapter in the book. It was about eighteen months from the day I first called on him in his office until the morning I last visited him in his highrise apartment, and between the two dates, during the series of conversations we carried on about his intriguing spy case of 1946, I saw him age and waste toward death. But even then, even on the last day I talked to him a couple of months before he died, he kept his enthusiasm for two activities that were central to his life. One was a good drink; at our final meeting, 11:30 on an early-autumn morning, he ordered his nurse to pour us a couple of strong Scotches. The other activity he held on to was conversation, plain old talk, reminiscences about past cases, trials he'd won, juries he'd enlightened, opposing counsel he'd routed. He gloried in talk, and from it there emerged a portrait of a counsel who'd taken from his profession joy and challenge in equal measure. He seemed all so typical of Canada's courtroom lawyers.

My favourite people.